FOUR PLAYS

The Storm
Too Clever By Half
Crazy Money
Innocent as Charged

First published in 1997 by Oberon Books Limited,
incorporating Absolute Classics, 521 Caledonian Road,
London, N7 9RH. Tel: 0171 607 3637 / Fax: 0171 607 3629

Cover design: Andrzej Klimowski and Richard Doust

Printed by Arrowhead Books Ltd, Reading

ISBN 1 899791 05 1

FOUR PLAYS

The Storm
Too Clever By Half
Crazy Money
Innocent as Charged

by

Alexander Ostrovsky

translated by Stephen Mulrine

4

CONTENTS

INTRODUCTION: ALEXANDER OSTROVSKY

Alexander Nikolaevich Ostrovsky was born in Moscow on the 31st of March, 1823, the son of a lawyer, whose busy practice among the merchant community, on the unfashionable south side of the river, had made him a very wealthy man. Following the early death of Ostrovsky's mother, his father remarried, and the young Ostrovsky spent much of his formative years wandering from one merchant's house to another, no doubt keeping out of his stepmother's way. A planned career in law came to an end in 1843, when Ostrovsky failed his resit examinations at Moscow University, but he was by then already besotted by the theatre, in particular the Maly, which had become a major civilising force in Russia, staging quality productions not only of Pushkin and Gogol, but also of Shakespeare, Molière, Goldoni, Schiller, etc.

Ejected from the university, Ostrovsky had to earn a living, and his father eventually obtained him a clerical post in the Moscow Commercial Court, where his intimate acquaintance with the domestic life of the city's rising merchant class, was now supplemented by their business dealings, at the sharp end of litigation. It was this same community, dominated by an extraordinary class of semi-barbarous self-made men, terrorizing workforce and family alike, which supplied the raw material for Ostrovsky's first decade as a working dramatist, beginning with the full-length *A Family Affair*, written in 1849, the same year as his father disinherited him for marrying beneath his station.

Ostrovsky's relationship with Nicholas I and the Tsarist censorship was no happier than Pushkin's had been, and the play, which made comedy out of the widespread abuse of the bankruptcy laws, was banned from the moment it was published. Nicholas himself wrote across the title page: 'Printed in vain – acting forbidden', and ordered his Minister of Education to read Ostrovsky a prepared lecture on the duties of the morally responsible dramatist. Ostrovsky was moreover placed under police surveillance, which lasted for years, and had the immediate effect of losing him his civil service post.

Forced to seek employment as a journalist, Ostrovsky continued to write, while his work circulated in a form of samizdat, clandestine readings in private houses and the like, to an extent that by 1851 he had become the country's most talked-about playwright, without a single public performance. *A Family Affair*, indeed, was not staged until 1858, during the reign of Nicholas' successor Alexander II, when the censor personally rewrote Ostrovsky's ending, to ensure that vice got its just deserts. By that time, however, Ostrovsky had firmly established himself in the theatre, with a two-volume collection of his works about to be printed. The publication in 1859, moreover, of Dobrolyubov's seminal review article "The Dark Kingdom", consolidated Ostrovsky's position as the first great social realist of the theatre, the sharp-eyed chronicler of Moscow mercantile life, its corrupt dealings and casual brutality.

In that same year, *The Storm*, widely regarded as Ostrovsky's masterpiece, was premiered in Moscow and St. Petersburg to instant critical acclaim, and celebrated by Dobrolyubov in a further article, *A Ray of Light in the Dark Kingdom*. The tragic action of *The Storm* takes place not in Moscow, but in rural Upper Volga, and concerns the doomed love of the married Katerina, in thrall to her ferocious mother-in-law, for the rather weak hero Boris, himself effectively a serf in his uncle's employ. Almost symmetrically paired, Boris' uncle Dikoi, and Katerina's mother-in-law Kabanova continue Ostrovsky's fascination with the phenomenon of the samodur, as he himself described it – the ignorant and uncultivated petty dictator who need only frown to strike terror into those forced to endure their tyranny. Katerina's eventual suicide, however, is rather the consequence of her own intense guilt feelings, the exalted spiritual plane on which she conducts her mental life, and among Ostrovsky's predominantly realist output, *The Storm* – which furnished the libretto for Janacek's opera Katya Kabanova – is justly distinguished for its lyric power and atmosphere.

After the success of the *The Storm*, Ostrovsky entered a period of increasing frustration with the censorship, and turned to writing history plays, on the model of Pushkin's *Boris Godunov*. In 1861, the abolition of serfdom began a process of far-reaching change in Russian society, as feudalism gave way to entrepreneurial capitalism, and Ostrovsky's later plays, upon his return to contemporary subject matter, reflect that process in the interaction of a rising class of adroit speculators, with a landed gentry in rapid decline. Two of the plays in this collection, *Too Clever By Half*, and *Crazy Money*, are concerned with the same social milieu, perceived from different angles.

Too Clever By Half, said to have been influenced by Sheridan's *School for Scandal*, is a devastating satire on Moscow's moribund high society, a closed circle of vain and gullible old women of both sexes, engaged in a rearguard action against new money and new ideas. As far as the sharpwitted and amoral Glumov is concerned, they are ripe for the taking, and by sedulous flattery and well-placed bribes, he manoeuvres himself to within a hair's-breadth of a huge fortune, coming unstuck only when his diary, in which he has recorded every detail of his nefarious scheme, falls into the wrong hands. Significantly, though, in Ostrovsky's world, the curtain falls on Glumov's dupes agreeing amongst themselves to reinstate him – he's simply too valuable to lose.

Ostrovsky's reluctance to provide either easy villains, or what would be termed in the Soviet era 'positive heroes' – when social realism turned into its opposite, Socialist Realism – was the cause of numerous run-ins with the censor, but it also characterises *Crazy Money*, written in 1870, and based on Shakespeare's *Taming of the Shrew*, which he had translated some years earlier. Ostrovsky's Petruchio, a provincial businessman named Vasilkov, represents the rising entrepreneurial class, the 'smart money', so to speak, cutting a swathe through the Moscow drones, living beyond their means on seemingly inexhaustible credit. Vasilkov achieves his dream of marrying a beautiful Moscow socialite, Lidiya, in fact as the result of a practical joke, engineered by another Glumov (perhaps the same one, a few years on), only to discover that he can't afford her extravagant life-style. Nor can anyone else, however, and the play concludes with Lidiya being forced to accept his offer of the post of housekeeper at his provincial estate, until she learns how to budget. Vasilkov bears more than a passing resemblance to Chekhov's Lopakhin, incidentally, but Ostrovsky's ending is not unambiguously happy, nor do his feckless 'grasshoppers' appear to suffer more than a temporary inconvenience.

Ostrovsky's dramatic output is vast by any standards, some fifty original plays, and over a score of translations. He also worked tirelessly on behalf of the theatre, and founded the Actors' Circle, along with the composer Nikolai Rubinstein, in 1865, helping to raise standards in both performance and repertoire. The Actors' Circle lasted until 1883, when it was succeeded by the Society of Literature and Art, which in turn paved the way for the great Moscow Art Theatre, and the achievement of Chekhov. Ostrovsky moreover obtained significant improvements in the lot of Russian playwrights, a subject on which he was well qualified to speak. At the height of his fame in the mid-1860's, for example, with some twenty-five successful plays behind him, a new script accepted by the monopoly Imperial theatres netted Ostrovsky a mere 100 roubles per act, and nothing at all outside of Moscow and St. Petersburg. Meanwhile a few star performers reputedly earned 10,000 roubles a year, and theatre managements grew rich on Ostrovsky's talent.

Not surprisingly, Ostrovsky wrote a number of plays about actors, among which *The Forest* is the best known. That strand of his work is here represented by *Innocent As Charged*, written in 1884, two years before his death. It is in many respects a classic melodrama, with a complex plot concerning an unmarried mother, Lyubov, who is abandoned by her lover at the very moment she learns that their infant son is dying. This painful tableau constitutes a prologue, and the remaining four acts of the play lead up to the discovery by Lyubov, seventeen years older and now a famous actress, that her long-lost son Grisha is alive, an embittered and misanthropic young actor in the provincial theatre company in which she is guesting. As with any melodrama, the plot audibly creaks from time to time, but it well merits its status in Russia as one of Ostrovsky's most popular plays, and the role of Lyubov/ Kruchinina shines out like a beacon, a genuinely moving expression of unselfish love.

In his country of origin, Ostrovsky's popularity has remained undimmed since the mid-19th century, not least among actors, for the meaty roles he offers, within an admirably even-handed ensemble; there are no spear-carriers in Ostrovsky, and few cardboard cut-outs. And while the realist world-view, underpinning Ostrovsky's drama, necessitates a certain detachment, it is not incompatible with intricate plotting, and downright theatricality, when the occasion demands.

In his own day, Ostrovsky's language was considered remarkable for its authenticity – the Russian of the Moscow streets and alleyways, the mudhole provincial villages – and that is still offered as a reason for his comparative neglect by the West. Indeed, it is extraordinary that an artist almost worshipped in his native country – the father of Russian drama, the theatrical peer of the great 19th century realist novelists – should be virtually unknown to English audiences. Certainly, his work is difficult to translate, but at its best it is both intensely Russian, and universal. Ostrovsky's best, moreover, is commonly estimated at around two-thirds of his output, a massive achievement by any standards.

Ostrovsky died on June the 2nd, 1886, typically hard at work revising his translation of Shakespeare's *Antony and Cleopatra*, but in many ways, Ostrovsky speaks more directly to us than ever before. In the present collection, for example, the gilded youth of *Crazy Money*, surfing the bubble economy, might pass for our contemporaries, and the place of women in society, as observed and analysed by Ostrovsky, is arguably of even more interest to our culture than his own. Before Ostrovsky, the Russian repertoire effectively consisted of three great plays – Pushkin's *Boris Godunov*, Griboedov's *Woe from Wit*, and Gogol's *Government Inspector*. After Ostrovsky, it could boast a treasure-house of outstandingly good plays, worthy of comparison with anything in the language then or since, and a freestanding monument, like the famous bronze statue of Ostrovsky outside his beloved Maly, to the lifetime effort of a truly great man of the theatre.

---o0o---

THE STORM

CHARACTERS

DIKOY   (Savyol Prokofyevich, a merchant, leading figure in the town)
BORIS   (Grigoryevich, his nephew, a well-educated young man)
KABANOVA   (Marfa Ignatyevna, a wealthy merchant's widow)
TIKHON   (Ivanych Kabanov, her son)
KATERINA   (His wife)
VARVARA   (Tikhon's sister)
KULIGIN   (A tradesman – a self-educated watchmaker, trying to
  discover the secret of perpetual motion)
KUDRYASH   (Vanya, a young man, Dikoy's clerk)
SHAPKIN   (A tradesman)
FEKLUSHA   (A pilgrim)
GLASHA   (A maid in the Kabanov house)
A Lady with Two Footmen, in her seventies, half-mad.
Townspeople

The action takes place in summer, in the town of Kalinov, on the
  banks of the Volga. Between Acts III and IV, ten days elapse.

Author's note: With the exception of Boris, all the characters wear
  Russian dress.

ACT ONE

The scene is a public park on the high bank of the Volga, and beyond the river, a rural landscape. There are two benches set amongst some shrubbery. Kuligin is sitting on one of the benches, gazing across the river, while Kudryash and Shapkin stroll back and forth.

KULIGIN: *(sings)* "Amid the peaceful valleys,
Atop the gentle heights .."

Oh, it's an absolute marvel, there's no other word for it. Hey, Kudryash! Just look at it, eh? Yes, my lad, I've been feasting my eyes on the Volga for fifty years now, and I still can't get enough.

KUDRYASH: Enough of what?

KULIGIN: That incredible view! It's sheer poetry! It rejoices the heart.

KUDRYASH: You think so?

KULIGIN: It's glorious! And all you can say is, 'You think so?'! You've either got tired of looking at it, or else you've no feeling for the beauty of nature.

KUDRYASH: Well, there's no point in talking to you anyway. The local eccentric, the mad scientist!

KULIGIN: A mechanic, a self-taught mechanic.

KUDRYASH: Same thing.

A silence.

KULIGIN: *(pointing off)* Look, Kudryash, over there – who's that waving his arms?

KUDRYASH: What, there? Oh, that's Dikoy swearing at his nephew.

KULIGIN: Huh – he's picked a fine place!

KUDRYASH: Any place'll do for him. He couldn't care less. He's got Boris in his clutches now, so he's taking his spite out on him.

SHAPKIN: Yes, you'll have a hard job finding a worse bully than our Mr Dikoy! He'll bite your head off as soon as look at you.

KUDRYASH: Loudmouthed peasant!

SHAPKIN: Kabanova's just about as bad.

KUDRYASH: Well, at least she does it in the name of morality – he's like a mad dog off the chain.

SHAPKIN: There's nobody to keep him in check, that's why he runs wild.

KUDRYASH: We need a few more lads like me, we'd soon sort him out.

SHAPKIN: Oh yes, and what would you do?

KUDRYASH: We'd give him the fright of his life, that's what.

SHAPKIN: How, exactly?

KUDRYASH: Well, we'd get four or five us in an alley somewhere, and have a little chat with him, man to man, to soften him up, like. And he wouldn't dare let out a squeak about our little lesson, he'd be looking over his shoulder after that, wherever he went.

SHAPKIN: No wonder he wanted to pack you off to the army.

KUDRYASH: Yes, well, he wanted to, but he didn't, so that goes for nothing. He won't send me, with that nose of his he's smart enough to know I'd make him pay. He might scare you people, but I can put him in his place.

SHAPKIN: Really?

KUDRYASH: What d'you mean, 'Really?' Everybody knows I'm a hard case, so why does he keep me on, eh? 'Cause he needs me, that's what. Anyway, I'm not scared of him, it's him should be scared of me.

SHAPKIN: So, he doesn't actually swear at you?

KUDRYASH: Listen, he can't help swearing. He can't breathe without it. But I don't let him away with it – he gives me one word, I give him ten back. He just spits, and walks away. No, you won't catch me grovelling to him.

KULIGIN: I see. So you take your example from him? You'd do better just to put up with it.

KUDRYASH: Oh yes, well, if you're so clever, why don't you teach *him* a bit of respect first, and then you can start on us. It's too bad his daughters are still in their teens, there's not one of them big enough yet.

SHAPKIN: Meaning what?

KUDRYASH: Well, I'd do him a favour, wouldn't I. I'm a right devil with the girls!

Dikoy and Boris go past. Kuligin doffs his cap.

SHAPKIN: *(to Kudryash)* Let's get out of his way, before he starts on us.

They withdraw.

DIKOY: So what did you come here for, eh? To sit twiddling your thumbs? Damn layabout! Go on, get the hell out of my sight!

BORIS: It's Sunday – what am I supposed to do?

DIKOY: You'd soon find something, if you were keen enough. If I've told you once, I've told you a dozen times, keep out of my bloody road! What's the matter, not got enough room, is that it? Dear God, I can't turn round but there you are! Go on, bugger off! What are you standing there for, like a lump of wood? I'm talking to you, are you deaf?

BORIS: And I'm listening, what else can I do!

DIKOY: *(glaring at Boris)* Oh, to hell with you. I can't be bothered even talking to you, you damned Jesuit, you make me sick! *(spits in disgust and stalks out)*

KULIGIN: I don't know why you have anything to do with him, sir, I really don't. You surely can't enjoy living with him, and taking that kind of abuse.

BORIS: Kuligin, how could I enjoy it! I've no choice.

KULIGIN: What d'you mean, no choice, sir, if you don't mind my asking? Tell us, if you can.

BORIS: Yes, why not. I take it you knew my grandmother Anfisa?

KULIGIN: I did indeed, sir.

BORIS: Well, she turned against my father because he married a noblewoman, so my parents went to live in Moscow. My mother used to say she couldn't live three days together here with her in-laws, life seemed so rough.

KULIGIN: Oh, it's a rough life here, sir, no other word for it. It takes some getting used to.

BORIS: Anyway, our parents gave us a good education in Moscow, spared themselves nothing for us. They sent me to the Commercial Academy, and my sister to boarding-school, then they both suddenly died of cholera, and my sister and I were left orphans. Later on we heard our grandmother here had also died, and willed us part of her estate, which my uncle would turn over to us when we came of age, but on one condition.

KULIGIN: And what was that, sir?

BORIS: That we treat him with respect.

KULIGIN: Which means, sir, that you're never likely to see your inheritance.

BORIS: Worse than that, Kuligin. He'll do nothing but taunt us, hurl all manner of abuse at us, whenever he takes a fancy, and he'll end up giving us nothing at all, or some piddling amount. Yes, and he'll tell everybody he's doing it out of charity, that we're not even due that much.

KUDRYASH: Well, that's the way our merchants go about their business, isn't it. And then again, even supposing you did treat him with respect, what's to stop him telling people you didn't?

BORIS: True enough. I mean, even now he says things like: "I've got children of my own, why should I give money to other people's? Why should I do my own kids down?"

KULIGIN: Looks like you're in a bad way, sir.

BORIS: If it was only myself, I wouldn't care. I'd just pack it all in and walk away. But I've got my sister to worry about. He was even on the point of sending for her, but my mother's family wouldn't hear of it, they wrote back and told him she was sick. God only knows what kind of life she'd have had here – it doesn't bear thinking about.

KUDRYASH: Well, it goes without saying – they haven't a clue how to treat people.

KULIGIN: So how d'you manage to live with him, sir? What's your situation like?

BORIS: Like nothing on earth. "You can stay here," he says, "but you'll do what you're told, and take what you're given." Meaning, in a year's time, he'll give me whatever he feels like.

KUDRYASH: Yes, that's him all over. None of us dare let out a squeak about money, he'll turn the air blue. "How the hell do you know what's in my mind!" he'll say, "You think you know what I've got in mind? Maybe I'm just in the right mood to pay you five thousand roubles, eh?" Yes, you try talking to him – he's never been in that sort of mood in his entire life!

KULIGIN: What can you do, sir? You've got to keep him sweet somehow.

BORIS: That's the whole point, Kuligin – it's quite impossible. Not even his own family can manage that, so what chance have I?

KUDRYASH: No, there's no pleasing him – it's his life's work, abusing people, especially when it comes to money. He won't settle a single bill without a fight. Quite often people are happy to give in, just to shut him up. Worst of all, is when somebody annoys him first thing in the morning – he'll pick holes in us the whole day then.

BORIS: You know, my aunt has to beg us every day, with tears in her eyes: "Don't make him angry, for God's sake! Don't annoy him, dears, whatever you do!"

KUDRYASH: Huh, fat chance! He's only got to pop down to the market, and that's it. He'll raise hell with all the traders. They can lose money on the deal, and he still won't leave without a swearing-match. And that's him set up for the whole day.

SHAPKIN: In a word – he's a maniac.

KUDRYASH: Oh, he's that all right!

BORIS: Yes, but the real trouble starts when somebody insults him, somebody he daren't abuse. Heaven help the family then!

KUDRYASH: Oh God, yes, that was so funny, that time on the Volga ferry, when some hussar swore at him. A sight for sore eyes, it was.

BORIS: Yes, well, it wasn't much fun for the people at home. For two weeks after that they had to hide in the attic and box-rooms.

KULIGIN: Hullo, what's this? They can't be coming out of vespers already, surely?

Several people pass by up-stage.

KUDRYASH: Right, come on, Shapkin, let's go for a drink. No point in standing around here.

They bow and exit.

BORIS: You know, it's terribly hard for me here, Kuligin, I can't get used to it. People keep giving me strange looks, as if I'm not wanted, as if I'm interfering somehow. I mean, I don't know the local customs – I know they're our own native Russian ways, but I can't seem to get used to them.

KULIGIN: And you never will, sir.

BORIS: Why not?

KULIGIN: 'Cause they're cruel ways, sir, terrible cruel in this town. You take the ordinary workers, sir – you'll find nothing but ignorance and stark poverty among them. And we'll never break out of that shell, sir, 'cause we'll never be able to earn more than our daily bread by honest toil. But if a man's got money, sir, he'll try to enslave the poor, so he can make even more money out of their unpaid labour. D'you know what that uncle of yours, Dikoy, said to the mayor? The peasants complained to the mayor that he hadn't paid them properly for their work. "Now, come on, Mr Dikoy," says the mayor, "Do the decent thing, settle up with your lads. I'm getting complaints about you every day." Well, your uncle claps the mayor on the shoulder, and he says, "Really, your Excellency, do we need to concern ourselves with this sort of rubbish? I deal with a great many people in the course of a year, as you know, and if I pay them all a kopeck or two short, well, that amounts to thousands, and that suits me just fine!" That's what he said, sir. And you should see how they behave amongst themselves, sir! They'll practically tear the business out of each other's hands, and not so much out of greed, as envy. They're at daggers drawn, the whole time. They'll sweet-talk some drunken clerk into those grand houses of theirs, sir, the sort of scribbler you can't see anything human in, some poor wretch with every trace of humanity disappeared, and for a small fee they'll get him to write the most fearful slanders about their neighbours, on official notepaper, too! And they start up lawsuits then, that drag on for years, causing no end of suffering. They're in and out of our court here, then they go to the district court, and of course the lawyers are delighted to see them, rubbing their hands with glee, they are. You know what they say, sir – a fairy-tale's soon done, but a lawsuit's never won. So the case drags on, gets more and more mixed up, and that suits them down to the ground, that's just what they want. "Well, this'll cost a fortune, " they'll say, "but it'll cost him a pretty penny too!" I tell you, for two pins I'd set all this down in verse...

BORIS: Do you write poetry?

KULIGIN: Oh, in the old style, sir. I'm a great reader of Lomonosov, Derzhavin... He was a wise man, Lomonosov, a real student of nature. And he was one of us, what's more, one of the common people.

BORIS: You should write it down. It would be very interesting.

KULIGIN: No, how could I, sir? They'd eat me alive, swallow me whole, they would. I get into enough trouble as it is, for my loose tongue, but I can't help it, I just love a good talk. I wouldn't mind telling you about family life here, sir, but maybe some other time. That's worth hearing too.

Enter Feklusha and another woman.

FEKLUSHA: It's bootiful, my dear, just bootiful! Absolutely lovely, what more can you say! It's the Promised Land you've got here, that's what it is. The merchant folks are right godfearing, just dripping with virtue, they are. Generous to a fault, filled with charity. Oh, I'm so pleased, my dear, I've got a lump in my throat, I'm so happy! And for helping us out, they'll be even more richly rewarded, 'specially that Kabanova woman.

They exit.

BORIS: Kabanova?

KULIGIN: Yes, Marfa Kabanova, sir. A right hypocrite. She'll do anything for a beggar, but she runs her own people ragged. *(a silence)* You know, what I'd really like, sir, is to discover the secret of perpetual motion.

BORIS: And what would you do with it?

KULIGIN: What wouldn't I do, sir! I mean, the English are offering
a million for it, and I'd use all that money for the good of society,
sir, to support the people. The common people need work –
they're ready and willing, and there's no work for them.

BORIS: And have you any hopes of finding the secret?

KULIGIN: Absolutely, sir! All I need now is a bit of money to build
my model. Anyway, goodbye, sir! *(exits)*

BORIS: *(alone)* It'd be a shame to disillusion him. He's a decent chap.
He has his dreams, and he's happy. As for me, it seems my young
life's to be ruined in this godforsaken hole. I go about half-dead as it it
is, and on top of that, I have to fill my head with this foolishness!
That's all I needed – a romantic attachment, for God's sake!
Downtrodden and bullied, and I have to fall in love! And with whom?
With a woman I'll never even have the chance to speak to. *(a silence)*
Yet I can't get her out of my mind, however much I want to. And
here she comes! With her husband, and her mother-in-law, besides.
God, what a fool I am. Well, just steal a glance at her, then go home...

> *He exits. From the opposite side, enter Kabanova, Tikhon,
> Katerina and Varvara.*

KABANOVA: And if you listen to your mother, you'll do exactly as
I've told you, the minute you get there.

TIKHON: Mama, how could I not listen to you?

KABANOVA: People've got no respect for their elders nowadays.

VARVARA: *(aside)* No respect for you? I'd like to see it.

TIKHON: Seems to me I don't dare make a move without your
permission, mama.

KABANOVA: Yes, I'd be more ready to believe you, if I didn't see
with my own eyes – and hear with my own ears – exactly what sort
of respect parents get from their children these days! You'd think
they'd at least remember the pain their poor mothers had to suffer,
bringing them forth.

TIKHON: Mama, I don't see...

KABANOVA: And if a mother says something hurtful now and again, something that dents your pride, well, I dare say you can put up with it, don't you think?

TIKHON: Mama, when have I ever not put up with it?

KABANOVA: Oh, yes, your mother's a foolish old woman – you young people are so clever, you shouldn't expect much from us old fools.

TIKHON: *(sighs, aside)* God almighty! *(to Kabanova)* Mama, I wouldn't dream of it!

KABANOVA: You know, it's love that makes parents so strict with you. It's love that makes them nag you, they only want you teach you what's right. Of course, that's not the fashion these days. So those same children spread wicked rumours – their mother's a shrew, she gives them no peace, she torments the life out of them. Oh, and God help her if she says anything to offend her daughter-in-law, the word fairly goes round, she's driving her into an early grave.

TIKHON: Mama, surely nobody's saying that about us?

KABANOVA: No, no, I haven't heard that, I won't tell a lie. But if I had heard it, I wouldn't be talking to you like this, you can be sure. *(sighs)* Oh, what a burden of sin we bear! And we can sin at any time – you get into a conversation, something close to your heart, next thing you flare up, and that's the sin of wrath. No, just go ahead and say what you like about me. You can't stop people talking – what they won't dare say to your face, they'll say behind your back.

TIKHON: God in heaven, if my tongue should wither...

KABANOV: That's enough, that's enough – don't swear any oaths! That's another sin! I've known it for a long time now, you care more for your wife than your mother. From the day you got married, I've never had the same affection.

TIKHON: Mama, I don't know what makes you say that.

KABANOVA: Just everything you do, my son, that's all! What a mother can't see with her own eyes, she knows in her heart, she can feel these things. Maybe it's that wife of yours turning you against me, I don't know.

TIKHON: No, of course it isn't, mama! How can you even think that?

KATERINA: Mama, you mean the same to me as my own mother, and Tikhon loves you too.

KABANOVA: Nobody asked for your opinion, so you can just keep quiet. You needn't bother trying to defend him, I won't harm him. He's my son, and never forget it. What are you springing to his aid for, anyway, making a fuss? You want everybody to see how much your love your husband, is that it? Yes, well, we know what you're like, showing off in front of people.

VARVARA: *(aside)* That's nice – a public lecture.

KATERINA: Mama, you've no right to say that about me. I'm the same anywhere, in company or alone – I don't try to show off.

KABANOVA: Anyway, I didn't mean to mention you – it just came out, that's all.

KATERINA: Even if it did just come out, why should you want to hurt me?

KABANOVA: Huh, touchy, isn't she. So, I've hurt her feelings now?

KATERINA: I'm sure nobody likes being falsely accused!

KABANOVA: Oh yes, I know you don't want to hear what I've got to say, but what else can I do? I'm not some stranger, my heart aches for you, Katerina. I've seen it coming for a while now, you want your own way. Well, you'll have to wait till I'm gone, then you can do what you like. Yes, you can do as you please then, you'll have no elders to watch over you. And maybe you'll remember me.

TIKHON: Mama, we pray for you day and night, that God'll grant you long life and prosperity, and success in all your business dealings.

KABANOVA: Oh, that's enough of that. Maybe you did love your mother once, when you were single, but I'm nothing to you now – you've got a young wife.

TIKHON: The one doesn't rule out the other, surely – my wife is my wife, all right, but I still respect my mother.

KABANOVA: And you'd give up your wife for your mother? I'll believe that when I see it.

TIKHON: Why should I give up either? I love both of you.

KABANOVA: Yes, yes, you can lay it on thick, but I can see I'm just a hindrance to you.

TIKHON: Well, you can think what you like, that's entirely up to you, but I can't understand why I was born to be so wretched, I can't do anything to please you.

KABANOVA: Huh, now he's acting the cry-baby. What are you whimpering about? What sort of husband are you? Just look at yourself. D'you think your wife'll fear you after this?

TIKHON: Why on earth should she fear me? She loves me, and that's good enough for me.

KABANOVA: Why should she fear you? Eh? Have you gone crazy or something? If she doesn't fear you, how's she going to fear me, eh? What sort of order will we have in the house then? She's your wife by law, isn't she? Or maybe the law doesn't mean anything to you. Well, if that's the case, you keep your foolish ideas to yourself. At least don't fling them around in front of her, and your sister, that's still a maid. She'll be getting married too, you know, listening to your stupid talk, and I doubt if her husband'll thank you for the lesson. You see now what kind of brains you've got, and you still think you can go your own way.

TIKHON: Mama, that's not true, I don't want to go my own way. I wouldn't know where to start.

KABANOVA: Oh yes, you think it's all kisses and cuddles with a wife. Never raise your voice to her, never threaten her?

TIKHON: Mama, I don't...

KABANOVA: What if she takes a lover, eh? Is that all right too? Eh? Well, come on!

TIKHON: Mama, for God's sake...

KABANOVA: Well, you're a fool. And there's no point in arguing with a fool. It's just another sin. *(a silence)* Right, I'm going home.

TIKHON: We'll be back soon. We'll just take a turn or two along the boulevard.

KABANOVA: Do what you like. Just don't keep me waiting, I can't stand that.

TIKHON: No, mama. God forbid.

KABANOVA: Yes, well, make sure you don't. *(exits)*

TIKHON: You see? You see what I have to put up with from mama because of you? God, what a life!

KATERINA: It's not my fault, is it?

TIKHON: I don't know whose fault it is.

VARVARA: No, you wouldn't, would you.

TIKHON: And the way she used to keep on at me: "Get married, get married, I want to see you a married man!" Now she never stops nagging, won't give me a minute's peace, and all because of you.

VARVARA: So why is it Katya's fault, eh? Mother keeps attacking her, and so do you. And you still say you love your wife? Honest to God, I can't bear to look at you!

TIKHON: Well, damn it, what am I supposed to do!

VARVARA: That's your business. You could keep your mouth shut, if you can't think of anything better! What are you standing there shuffling your feet for? I can see what's on your mind.

TIKHON: What's that, then?

VARVARA: You know perfectly well – you want to go off to Dikoy's place, have a drink with him, right?

TIKHON: Yes, that's right, sister of mine.

KATERINA: Tisha, you'd better not stay long, or mama'll start nagging you again.

VARVARA: Oh, yes, you'd better be quick, or you'll get what for!

TIKHON: As if I don't know.

VARVARA: And we don't fancy getting a roasting on your account either.

TIKHON: I'll be back in a second. Wait here for me. *(exits)*

KATERINA: You feel sorry for me, Varya, don't you.

VARVARA: Of course I do.

KATERINA: So, that means you do like me? *(kisses her impulsively)*

VARVARA: Why on earth shouldn't I like you?

KATERINA: Oh, thank you! You're so kind, I'm so terribly fond of you. *(a silence)* D'you know what's just come into my head?

VARVARA: What?

KATERINA: I wonder why people can't fly?

VARVARA: I don't know what you're talking about.

KATERINA: I'm saying, why can't people fly like birds? You know, I sometimes feel as if I am a bird. When you're standing on a hill, something makes you want to fly. See, if I could just take a little run, spread out my arms, and fly away. Shall I give it a try? *(makes to run)*

VARVARA: Heavens above, what's got into you!

KATERINA: *(sighs)* Oh, I used to be so full of life. I'm fading away in your house.

VARVARA: You think I haven't noticed?

KATERINA: When I think of how I was... I hadn't a care in the world, I was as free as a bird. Mama absolutely doted on me, she used to dress me up like a little doll, and never made me do housework – I could do whatever I liked. You know how I lived when I was a girl? I'll tell you. I used to get up early in the morning, and in the summer, I'd go down to the spring to wash, and bring back a pail of water, for all the flowers in the house. We had lots and lots of flowers. Then mama and I would go to church, along with all the pilgrims – our house was always full of pilgrims and pious old ladies. And when we got back from church, we'd sit down at some work or other, mostly embroidery – gold thread on velvet – and the pilgrims would tell us stories, about where they'd been, and what they'd seen, the lives of the different saints, or else they'd sing hymns. And that's how we'd pass the time until dinner. After that the old women would have a nap, and I'd go for a walk

round the garden. Then in the evening, we'd go to vespers, and
there'd be more stories and songs. It was so beautiful!

VARVARA: Well, we do the same things here.

KATERINA: Yes, but it's as if it's against your will. And I used to adore
going to church. It felt just like going to heaven, I wouldn't see
anybody, or be aware of the time passing, I wouldn't even hear when
the service ended. It was as if it was all over in a second. Mama told
me that people used to stare at me, wondering what had happened.
But you know, on a sunny day, the light would stream down from
the church dome in a sort of column, and the smoke from the
incense looked like clouds, and it was as if I could see angels in that
column of light, flying and singing, And sometimes I'd get up in the
middle of the night – we had little icon lamps burning all through the
house – and I'd kneel before one of the icons and pray until morning.
Or else I'd go out into the garden early, just as the sun was rising,
and kneel down and pray and weep, I don't even know myself why,
but that's how they would find me. What I was praying for, what I
wanted from God, I can't imagine – I had everything I needed then, I
was so happy. Oh, and such dreams I used to have, Varya dearest,
such beautiful dreams! Golden temples, strange and wonderful
gardens, filled with unseen voices singing, and the scent of cypress
wood, and mountains and trees like nothing on earth, as if they were
painted on a holy icon. And it was as if I was flying, flying through
the air. I still have dreams now, but not often, and never like those.

VARVARA: What do you dream now?

KATERINA: *(after a silence)* That I'm going to die soon.

VARVARA: Heavens, don't say that.

KATERINA: No, I know I'm going to die. Oh, dearest Varya, something
terrible is happening to me, something very strange. I've never felt
like this before, it's extraordinary, something deep inside me. It's as
if I was starting life all over again, or else... oh, I don't know.

VARVARA: What could it be?

KATERINA: Varya, I think it's something bad – oh, I feel so afraid,
so terribly afraid! It's as if I'm standing on the edge of an abyss,
and someone's pushing me over, and I've nothing to hold onto.

VARVARA: Katya, what is it? Are you all right?

KATERINA: Yes, I'm fine... I wish I were sick, it wouldn't be so bad.
I keep having these strange thoughts, I can't get them out of my
mind. I try to think of something else, but I can't get rid of them –
I try to pray, but I just can't. I can form the words with my lips,
but my mind's somewhere else. It's as if the devil's whispering in
my ear, frightful things, unspeakable. And I start imagining things
that make me feel ashamed of myself. What's wrong with me,
Varya? Something terrible's going to happen, I know it. I can't
sleep at night, I hear whispering the whole time, so gentle and
caressing, like the murmuring of a dove... Oh, Varya, I no longer
dream of heavenly trees and mountains – it's as if someone 's
holding me in his arms, so tightly, and leading me away
somewhere, and I'm going with him – yes, I go with him and...

VARVARA: And?

KATERINA: Oh, God, why am I telling you this? You're still a maid.

VARVARA: You can tell me. I'm worse than you.

KATERINA: Oh, how can I? I'm so ashamed!

VARVARA: Why should you be? Tell me, Katya.

KATERINA: I feel so cramped at home, so stifled, sometimes I just
want to escape. And sometimes I think, if I had my way, I'd be
sailing down the Volga right now, in a little boat, singing songs, or
else racing along in a fine troika, huddled up close to...

VARVARA: Someone other than your husband.

KATERINA: How did you know?

VARVARA: As if I don't know!

KATERINA: Oh, Varya, I have such sinful thoughts! I'm so wretched,
you've no idea how I've wept, how hard I've tried to get rid of
these feelings, but I can't put them out of my mind, I just can't. I
mean, it's wicked, isn't it, it's a terrible sin if I love someone else.

VARVARA: Who am I to judge? I've enough sins of my own.

KATERINA: What am I going to do? I haven't the strength, Varya,
where can I go? I'm so unhappy I could do something desperate!

VARVARA: Katya, don't be silly! What's the matter with you? Just wait, my brother's leaving tomorrow, we'll think of something then. You might even be able to see each other.

KATERINA: No, no, I can't! Good God, what are you saying!

VARVARA: What are you so afraid of?

KATERINA: Varya, if I met with this man even just once, I'd run away from home and never come back, not for anything in the world.

VARVARA: Well, let's just wait and see, shall we.

KATERINA: No, no, don't even mention it, I don't want to hear!

VARVARA: You surely don't want to fade away? You could die of a broken heart, and no-one'd care. D'you think they'd care? So why torture yourself?

> *Enter a Lady walking with a stick. She is accompanied by two Footmen, wearing three-cornered hats.*

LADY: Well, well, my beauties – what's going on here? Waiting for your young men, are you, your lovers? Having a good time? High spirits? Rejoicing in your beauty, eh? Well, there's where beauty leads... *(points to the Volga)* Down there, yes, to the very depths!

> *Varvara laughs.*

What are you laughing at? There's no reason for joy. You'll all burn in the eternal fires! All of you, in boiling pitch for evermore! Oh yes, that's where all your beauty leads. *(exits)*

KATERINA: Oh God, she's given me such a fright, I'm trembling all over – it's as if she's foretold my future.

VARVARA: *(calling after her)* You don't scare us, you old hag!

KATERINA: What was it she said? What did she say?

VARVARA: Nothing, it was all nonsense. That's just what you need, listening to people like her. She says that to everybody. I mean, she's been sinning her whole life, you should hear the tales they tell about her! Now she's at death's door, so she's scared, and she's trying to frighten other people, with what frightens her. All the little boys in town hide from her – she threatens them with that stick of hers and shouts: "You're all going to burn in hell-fire!"

KATERINA: Oh, don't, don't, I think my heart's stopped.

VARVARA: You're not scared of that old fool?

KATERINA: Yes, I'm scared – I'm terrified! I can still see her, right before my eyes.

A silence.

VARVARA: I wonder what's keeping my brother? Looks like there's a storm on the way.

KATERINA: A storm? We'd better go home! Let's run, hurry!

VARVARA: Katya, what's the matter with you, are you mad? You don't dare go home without Tisha.

KATERINA: No, let's go home now! Never mind about him.

VARVARA: What are you so scared of? The storm's still miles away.

KATERINA: Well, if it's a long way off, we can wait a little while, but we really ought to start walking. Let's go, please.

VARVARA: Look, if something's going to happen, you won't be any safer at home.

KATERINA: All the same I'd feel better, more at ease. At least I can pray there, before the holy icons.

VARVARA: I'd no idea you were so frightened of storms. They don't bother me in the least.

KATERINA: Of course I'm frightened. Everybody should be. It's not so terrible to be killed, it's the fact that death can take you unawares, just the way you are, with all your sins on your conscience, all your wicked thoughts. I'm not afraid to die, but when I think I might suddenly find myself standing before God, just as I've been standing here with you, after everything we've said... well, that really scares me. The thoughts I have! That dreadful sin... I'm terrified even to mention it.

A peal of thunder.

Oh!

Enter Tikhon.

VARVARA: Here's Tisha now. *(to Tikhon)* Come on, hurry up!

Another peal of thunder.

KATERINA: Oh, hurry, hurry!

END OF ACT ONE

ACT TWO

The scene is a room in the Kabanov house. Glasha is tying up clothes into a bundle, when Feklusha enters.

FEKLUSHA: Oh, you poor dear, you're always working. What's that you're doing?

GLASHA: I'm getting the master's things ready for the road.

FEKLUSHA: You mean our dear boy's going someplace?

GLASHA: Yes, he is.

FEKLUSHA: And will he be gone long?

GLASHA: No, not long.

FEKLUSHA: Well, I wish him a safe journey. Will his wife start howling to see him go, d'you think?

GLASHA: I don't know, I couldn't tell you.

FEKLUSHA: She like a good howl, does she?

GLASHA: Can't say as I've heard her.

FEKLUSHA: Oh, I like a good howl, my dear, I truly do, that's what I like to hear, yes! *(a silence)* Listen, I tell you, you want to keep an eye on that beggar-woman, afore she swipes something.

GLASHA: God, I can't make you people out, you do nothing but tell tales on each other – why can't you live at peace? You do pretty well in this house, to my way of thinking, all you travelling folk, and yet you're like cat and dog the whole time. Have you no fear of sin?

FEKLUSHA: You can't live in this world, my dear, without sin. And I'll tell you this much – simple folks like you has only one devil to work on you, whereas folks like us, godfearing travellers, well, we've got as many as six, or a dozen devils set on us, and we've got to fight 'em all off. It's hard work, my dear, believe me.

GLASHA: So why have you got so many?

FEKLUSHA: Well, Satan does it out of hate, my dear, 'cause we're leading a righteous life. And I'm not a troublemaker, my dear, I'm innocent of that sin. But one fault I do have, to be sure, and I know what it is – I love to eat. Well, what if I do? The Lord provides for me in my infirmity.

GLASHA: So, you've travelled a fair bit, Feklusha?

FEKLUSHA: No, my dear, I haven't. I can't go far on account of my infirmity. But I've heard a lot, oh yes. They say there's even some countries as has no Christian tsar to rule 'em, but is ruled by sultans and suchlike. And in one of them countries, Sultan Makhnut the Turk sits on the throne, and in another one, Sultan Makhnut the Persian, and they sit in judgment on the people, my dear, and all the judgments they make, well, they're all wrong. I mean, they can't make even one right judgment, my dear, 'cause the good Lord's set limits on them. You see, all our laws is just, my dear, and theirs is unjust. Whatever comes out one way by our laws, comes out the opposite by theirs. And all the judges in these countries is unjust too – oh yes, my dear, and that's why the people write in their petitions: "Judge me, thou unrighteous judge!" And there's another country where the people all has heads like dogs.

GLASHA: Dogs' heads? Why's that, then?

FEKLUSHA: It's 'cause they're infidels, of course. Well, anyway, my dear, I'm off to take a turn round the merchants' houses, see if they've got anything for us poor people. 'Bye for now!

GLASHA: Goodbye!

Feklusha exits.

Well, fancy that – all those countries! The world's full of wonders, right enough. And we're stuck here, and we don't know nothing. It's just as well there's some good people about, or we'd never hear what's happening in the wide world. If it weren't for them, we'd stay fools till our dying day.

Enter Katerina and Varvara.

VARVARA: Take that bundle out to the cart, Glasha, the horses are ready. *(to Katerina)* You were married off too soon, you'd no chance to have a good time when you were single, that's why your heart hasn't settled yet.

Glasha exits.

KATERINA: And it never will settle.

VARVARA: Why not?

KATERINA: Because that's how I'm made – hot-blooded. I
remember when I was no more than six – you wouldn't believe
what I did! Someone had upset me at home, and it was evening,
already dark, and I ran out to the Volga, climbed into a boat, and
shoved off from the bank. They found me next morning, six or
seven miles downstream!

VARVARA: Anyway, didn't the young lads give you the eye?

KATERINA: Ho, didn't they just!

VARVARA: And what about you? Weren't you in love with anybody?

KATERINA: No, I just laughed at them.

VARVARA: You know, Katya – you're not in love with Tikhon.

KATERINA: What do you mean? I feel sorry for him.

VARVARA: No, you don't love him. If you feel sorry for him, that
means you don't love him. There's nothing there, if you want the
truth. And it's no use trying to hide it from me. I noticed a long
time ago you were in love with another man.

KATERINA: *(alarmed)* How could you have noticed?

VARVARA: Oh, Katya, don't be ridiculous. I'm not a child. I mean,
there's the first sign – the minute you see him, your whole
expression changes. And that's not the only sign...

KATERINA: Well, who is he?

VARVARA: You know perfectly well. Why should I name him?

KATERINA: No, tell me! Tell me his name!

VARVARA: It's Boris... Boris Grigorich.

KATERINA: Oh, Varya, yes, yes – that's him! Oh, Varya, for God's
sake, please don't...

VARVARA: As if I would! No, no – just watch out you don't give yourself away.

KATERINA: I can't deceive anybody, I've no idea how to hide anything.

VARVARA: Well, you can't get by without deception. Just remember where you're living. Our entire household is built on lies. I never used to lie, but I learned how, when I had to. Listen, Katya, I saw him when I was out last night, and spoke to him.

KATERINA: Well?

VARVARA: He sends his regards. And he said it was a pity there was nowhere you could meet.

KATERINA: Where on earth should we meet? What for?

VARVARA: He looked so lonely...

KATERINA: No, don't talk to me about him, please – don't say any more. I don't want to know him. I'm going to love my husband. Oh, Tisha darling, I wouldn't change you for anyone. I didn't even want to think about this, you're getting me all confused.

VARVARA: Well, don't think about it. No-one's forcing you.

KATERINA: You've no feeling for me at all. Don't think about it, you say, but you yourself bring it up. D'you suppose I want to think about it? But what can I do if I can't get him out of my mind? It doesn't matter what I try to think about, he's there all the time, in my mind's eye. I wish I could control myself, but I just can't. I'll tell you something, Varya – Satan tempted me again last night. I almost ran out of the house.

VARVARA: God help you, Katya, you're so mixed up. As far as I'm concerned, you do what you like, as long as it's kept well hidden.

KATERINA: No, I don't want to be like that. That's a fine thing! I'd rather just put up with it, for as long as I can.

VARVARA: And when you can't, what'll you do then?

KATERINA: What'll I do?

VARVARA: Yes, what'll you do?

KATERINA: I'll do whatever I want.

VARVARA: Huh, you try it, they'll eat you alive in this place.

KATERINA: Will they now? Well, I'll just walk out, and disappear.

VARVARA: And where will you go? You're a married woman.

KATERINA: Oh, Varya, Varya, you really don't know me, do you. I mean, God forbid that it should ever happen, but if life becomes truly unbearable, nothing on this earth will keep me here. I'll jump out of a window, or throw myself into the Volga. If I don't want to live here, then I won't, no matter what.

   A silence.

VARVARA: Listen, Katya – once Tikhon's gone, let's sleep in the garden tonight, in the summerhouse.

KATERINA: Why?

VARVARA: Well, why not? What difference does it make?

KATERINA: I'm frightened. I don't like sleeping in a strange place.

VARVARA: What's to be frightened of? Glasha'll be with us.

KATERINA: I don't know, I'm a bit uneasy. Oh, all right.

VARVARA: I wouldn't have asked you, but mama won't let me go alone, and I've got to.

KATERINA: Why have you got to?

VARVARA: *(laughs)* Well, you and I'll be telling fortunes there.

KATERINA: You're joking, surely.

VARVARA: Of course I am. You didn't think I was serious?

   A silence.

KATERINA: Where on earth's Tikhon?

VARVARA: What d'you want with him?

KATERINA: I'm just wondering. I mean, he'll be leaving soon.

VARVARA: He's sitting cooped up with mama. She'll be eating into him now, like rust into iron.

KATERINA: What on earth for?

VARVARA: For nothing – she'll be teaching him the facts of life, same as usual. Heavens, he'll be gone two weeks, that's two weeks out of her sight! Just think! She'll have palpitations, worrying about him off on his own. So now she'll be giving him his orders, full of threats and menaces, and then she'll make him kneel down in front of an icon, and swear to God that he'll do exactly as she commands.

KATERINA: So he'll still be tied to her apron-strings.

VARVARA: Oh, absolutely. The minute he's out of her sight, he'll start drinking. He'll be listening to her now, and wondering how to get out of her clutches.

Enter Kabanova and Tikhon.

KABANOVA: Now, do you remember what I've told you? See you do remember – get it into your thick skull!

TIKHON: I'll remember, mama.

KABANOVA: Well, that's everything ready now. The horses are waiting, all you've got to do is say goodbye, and be off.

TIKHON: Yes, mama, it's time I was going.

KABANOVA: Well?

TIKHON: What is it, mama?

KABANOVA: What are you standing there for? Don't you know the drill? Give your wife her orders, tell her what she's to do while you're away.

TIKHON: Well, I mean, she knows, mama.

KABANOVA: Are you still arguing! Go on, instruct her! So I can hear too, I want to hear your orders! Then when you come home, you'll be able to ask whether she's carried them all out.

TIKHON: Katya, you've to do what mama tells you.

KABANOVA: Tell her she's not to be rude to her mother-in-law.

TIKHON: And don't be rude.

KABANOVA: She's got to respect her mother-in-law, like her own mother.

TIKHON: Katya, you've to respect mama, like your own mother.

KABANOVA: And not to sit doing nothing, as if she was a grand lady.

TIKHON: And see you work around the house while I'm away.

KABANOVA: And not to sit gazing out of the window.

TIKHON: Mama, when does she ever...

KABANOVA: Go on, go on!

TIKHON: And don't look out of the window.

KABANOVA: And not to make eyes at all the young lads while you're away.

TIKHON: Oh, mama, for heaven's sake!

KABANOVA: Will you never learn! Do what your mother tells you, it's your duty. It's just as well to get these things straight.

TIKHON: *(embarrassed)* And don't be making eyes at the lads.

Katerina glares at him indignantly.

KABANOVA: Right, you can say your piece now in private, if you have to. Come along, Varya!

They exit. Tikhon and Katerina stand as if in a daze.

TIKHON: Katya! Katya, you're not angry with me, are you?

KATERINA: No.

TIKHON: Then why are you being like this? Katya, forgive me.

KATERINA: It's not you. Tisha, she's really hurt me!

TIKHON: Katya, you take everything too much to heart – you'll fall into a consumption if you don't watch out. Don't even listen to her! I mean, she's always got to say something. Let her say what she likes, it'll go in one ear and out the other. Anyway, goodbye, Katya...

KATERINA: Tisha, don't go! For God's sake, don't leave me! Please, darling, don't go!

TIKHON: Katya, I've got to. Heavens, mama's sending me, how can I not go!

KATERINA: Well, take me with you then, please!

TIKHON: I can't.

KATERINA: Tisha, why not? Why can't you?

TIKHON: What fun would that be, dragging you along? I get enough of you women at home, I'm worn out! I can hardly wait to clear off, and here you're still hanging onto me.

KATERINA: Have you really stopped loving me?

TIKHON: No, of course I haven't. But you could have the most beautiful wife in the world, and you'd still want to escape from this prison! You just think, Katya – I may be no great shakes, but I'm a man all the same, and to live my whole life like this, the way you see, well, you'd want to run away from any wife. And now I know I've got two whole weeks, with no threat hanging over me, no chains round my feet, why I should care about a wife?

KATERINA: And how am I supposed to love you, when you say things like that?

TIKHON: What've I said? What else d'you expect me to say? Eh? What are you afraid of? It's not as if you'll be on your own, you'll be staying with mama.

KATERINA: Don't even mention her to me, don't twist the knife in my heart! Oh, God help me! Oh, I'm so miserable, what am I going to do? Who can I turn to? Save me, blessed saints!

TIKHON: Katya, for God's sake!

KATERINA: Oh, Tisha darling, if you'd only just stay, or take me with you, I'd love you so much, I'd do anything for you, darling, please!

TIKHON: I can't figure you out, Katya, I really can't. One minute I can't get a word out of you, never mind loving, next minute you're all over me.

KATERINA: Tisha, don't leave me, you don't know what you're doing! Something dreadful's going to happen! Something really awful!

TIKHON: Well, that can't be helped, can it. That's just too bad.

KATERINA: Tisha, listen, I know what to do – you make me swear a terrible oath!

TIKHON: An oath? What do you mean?

KATERINA: Like this, listen – I'm to swear that while you're away, I won't speak to any strange man, not on any account, I won't meet anybody, I won't even dare think about anybody, except you, Tisha.

TIKHON: What on earth for?

KATERINA: Tisha, just put my mind at ease, do me this one favour, please.

TIKHON: Katya, you can't commit yourself to something like that. All sorts of ideas come into a person's head.

KATERINA: *(falls to her knees)* May I never see my mother and father again! May I die unrepentant, if I even...

TIKHON: *(lifting her up)* Katya, what are you doing! For God's sake! That's sinful! I don't want to hear it!

> *Kabanova is heard off-stage: "It's time you were going, Tikhon!" Enter Kabanova, Varvara and Glasha.*

KABANOVA: Right, Tikhon, time you were off, and Godspeed. Sit down, everybody!

> *They all sit in silence a few moments.*

Now, say goodbye!

TIKHON: Goodbye, mama!

KABANOVA: *(points to the ground at her feet)* Aren't you going to bow?

Tikhon bows, then kisses his mother.

Say goodbye to your wife.

TIKHON: Goodbye, Katya.

Katerina falls on his neck.

KABANOVA: What on earth are you doing, you shameless creature!
It's not a lover you're parting with, it's your husband, your lord
and master! Don't you know anything? Bow to him, go on!

Katerina bows.

TIKHON: Goodbye, dear sister. *(kisses Varvara)* Goodbye, Glasha.
(kisses Glasha) Goodbye, mama. *(bows to her)*

KABANOVA: Goodbye. The longer the leave-taking, the longer the
weeping.

Tikhon exits, followed by Katerina, Varvara and Glasha.

These young people, huh! It'd make you laugh, just looking at
'em. Oh yes, if they weren't my own, I'd die laughing. They don't
know nothing, they've no idea of what's right. Don't even know
how to say a proper goodbye. Just as well they've got old 'uns at
home, to keep 'em in order, while they're still alive. Silly fools that
they are, they want their own way, yes, and when they get it, well,
you see what a mess they make, it's a disgrace – decent people just
laugh at 'em. There's some as'll feel sorry for 'em, of course, but
most folks just laugh, and no wonder. They invite people, and
they've no idea how to sit them at table – half the time they'll even
forget their own kith and kin. Ridiculous, that's what it is! Yes, the
old ways is dying out. There's some houses you wouldn't set foot
in these days. And if you should do, why, you'd spit in disgust and
clear off out, as quick as you like. As for what'll happen, who'll
keep the world upright, once the old folks dies off, God only
knows. Well, I won't be around to see it, I'm glad to say.

Enter Katerina and Varvara.

Huh, so much for all your bragging about how much you love
your husband! I can see what your love's worth now. Any decent
wife as'd just seen off her man would've lain on the porch and
howled for an hour and a half, but not you, obviously.

KATERINA: Why should I? Anyway, I don't know how. And I don't want to make a fool of myself.

KABANOVA: There's no great art to it. If you really loved him, you'd soon learn it. And if you don't know what's what, you might at least have the decency to make a show, but no, it's all just words with you. Well, I'm off now to say my prayers, and mind you don't disturb me.

VARVARA: I think I'll go out, mama.

KABANOVA: *(affectionately)* And why shouldn't you? Off you go, my dear, enjoy yourself while you still can. You'll be stuck at home soon enough.

Kabanova and Varvara exit.

KATERINA: The house'll be as silent as the grave now. Oh, it's so boring! If only there were some children – anybody's children. What a pity I have none of my own – at least I could sit and play with them. I love talking with children – they're such angels. I wish I'd died when I was little. I'd have been able to look down from heaven and take pleasure in everything I saw. Or else I could fly wherever I wished, invisible. I'd fly down into the fields, and flutter on the breeze from one cornflower to the next, like a butterfly. I know what I'll do. I'll make a vow, and start work on some task or other, I'll go to the shops and buy some linen to make shirts, then I'll give them away to the poor. They'll pray to God for me. Varya and I'll sit together sewing, and we won't even notice the time passing. Tisha'll be home before we know it.

Enter Varvara.

VARVARA: *(puts on her headscarf at a mirror)* I think I'll go for a walk now. Glasha's going to make up beds for us in the garden, mama's allowing her. There's a little gate beyond the raspberry bushes, and mama always keeps it locked, and hides the key. I've managed to get hold of it, and put another key in its place, so she won't notice. Here, take it, it might come in handy. If I see him, I'll tell him he's got to come to the gate.

KATERINA: *(alarmed, refuses the key)* What for? No, I don't need it! Keep it!

VARVARA: Well, if you don't want it, I do. Go on, take it, it won't bite.

KATERINA: Heavens, what are you up to, you shameless creature? How can you? What are you thinking of? Varya, for God's sake!

VARVARA: Oh, I can't be bothered arguing – I haven't got the time. I'm going for a walk. *(exits)*

KATERINA: What is she doing? Just exactly what is she up to? She's crazy, she really is. And look at this – this is my destruction! I'll get rid of it, I'll throw it away, I'll fling it in the river where no-one'll ever find it. Oh God, it's burning my fingers like a hot coal. Yes, that's how women like us are ruined. You think it's fun, being imprisoned like this? All kinds of ideas come into your mind. And if an opportunity arises, well, some women would be delighted – they'd jump at the chance. But how can they do that, without thinking, without weighing the consequences? One fatal step, that's all it takes. Then you'll spend the rest of your life weeping, torturing yourself. Imprisonment will seem even more bitter. And it *is* bitter, oh God, it's a hard, bitter thing, never to be free! Who wouldn't weep? And no-one weeps more than a woman. Look at me now. I go on living, and suffering, without ever seeing a chink of light. And I never shall, I know that. The longer I live, the worse it'll get. And now I have this sin on my conscience. If it weren't for my mother-in-law!... She's crushed my spirit. Because of her I've grown to loathe even her house – the very walls disgust me. *(looks at the key)* Get rid of it? Of course, I must get rid of it. How did it come to fall into my hands? To tempt me – to tempt me to my ruin. Oh God, someone's coming. My heart's starting to pound. *(puts the key in her pocket)* No. There's no-one there. Why was I so frightened? And I've hidden the key. Well, it seems I knew what to do. Obviously, it's what fate itself wants. Anyway, where's the harm in just looking at him, just once, from a distance. Or if I even spoke to him, what's so terrible about that? All right, I did promise my husband... but Tisha himself didn't want me to. And maybe I'll never have a chance like this again. Yes, you'll feel sorry for yourself then – you had the chance, and you didn't take it. What am I saying? Why am I trying to deceive myself? I'd gladly die, if I could even just see him. Who am I putting on this act for? Get rid of the key? No, not for anything in the world! It's mine now – and I'll see Boris tonight no matter what happens! Oh, if only the night would come quickly!...

ACT THREE

SCENE ONE

The street outside the Kabanov house. Kabanova and Feklusha are stting on a bench in front of the gate.

FEKLUSHA: Yes, these are the last days, ma'am – we're in the last days now, all the signs are there, it's the end of the world. It's still quiet in your town, ma'am, a paradise on earth, but it's absolute bedlam in some places – noise and rushing around, carriages everywhere, people driving back and forth non-stop.

KABANOVA: Well, we're in no hurry to get any place, my dear – we take our time.

FEKLUSHA: No no, ma'am, the reason your town's so quiet, is that so many people – take your goodself, for instance – are adorned with virtue, like a garland of flowers. That's why everything's so peaceful, and orderly. I mean, what's all this rushing around signify, eh? It signifies vanity, that's what! You just look at Moscow – people running here, there and everywhere, and they haven't a clue what for. That's vanity, that is. They're a vain people, ma'am, that's why they can't sit still. Yes, they think they're running after business, some poor wretch, in a tearing hurry, he doesn't even see people in the street, he imagines he's wanted some place, and then when he gets there it's all just a dream, there's nothing for him. And he goes into a decline. Another one'll think he's catching up on some acquaintance, and of course somebody else, looking on from the side, as it were, can see there's nobody there at all, it's vanity as makes him think different. You know, vanity's like a kind of fog. I mean, even on a lovely night like this, there's not many people in this town as'll sit for a while outside their gate. In Moscow, though, they'll be having a high old time, dancing and playing games, and the noise on the streets, well, you wouldn't believe – it'd give you earache. And if that's not bad enough, ma'am, they've got one of them fiery dragon things harnessed up. And all for the sake of speed.

KABANOVA: So I've heard, my dear.

FEKLUSHA: Well, I've seen it with my own eyes, ma'am. Of course, some folks, on account of vanity, thinks it's an engine they're looking at, they even call it an engine. But I've seen the way it runs along on its paws, like so... *(spreads open her fingers to demonstrate)* And it roars, too, decent people can hear it.

KABANOVA: Well, you can call it whatever you like – call it an engine
if you want – people are stupid, they'll believe anything. But I
wouldn't ride on one, suppose you were to shower me with gold.

FEKLUSHA: God forbid, ma'am! May the Lord preserve us from
that extremity. And there was something else, ma'am – a certain
vision I had in Moscow. I was walking along one morning early,
the sun was just coming up, and I sees on top of this great tall
building, up on the roof, ma'am, I sees this creature standing
there, with a black face. I'm sure I don't need to tell you who he
was! And he was doing something with his hands, like as if he was
scattering something, only there was nothing there. But I was onto
it right away, ma'am – he was sowing tares, ma'am, the seeds of
sin, and of course they're invisible, folks can't see them later on in
the day, but they pick them up, 'cause of vanity. Yes, that's why
they rush around so much, that's why Moscow women are so
skinny. Their bodies don't ever get fat, ma'am, and it's like as if
they've lost something, they're looking all over the place, and
they've got such long faces, it's really pitiful.

KABANOVA: Well, I don't doubt it, my dear. Nothing surprises me
these days.

FEKLUSHA: No, these are difficult times, ma'am, that's for sure.
And time itself's not what it used to be. It's getting shorter.

KABANOVA: What d'you mean, getting shorter?

FEKLUSHA: 'Course we don't notice it, ma'am, blinded by our
vanity, but there's clever people as have actually observed it –
time's getting shorter. Used to be summers and winters dragged
on for ever, you couldn't wait till they was ended, but now, you've
hardly clapped eyes on 'em, and they've flown past. I mean, the
days and hours is still the same, but the actual time, 'cause of our
sins, is getting shorter. Least, that's what the wise men are saying.

KABANOVA: And things'll get worse, my dear.

FEKLUSHA: Well, I only hope we're not here to see it, ma'am.

KABANOVA: Who knows? We might be.

Enter Dikoy.

KABANOVA: Well then, neighbour, what are you doing wandering
around at this hour?

DIKOY: And who's going to stop me?

KABANOVA: Who'll stop you? Who'd want to?

DIKOY: Right, so there's no argument. You think I'm under
somebody's thumb, eh? Like yours, for instance? What are you
doing out here anyway? What the hell d'you think you're playing at?

KABANOVA: Now look here, don't you go shouting your head off at
me! Find somebody a bit cheaper, 'cause I'll cost you dear, I can
tell you. Go on, get on your way, wherever you were going. Come
on, Feklusha, let's go indoors. *(stands up)*

DIKOY: No, wait, neighbour, hold on. Don't be angry. You'll get
home in plenty of time, it's not as if it was miles away, it's just there.

KABANOVA: Well, if you've some business to discuss, keep your
voice down, and talk sense.

DIKOY: No, I've no business – I'm a little bit drunk, that's all.

KABANOVA: Huh, and you want me to praise you for that?

DIKOY: I'm not looking for praise, or abuse. I'm drunk, and there's
an end to it. There's nothing I can do about it till I sleep it off.

KABANOVA: Then clear off and go to bed.

DIKOY: Clear off where?

KABANOVA: Home, where d'you think?

DIKOY: And suppose I don't want to go home?

KABANOVA: And why not, may I ask?

DIKOY: 'Cause there's a fight going on.

KABANOVA: And who's likely to be fighting there? You're the only
fighter in that place.

DIKOY: Well, what if I am a fighter? What's up with that?

KABANOVA: Eh? Oh, nothing. But it's no great honour, either,
when you spend your whole life fighting with women. So there.

DIKOY: Well then, they ought to do what I tell them. Or maybe you think I ought to do their bidding?

KABANOVA: I'm surprised at you, neighbour – all those people in that house of yours, and they can't seem to please just one man.

DIKOY: Yes, fancy that!

KABANOVA: Anyway, what is it you want?

DIKOY: I want you to talk to me, till I calm down, that's what I want. You're the only one in this whole town as knows how to talk to me.

KABANOVA: Feklusha, go and tell them to fix us something to eat.

Feklusha exits.

We'll have a sit-down.

DIKOY: No, I don't want to go inside, I'm worse when I sit down.

KABANOVA: So what's made you so angry?

DIKOY: It's been like that since first thing this morning.

KABANOVA: Somebody asked you for money, I suppose.

DIKOY: Damn right – they ganged up on me, the buggers – they've been pestering me one after another the whole day.

KABANOVA: Well, they must have good reason.

DIKOY: I know, I know, but what can I do about it, with the sort of temper I've got – what d'you suggest? I mean, I know I've got to hand it over, but I just can't do with a good grace. You're a friend of mine, right? Well, if I owed you money, and you was to come and ask me for it, by God I'd curse you out. I'd give you it, for sure, but I'd curse you out first. It's like you've only got to mention money to me, and my whole insides goes on fire, and that's the truth. And at times like that, well, I'll curse people out for no reason.

KABANOVA: You've got no elders to keep you down, that's why you're such a bully.

DIKOY: Now just be quiet, neighbour, and you listen to me. I'll tell you the kind of things as happen. One time it was Lent, and I was fasting, getting ready for confession, and damn me if Satan himself didn't send some miserable peasant after me, wanting his money for hauling wood. Yes, at a time like that he turns up, just to make me sin. And by God, I sinned all right! I swore like a trooper, I did, you wouldn't believe it, I damn near gave the man a beating. That's the sort of temper I've got, you see? And I had to beg his forgiveness afterwards, go down on my knees, I truly did. That's the God's truth, I got down on my knees to that peasant. That's what that temper of mine does to me: right there in the yard, on my knees in the mud, bowing down in front of everybody.

KABANOVA: So why d'you work up a temper on purpose then, eh? That's not nice, neighbour.

DIKOY: What d'you mean on purpose?

KABANOVA: I've seen you, I know. The minute you see somebody's wanting something, you take it out deliberately on your own family, you fly at them to stir up your rage, 'cause you know right well nobody'll come near you in that mood. And that's a fact, neighbour.

DIKOY: Well, what of it? Nobody likes giving money away.

Enter Glasha.

GLASHA: Supper's on the table, ma'am.

KABANOVA: Anyway, come on in, neighbour. Let's eat what the good Lord has provided.

DIKOY: All right.

KABANOVA: Be my guest.

She allows Dikoy to go first and follows him out. Glasha stands by the gate, her arms folded.

GLASHA: That's surely Boris Grigorich. Is he looking for his uncle? Maybe just out for a walk? Yes, out for a stroll, most like.

Enter Boris.

BORIS: My uncle isn't here, is he?

GLASHA: He is. D'you want to see him?

BORIS: No no, I've been sent to find out where he is, that's all. If
he's here, let him stay, who cares? They're delighted to see the
back of him at home.

GLASHA: He ought to be married to my mistress, she'd soon cut
him down to size. Anyway, I shouldn't be standing here, talking to
you. Goodbye. *(exits)*

BORIS: Oh God, if I could only see her, even just for a second! I can't
go into her house – they don't welcome uninvited guests. What a
life! Here we are living in the same town, practically next door, and
we see each other once a week, at church, or in the street, and that's
all. When a woman gets married here, she might as well be in her
grave, it's the same thing. It'd be easier for me if I didn't see her at
all. Seeing her this way, once in a while, and always in public, always
a hundred pairs of eyes trained on us... it just breaks the heart. I
don't know what to do with myself. Whenever I go out for a walk I
end up here, at her gate. Why should I come here? I can't ever see
her, and anyway, people would talk, and she'd get into trouble. God,
what a town I've landed in.

Kuligin enters, comes towards him.

KULIGIN: Well, sir – out for a walk?

BORIS: Yes, just taking a stroll, it's such a fine evening.

KULIGIN: It is indeed, sir, lovely evening for a stroll. It's so quiet,
the air's splendid, the smell of the flowers coming off the meadows
over the Volga, the clear sky...

There stood infinity, with stars replete,
Unnumbered stars – unfathomable deep!

Let's go for a walk on the boulevard, sir – there won't be a soul
there now.

BORIS: Yes, let's.

KULIGIN: You see the kind of town we have, sir? They've made a
boulevard, and nobody uses it, except on Sundays, and then it's only
for show – yes, they'll walk along it then, to parade their new clothes.
We're not likely to run into anybody but the odd drunken clerk,
staggering home from the pub. And poor folks don't have time for
walks, sir, they've got to work night and day. They're lucky if they get
three hours sleep of a night. As for the rich – well, you'd think they'd

be out, wouldn't you, for a breath of fresh air. No, not them. They've locked their gates long ago, sir, and turned the dogs loose. And you think they're at some useful business, or praying to God, maybe? No, sir! And it's not 'cause of thieves they've locked themselves in, but so people won't see how they terrorise their servants, yes, and bully their own families. Oh yes, there's plenty of tears shed behind those gates, unseen and unheard! Still, I don't have to tell you, sir. You've seen it for yourself. And the sort of drunkenness and debauchery that goes on behind those locked doors, sir – all done on the quiet, so nobody ever gets wind of it – well, only God sees that! You can have a look at me in company, they say, or on the street, but my family's none of your business – I've got bolts and bars, yes, and vicious dogs to keep that private, that's my secret! But we know all about these secrets – there's only one person gets any joy from secrets like that, and the rest can howl at the moon. And just what exactly is it, that private life? As if we don't know – robbing orphans, their own kith and kin, nephews, beating servants senseless, so they won't dare utter a squeak about what's going on. Yes, that's their secret, the sum total. Well, let them do what they like. D'you know, sir, the only people you'll see enjoying themselves in our town? The young lads and lasses – yes, they'll steal an hour or two from sleep, to go out for a walk together. Look, there's a young couple now.

Kudryash and Varvara appear. They stop to kiss.

BORIS: They're kissing.

KULIGIN: Well, we don't mind that here.

Kudryash exits, and Varvara walks up to her own gate and beckons to Boris. He approaches.

I'll go down to the boulevard, sir, and leave you in peace. I'll wait for you there.

BORIS: Thanks, I won't be a minute.

Kuligin exits.

VARVARA: *(covers her face with her headscarf)* Do you know the gully at the back of the Kabanovs' garden?

BORIS: Yes.

VARVARA: Come there later tonight.

BORIS: Why?

VARVARA: Are you stupid? Just come, you'll find out why. Anyway, you'd better go now – Kuligin's waiting for you.

> *Boris exits.*

And he didn't even recognise me! He'll be racking his brains now. Well, when the time comes, Katerina won't be able to resist, she'll jump at the chance! *(exits through the gate)*

SCENE TWO

Night. A gully, overgrown with bushes; at the top end, the Kabanovs' garden fence and wicket gate, and a path leading down from it. Kudryash enters with a guitar.

KUDRYASH: Nobody here. Where on earth is she? Well, I'll just have a seat while I wait. Yes, let's sing a song to pass the time...

Oh, a Cossack to water his horse has led,
A brave Don Cossack, stood by the gate,
Stood by the gate, and one thought in his head,
One thought in his head, kill the wife he hates,
And his wife, his poor wife, how she begs her man,
Kneels down before him, fleetfooted and strong:
'Show mercy , dear husband, as only you can.
Kill me not yet, you may kill me ere long,
Kill me this midnight, let our little ones sleep,
Let our dear little ones their innocence keep...'

> *Enter Boris.*

KUDRYASH: Well, look who it is! Meek and mild, and here he's out on the tiles too.

BORIS: Is that you, Kudryash?

KUDRYASH: It is indeed, sir.

BORIS: What are you doing here?

KUDRYASH: Me? Well, I must've a good reason, sir, or I wouldn't be here. So what on earth brings you here?

BORIS: Look, Kudryash, I've got to stay here, and well – if it's all the same to you, I'd rather you found another spot.

KUDRYASH: No thanks, sir – I can see this is your first time here, but I've practically worn this seat out, and beaten my own little path to this place. I'm quite fond of you, sir, and I'm willing to oblige you, but you'd best not bump into me on this road at night, or God forbid, you'll get something you hadn't bargained for. Persuasion's better than money, they say.

BORIS: Vanya, what's got into you?

KUDRYASH: What's all this Vanya stuff? All right, my name's Vanya, but you'd better clear off, that's all I've got to say. Find somebody of your own, have a good time with her, and it's nobody else's business. But keep your hands off other people's! That's not done around here, unless you want your legs broke. If it was mine – well, I don't know what I'd do – cut your throat, most like!

BORIS: You've no need to get angry with me. I've no intention of stealing your girl. I wouldn't even have come here, if I hadn't been told to.

KUDRYASH: So who told you?

BORIS: I couldn't make out, it was too dark. A young woman stopped me in the street and told me I should come here without fail, behind the Kabanovs' garden, where the path is.

KUDRYASH: Who on earth could it have been?

BORIS: Listen, Kudryash – if I tell you something in private, you won't spread it around?

KUDRYASH: Go ahead, you needn't worry. Your secret's safe with me.

BORIS: I don't know anything here, about your local ways and customs, but the fact is...

KUDRYASH: You've fallen in love, right?

BORIS: Yes.

KUDRYASH: Well, there's nothing wrong with that. We're pretty free about these things. The girls round here do what they like, their folks don't interfere. It's only the married women as sits locked up at home.

BORIS: That's just the trouble.

KUDRYASH: Don't tell me you've fallen for a married woman?

BORIS: I have indeed, Kudryash.

KUDRYASH: Oh God, sir, you'd best drop her.

BORIS: That's easy to say, drop her. Maybe it doesn't matter to you – drop this one, pick up that one – but I can't do that. Once I've fallen in love...

KUDRYASH: Sir, you don't know what that means – you'll ruin her completely, is that what you want?

BORIS: No, no, God forbid, never! No, Kudryash, how could I? D'you think I want to ruin her? I only want to see her, that's all – just to see her.

KUDRYASH: Ah yes, sir, but you can't be sure of yourself, can you. And you know what people are like round here. They'll eat her alive, they'll drive her into an early grave.

BORIS: Don't say that, Kudryash, please, you're scaring me.

KUDRYASH: So, does she love you?

BORIS: I don't know.

KUDRYASH: Well, have you met her any time?

BORIS: Only once, when I was at her house with my uncle. And I see her at church, and now and again on the boulevard. Oh, Kudryash, if you could just see her at her prayers. Such an angelic smile on her lips, it's as if her whole face is lit up.

KUDRYASH: That must be Tikhon Kabanov's young wife, right?

BORIS: Yes, it is.

KUDRYASH: Well, well, so that's how things stand, eh? Allow me to congratulate you, sir.

BORIS: On what?

KUDRYASH: What d'you think? If she's invited you to come here, that means your little affair's moving along nicely.

BORIS: Did she really invite me?

KUDRYASH: Well, who else?

BORIS: No, you must be joking. It's not possible.

KUDRYASH: What's the matter with you?

BORIS: I think I'll go mad with joy.

KUDRYASH: Good God, you've got nothing much to go mad about. Just be careful you don't make trouble for yourself, yes, and ruin her into the bargain. That husband of hers might be an idiot, but her mother-in-law's a holy terror.

Varvara enters through the wicket gate, singing.

VARVARA: Across the river, the rapid river,
My Vanya must ply,
My darling Vanya, 'cross the river...

KUDRYASH: Fine goods for to buy... *(whistles)*

Varvara comes down the path, her face hidden by a scarf, and approaches Boris.

VARVARA: Wait here, my lad, and something might turn up. *(to Kudryash)* Let's walk down to the Volga.

KUDRYASH: What on earth's kept you all this time? Keeping me waiting, indeed! You know I don't like that.

Varvara puts her arm around him and they walk off.

BORIS: This is like some kind of dream! This night, these songs and meetings. Young people walking arm in arm. This is all so new to me, such joy, it's wonderful. And here I am waiting too. But what I'm waiting for I've no idea, I can't imagine, yet my heart is pounding and every fibre of my being is trembling. I can't even think what I'm going to say to her, I can scarcely breathe, and my knees are giving way beneath me. Oh God, this foolish heart of mine – once it's set aflame, nothing will put it out. Wait, someone's coming!

Katerina comes quietly down the path, her face concealed by a large white scarf and her eyes downcast. A silence.

Katerina Petrovna, is that you? I don't even know how to thank you. Oh, Katerina, if you only knew how much I love you! *(tries to take her hand)*

KATERINA: *(alarmed)* No, don't touch me, don't touch me!

BORIS: Don't be angry.

KATERINA: Go away! Get away from me, you wretched man. I'll never be forgiven for this sin, you know that, however much I pray. It lies like a stone on my heart.

BORIS: Please, don't send me away!

KATERINA: Why have you come here? To ruin me? I'm a married woman, I've got to live with my husband until death do us part.

BORIS: But you yourself asked me to come.

KATERINA: Don't you understand? You're my enemy. Till death do us part!

BORIS: I wish I'd never set eyes on you.

KATERINA: Oh God, what have I done? What am I storing up for myself?

BORIS: Katerina, keep calm. Sit down.

KATERINA: Why do you want to ruin me?

BORIS: How can I want to ruin you when I love you more than anything on this earth, more than my very self?

KATERINA: No, no, you've destroyed me!

BORIS: Katerina, do you really think I'm evil?

KATERINA: No, no, you've destroyed me, you've ruined me!

BORIS: God forbid such a thing, Katerina. I'd rather destroy myself!

KATERINA: But you've already ruined me – why else would I leave the house at night to come to you?

BORIS: You did that of your own free will.

KATERINA: I have no free will. If I had any will of my own I wouldn't have come. It's your will I obey now, can't you see?

She suddenly flings herself into his arms.

BORIS: Oh, my life!

KATERINA: You know something? I want to die now, this very moment.

BORIS: Why die, when life is so sweet?

KATERINA: No, there's no life for me. I know that already.

BORIS: Katerina, please don't say things like that, don't make me sad...

KATERINA: It's easy for you, you're a free man, but I...

BORIS: No-one will ever know about our love. I'll be careful for your sake, you must believe me.

KATERINA: Why should you care about me? I've no-one to blame but myself. I've done this of my own accord. No, don't feel sorry for me, go ahead and ruin me! Let them all know, let them all see what I'm doing! If I'm not afraid to commit this sin, why should I fear their judgment? People say it's even easier, when you have to suffer here on earth for your sins.

BORIS: Anyway, let's not think about that, when we're so happy now.

KATERINA: Yes! Yes! I'll have plenty of time to think later, yes, and to weep.

BORIS: And I was so afraid you were going to send me away.

KATERINA: Send you away? How could I, with my woman's heart? If you hadn't come to me, I think I'd have come to you myself.

BORIS: I had no idea you loved me.

KATERINA: I've loved you for a very long time. It's as if you came here to be my downfall. The moment I saw you I was no longer my own person. From that very first moment, you only had to beckon and I'd have followed you to the ends of the earth, without so much as a backward glance.

BORIS: Will your husband be gone for long?

KATERINA: Two weeks.

BORIS: So we'll see a good deal of each other. We'll have plenty of time.

KATERINA: Yes, we shall. And then... If they lock me up, that'll be my death. But if they don't, I'll surely find some way of seeing you.

Enter Kudryash and Varvara.

VARVARA: Well, have you two managed to agree?

Katerina hides her face against Boris' chest.

BORIS: We have.

VARVARA: Well, you go for a walk and we'll wait here. Vanya'll give a shout when it's time to go.

Boris and Katerina exit. Kudryash and Varvara sit down on a stone.

KUDRYASH: That was a smart idea you two had, slipping through the garden gate. Very convenient for us lads.

VARVARA: It was my idea.

KUDRYASH: Anyway, it was nicely done. You're sure that mother of yours won't catch on?

VARVARA: Her? No, it'd never enter her head.

KUDRYASH: And what if it should, just out of spite?

VARVARA: No, she sleeps like a log the first half of the night – she doesn't start to wake up till morning.

KUDRYASH: Yes, that's all you know, but supposing the devil gives her a shake?

VARVARA: So what? The gate's locked from the inside, from the garden side, she'll just keep knocking and eventually go away. And in the morning we'll tell her we were so sound asleep we couldn't hear her. Anyway, Glasha's keeping an eye out, she'll give us a shout if anything happens. You've got to take precautions, you know. You need to be careful, or you can get into serious trouble.

Kudryash strums a few chords on his guitar, and Varvara lays her head on his shoulder. He pays her no attention, goes on softly playing.

VARVARA: *(yawns)* I wonder what time it is?

KUDRYASH: It's after twelve.

VARVARA: How d'you know?

KUDRYASH: The watchman rang his bell.

VARVARA: It's time we were going. Give those two a shout. We'll come earlier tomorrow, have a bit more time.

KUDRYASH: *(whistles, and starts singing loudly)*
   Time to go home, time to go home,
   Not for me, I'd much rather roam!

BORIS: *(off-stage)* I can hear you!

VARVARA: Well, goodbye then. See you come a bit earlier tomorrow. *(calls to Boris and Katerina)* You'd better say goodbye now – you're not parting forever, you'll see each other tomorrow.

Katerina comes running up, followed by Boris.

KATERINA: *(to Varvara)* Come on, let's go now. Goodbye!

BORIS: Till tomorrow!

KATERINA: Yes, till tomorrow! And you can tell me what you dream about tonight!

BORIS: Yes, I shall!

KUDRYASH: *(singing and playing his guitar)*
   Have fun, sweet maiden, while you may,
   This evening till the close of day;
   Sweet maiden, what you will, you may,
   This evening till the close of day...

VARVARA: Oh yes, my love, and while I may,
   I'll love until the break of day,
   For I shall love you while I may,

This evening till the close of day... *(exits)*

KUDRYASH: And not until the dawn's bright glow,
Only then I'll homeward go...

END OF ACT THREE

ACT FOUR

In the foreground is a narrow vaulted gallery of an ancient building, now beginning to crumble, with weeds and bushes springing up here and there. Through the arches can be seen the banks of the Volga, and beyond. A few strollers pass by on the other side of the arches.

1ST MAN: That's the rain coming on, d'you think there's a storm brewing?

2ND MAN: Yes, look at it.

1ST MAN: Just as well we've got somewhere to shelter here.

They walk underneath the arches.

WOMAN: Heavens, what a crowd of people on the boulevard! It's Sunday of course, they're taking the air. And the way these merchants' wives are dressed up!

1ST MAN: They'll be looking for a place to hide in a minute.

2ND MAN: Yes, you'll see, they'll come rushing in here now.

1ST MAN: You know, there used to be paintings on these walls. You can still make them out in places.

2ND MAN: Yes, of course there were. It's only natural they'd be painted. Only now, you see, it's all been let go, it's falling apart, weeds growing everywhere. They never put it right after that big fire. You won't remember the fire, it'd be about forty year ago now.

1ST MAN: So what d'you reckon would've been painted here, friend? It's quite difficult to make it out.

2ND MAN: Well, that's the fires of Hell, isn't it.

1ST MAN: You don't say!

2ND MAN: And that's people going into 'em, from all walks of life.

1ST MAN: Right, right, I can see that now.

2ND MAN: All classes of people, too.

1ST MAN: And black people?

2ND MAN: Oh yes.

1ST MAN: And what's this, friend?

2ND MAN: That's the great Lithuanian disaster. A great battle, you see? That's us fighting the Lithuanians.

1ST MAN: So what's Lithuanians?

2ND MAN: Well, Lithuanians is... Lithuanians, my friend.

1ST MAN: They say they fell on us right out of the sky.

2ND MAN: Well, that I couldn't say. Maybe it was out of the sky.

1ST MAN: You're surely not going to argue? Everybody knows they came out of the sky – there's graves piled high with 'em, marking the spot where the battle was.

2ND MAN: Anyway, there you are, friend. That's exactly how it was.

Enter Dikoy, followed by Kuligin, hatless. Everyone bows to Dikoy, and assumes a respectful pose.

DIKOY: Damn it to hell, I'm wet through! *(to Kuligin)* Get out of my sight, go on, bugger off! Stupid creature!

KULIGIN: But, sir, please, your honour – don't you see it would be of benefit to the whole community?

DIKOY: Go to hell! What benefit? Who needs your benefit?

KULIGIN: Why, you yourself, your honour – and we could erect it here on the boulevard, on this open space. And as for the cost, well, it'd be practically nothing: a little stone pillar, with a little bronze table, round like this, and a style to cast a shadow, absolutely straightforward, couldn't be simpler. And I'll assemble it all myself, sir, and carve the numbers, too. So now when your honour goes for a walk, or if other people do likewise, they can come up here and see what time it is. I mean, this is a lovely spot, sir, with a fine view and everything, but it's a bit bare. And there's people passing through the town too, your honour, as comes here to look at the view, and it'd be an ornament for them, something nice to look at.

DIKOY: Why d'you keep bothering me with this drivel? Maybe I don't even want to talk to you. You should find out if I'm in the mood to listen or not, you old fool. D'you think I'm your equal or something? Good God, this is really important business he's found! And so he marches straight up and pokes his ugly snout into mine, wants a discussion, no less!

KULIGIN: I'm sorry, sir, but if it had been my own business, yes, I would've been at fault. But it's for the general good, your honour. And what's ten roubles for the whole community? That's all we need, sir, nothing more.

DIKOY: Maybe you're out to steal it for yourself, who knows?

KULIGIN: Your honour, I'm offering my labour free of charge, how can I be stealing it? And everybody knows me besides, nobody has a bad word to say about me.

DIKOY: Fine, let them know you, I don't want to.

KULIGIN: Sir, why should you insult an honest man?

DIKOY: What, you think I'm accountable to you? I'm accountable to nobody, not even a damn sight bigger than you. I'll think whatever I like about you, and that's that. You might be an honest man to other people, but as far as I'm concerned you're a scoundrel, and there's an end to it. Is that what you wanted to hear from me? Well, you listen to this – I say you're a villain, through and through. Now what are you going to do – sue me? Well, you just remember, you're nothing but a worm. If I feel like it, I'll spare you – if I don't, I'll crush you underfoot!

KULIGIN: Well, God have mercy on you, sir – I'm a poor man, true enough, you can easily insult me, but let me tell you this, your honour: Virtue deserves respect, even in rags and tatters!

DIKOY: Don't you dare talk back to me, d'you hear!

KULIGIN: I'm not talking back to you, sir. I only brought this up in case you might some day want to do something for the town. You've got the means, your honour, if you only had the will to do a good deed. I mean, take our present condition – we have thunderstorms all the time, and yet we don't put up lightning rods.

DIKOY: Worthless rubbish!

KULIGIN: They're not rubbish, sir, there's been experiments.

DIKOY: What sort of lightning rods are you talking about?

KULIGIN: Steel ones, sir.

DIKOY: So? Go on!

KULIGIN: Steel rods.

DIKOY: Yes, yes, rods, I heard you, you stupid cretin! Rods, you say – so what else? Is that all?

KULIGIN: That's all, sir.

DIKOY: Really? So what's a thunderstorm in your opinion? Eh? Come on, out with it!

KULIGIN: Electricity, sir.

DIKOY: Elastricity, what the hell's that! And you tell me you're not a scoundrel? Storms are sent to us for a punishment, to make us think twice, and you'd have us try and escape them, God forbid, with your damn rods and feelers! What are you, some sort of heathen? Eh? Is that what you are, a heathen? A bloody Tartar?

KULIGIN: Forgive me, your honour, but in the words of the poet Derzhavin:
What though my body to dust decay,
My mind the thunder does obey!

DIKOY: You ought to be hauled up in front of the mayor for words like that, he'd soon sort you out! Hey, citizens! Decent people – just listen to what this man's saying!

KULIGIN: Oh, what's the use, I give up. But one of these days, when I've got money, then I'll speak out. *(exits)*

DIKOY: What, are you going to steal it from somebody? Hold him, don't let him get away! Miserable two-faced peasant! Dear God, how are you supposed to stay human with people like that around? *(to the bystanders)* You too, you swine, you'd drive anybody to sin! I'd no intention of losing my temper today, but he's just infuriated me, it's as if it's deliberate. Damn him to hell! Well, has it stopped raining or what?

1ST MAN: I think it's stopped, sir.

DIKOY: You think? Well, go and have a look, you bloody idiot. Huh, he thinks!

1ST MAN: *(emerging from under the arches)* It's stopped.

> *Dikoy exits, followed by the others. The stage is deserted a few moments, then Varvara runs on beneath the arches. She hides, and peeps out now and again.*

VARVARA: I think it's him!

> *Boris crosses upstage.*

Psstt! Come over here!

> *She beckons to him and Boris approaches.*

What are we going to do about Katerina? Tell me, for God's sake.

BORIS: What's happened?

VARVARA: Only a disaster, that's all. Her husband's come back, haven't you heard? They weren't expecting him, but he's back home now.

BORIS: I didn't know.

VARVARA: She's just about out of her mind.

BORIS: So I've enjoyed my little bit of life for ten short days, while he's been away. Now I won't even be able to see her!

VARVARA: Shame on you! You listen to me – she's trembling all over, it's as if she's been stricken with a fever. She's white as a sheet, rushing around the house, as if she's searching for something, and her eyes staring like a madwoman's. She started crying this morning, and she's still sobbing! God in heaven, what am I going to do with her?

BORIS: Maybe it'll pass over.

VARVARA: No, not a chance. She doesn't even look at her husband. And mama's begun to take notice, keeps giving her filthy looks, and that only makes her worse. It's torture even to look at her. And I'm frightened too.

BORIS: What are you frightened of?

VARVARA: Oh, you don't know Katerina. That's a strange one
we've got, I tell you. She's capable of anything. You've no idea
what she'll do.

BORIS: Oh, my God! What are we going to do? Couldn't you have
a quiet talk with her? Surely you can bring her round?

VARVARA: I've tried, I've tried. She won't listen. There's no point
in going near her.

BORIS: So, what d'you think she might do?

VARVARA: She'll throw herself at her husband's feet and tell him
everything, that's what. And that's what I'm afraid of.

BORIS: No, that's not possible, surely?

VARVARA: Anything's possible with her.

BORIS: Where is she now?

VARVARA: She's gone out for a walk along the boulevard with Tisha, and
mama's with them. You could go there if you want. No, on second
thoughts you'd better not – she might lose her head completely.

A rumble of thunder in the distance.

Is that a thunderstorm? Yes, there's a spot of rain. And look,
there's a crowd of people coming. Hide yourself somewhere, and
I'll stay out here in the open, so they won't get any ideas.

A group of people enter.

1ST MAN: That young woman must be pretty scared, if she's in
such a hurry to hide from the storm.

WOMAN: She can hide all she likes, there's no escaping your fate,
what's written down for you.

KATERINA: *(runs on)* Oh, Varya! Varya!

VARVARA: Stop, stop, what's the matter with you?

KATERINA: Oh Varya, this is the end for me.

VARVARA: Katya, talk sense! Try and think straight, for heaven's sake!

KATERINA: No, no, I can't! I can't do anything, I'm in a dreadful state, my heart's breaking.

KABANOVA: *(entering)* What I say is a person's got to live right, so they're ready for anything. Then they'd have nothing to fear.

TIKHON: And just exactly what sins can she have, mama, eh? The same as the rest of us, I reckon – it's just her nature to be fearful, that's all.

KABANOVA: And how do you know? You can't see into other people's souls.

TIKHON: *(jocularly)* Oh well, of course, while I was away, that's different, but now I'm home, surely...

KABANOVA: Maybe it was while you were away.

TIKHON: Right then, Katya, you'd better confess your sins. You can't hide them from me, you've been up to mischief, and I know all about it.

KATERINA: Oh, my darling!

VARVARA: Stop pestering her, will you! Can't you see it's been hard enough for her with you away?

Boris emerges from the crowd and bows to Tikhon. Katerina cries out.

TIKHON: What are you so frightened about? He's not a stranger, you know. This is a friend of mine. So – how's your uncle these days?

BORIS: He's well, thank God.

KATERINA: *(to Varvara)* What more does he want of me? Isn't it enough that I'm suffering such torment? *(presses herself to Varvara and begins sobbing)*

VARVARA: *(loudly, so her mother will hear)* Huh, we're at our wits' end, we don't know what to do with her, and now complete strangers come poking their noses in!

She gestures to Boris, who withdraws to the far exit. Meanwhile Kuligin steps out into the midst of the crowd, begins addressing them.

KULIGIN: Now then, good people, what is it you're afraid of? Every blade of grass, every flower now rejoices, and here we are in hiding, as if we fear some terrible calamity. Is the storm going to kill us? No, it's not a threat, but a blessing! Yes, a blessing. But you see a threat in everything. When the Northern Lights are shining, we ought to admire them, and marvel at God's infinite wisdom: 'Tis daybreak now in the midnight lands! But you all take fright, and imagine it's an omen of war or death. And when a comet passes by – so beautiful you can't take your eyes off it – we've got used to seeing the stars, they're all the same, but this is absolutely new, and you should gaze on it, yes, and wonder! No, you're too afraid – one glance at the sky, and you're shaking in your shoes! You've managed to turn everything into some sort of bogey. Honestly, what people! Well, look, I'm not afraid. Let's go, sir.

BORIS: Yes, let's. It's more frightening here than outside.

They exit.

KABANOVA: Well, well, that's some fine speech he's delivered. If this is what we've got to listen to, then there's no more to be said. We've come to a pretty pass these days, when teachers like that appear amongst us. If an old man thinks those sort of things, what can we expect from the young?

WOMAN: Look, the whole sky's covered up, it's as if somebody's put a hat on it.

1ST MAN: Look, see, brother, it's as if that cloud's spinning like a ball, with some sort of creature whirling around inside it. And it's creeping towards us, closer and closer, like a living thing!

2ND MAN: Mark my words, friend, this storm hasn't come for nothing. That's the truth I'm telling you, 'cause I know. It's either come to kill somebody, or burn down somebody's house – you just wait and see, yes! Look at the colours, they're not normal, see.

KATERINA: What's that they're saying? They're saying somebody's going to be killed.

TIKHON: Oh, forget it, they say the first thing that comes into their heads.

KABANOVA: And don't you dare criticise your elders! They know better than you. Old people know all the signs. An old man doesn't waste his words.

KATERINA: Tisha, I know who the storm's going to kill.

VARVARA: *(aside, to Katerina)* Shut up, for God's sake!

TIKHON: How do you know?

KATERINA: It's going to kill me. Oh God, Tikhon, pray for me!

> *Enter a Lady with two Footmen. Katerina cries out and tries to hide in the crowd.*

LADY: What are you hiding for? There's no point in hiding. You're frightened, of course you are – you don't want to die. Yes, you want to live! And why shouldn't you, a beautiful young woman like you? Ha ha ha! Beauty, indeed! You should pray God to take away your beauty. It's the ruin of us women, beauty is. You ruin yourself, you tempt other people, that's all the joy you'll get of your beauty. You'll lead people into sin, time and time again. Foolish young men fight duels, pierce each other's bodies with swords. What joy! Old men, men grown old in piety, forget about death, tempted by a pretty face. And who'll answer for it? You will, it's you who are to blame! Far better your pretty face was at the bottom of the river! Go, hurry, hurry! What are you hiding for, you foolish girl? You can't escape God. *(a thunderclap)* You'll all burn forever in the eternal fire! *(exits)*

KATERINA: Oh God, I'm dying!

VARVARA: For God's sake, Katerina, what are you torturing yourself for? Go off and say a prayer somewhere, you'll feel better.

> *Katerina goes up to the wall, kneels, then instantly springs to her feet again.*

KATERINA: Oh, my God! It's Hell! Hell! The fires of Hell!

> *Kabanova, Tikhon and Varvara gather round her.*

My heart's bursting! I can't stand it any longer! Mama! Tikhon! I've sinned before you and before God! Didn't I swear to you that I wouldn't look at anybody while you were away? Don't you remember? And you know what I've done, vile wretch that I am, you know what I've been doing while you were away? That very first night, I slipped out of the house...

TIKHON: *(distracted, in tears, tugs at her sleeve)* No, no, Katya, don't say another word! For God's sake, mama's here!

KABANOVA: Come on, out with it – finish what you've started.

KATERINA: Those ten nights, Tikhon, every one of them, I went with him...

She breaks down sobbing. Tikhon makes to embrace her.

KABANOVA: Don't touch her! Went with whom?

VARVARA: She's making it up, she doesn't know what she's saying.

KABANOVA: Shut up, you! Well, this is very nice. Come on, who was it?

KATERINA: It was Boris Grigorich.

A clap of thunder. Katerina shrieks and faints in her husband's arms.

KABANOVA: Well, son – you see what all your freedom leads to? I warned you, but you wouldn't listen. And now you've got what was coming to you.

END OF ACT FOUR

ACT FIVE

The setting is the same as in Act One. Twilight. Kuligin is sitting on a bench, singing, as Tikhon comes along the boulevard.

KULIGIN: The shades of night have covered o'er the skies,
   As weary people all now close their eyes...

(catches sight of Tikhon) Good evening, sir. Are you going far?

TIKHON: Home, that's all. You'll have heard about my misfortune, neighbour? The whole family's in a mess.

KULIGIN: I did hear about it, sir.

TIKHON: You know I went to Moscow? Well, before I left, mama read me a long lecture about how I was to behave, but the minute I got out of that place I started raising hell. I was just so overjoyed at being free. I was drinking the whole road to Moscow, and the same when I got there, and that's a power of drink, I can tell you. A whole year's worth of hell-raising! I didn't give so much as a thought to them back home. And if I had, it would never have entered my mind, what was going on here. You know what I mean?

KULIGIN: Yes, I've heard, sir.

TIKHON: And now I'm absolutely miserable. My whole life's ruined, and what for? For nothing, nothing worth a light.

KULIGIN: Your mother's a very hard woman, sir.

TIKHON: She is that. And she's the cause of it all. But why am I the one to suffer, tell me that, sir, eh? I've just looked in at Dikoy's place, and well, we had a few drinks – I thought I'd feel better but no, I feel even worse, Kuligin. I mean, what my wife's done to me... it couldn't be worse.

KULIGIN: It's a difficult business, sir. It's not easy to pass judgment.

TIKHON: Eh? No, come on – there's nothing worse than what she's done. Killing's too good for her. Mama says she ought to be buried alive, to make her suffer. But I love her, I can't bear to lay a finger on her. I had to beat her a little, 'cause mama ordered me to, but I feel so sorry for her, can you understand that, Kuligin? Mama's just about eating her alive, and she goes around like a ghost, not saying a word. Does nothing but cry all the time, she's melting away like wax. I tell you, it's killing me just to look at her.

KULIGIN: If only there were some way you could make it up between you, sir. If you could just forgive her, and never cast it up again. After all, it's not as if you're without sin yourself.

TIKHON: You can say that again!

KULIGIN: But you'd never want to reproach her with it, sir, not even when you were under the influence. She'd be an excellent wife to you, sir – you can see for yourself, the very best.

TIKHON: Kuligin, you don't understand – I wouldn't mind at all, but it's mama, and there's no way she'll come round.

KULIGIN: Well, it's about time you lived by your own counsel, sir.

TIKHON: Yes, well, how am I to cut loose, tell me that? I haven't got a mind of my own, they say, so I've got to mind other people. I'll just poison what's left of me with drink, then mama can nurse me, like an idiot.

KULIGIN: Oh, sir, this is terrible, terrible! And what about Boris Grigorich, what's happened to him?

TIKHON: He's going off to Tyakhta, to live among the Chinese, the swine. His uncle's sent him to some merchant he knows there, to work in his office. He'll be gone for three years.

KULIGIN: And how's he taking it, sir?

TIKHON: Well, he's in a state too, crying and so forth. His uncle and me gave it to him hot this morning, swore at him something awful – he didn't say a word, like as if he'd turned into some dumb animal. Do what you like to me, that's all he says, only don't torture her. He feels sorry for her too.

KULIGIN: He's a good man, sir.

TIKHON: Well, he's packed to go now, and the horses are ready. He looks heartbroken, terrible. I can see he's desperate to say goodbye to her. Huh, there's no chance of that. He's done enough harm. I mean, he's my sworn enemy, Kuligin, isn't he. He ought to be hung, drawn and quartered, so's he'd know...

KULIGIN: We're commanded to forgive our enemies, sir.

TIKHON: Yes, well, you go and tell that to mama, see what she
says. Anyway, neighbour, that's our whole family split up now.
We're not like kinfolk now, more like mortal foes to one another.
Mama kept on nagging Varya, till she couldn't stand it any longer,
and you know what she's like, she just up and walked out.

KULIGIN: Where's she gone?

TIKHON: Who knows? They say she's run off with Kudryash, that
Vanya creature, and he's not to be found anywhere either. I'll tell
you straight, Kuligin, this is all mama's fault, 'cause she started
bullying Varya, and tried to keep her under lock and key. "Don't
you dare lock me up," she says, "or it'll be the worse for you!"
Well, that's just what's happened. And what am I to do now, tell
me? How am I going to live now, Kuligin, advise me? I can't abide
that house, it's disgusting, I'm ashamed to meet people, I can't do
a stroke of work, my hands just drop. And here I am on the road
home – d'you think I'm happy about that?

Enter Glasha.

GLASHA: Master Tikhon, sir!

TIKHON: What is it now?

GLASHA: There's trouble at home, master!

TIKHON: God almighty, it's one thing after another. What's up
now, tell me?

GLASHA: It's your good lady, sir...

TIKHON: What is it? She's not dead, is she?

GLASHA: No, sir, no – she's gone off somewhere and nobody can
find her. We've searched high and low, sir, we're worn out.

TIKHON: I'd better go and look for her, Kuligin. You know, what
I'm scared of is that she might do herself an injury out of sheer
misery. God, she's so wretched unhappy, it'd break your heart
even just to look at her. *(to Glasha)* Couldn't you have kept an eye
on her? Has she been gone long?

GLASHA: No, just a little while, master. It's our fault, we weren't watching, but you can't stand guard over somebody every minute.

TIKHON: Well, come on, then, what are you hanging about for, get moving!

Glasha exits.

Come on, Kuligin, we'll go too.

They exit. The scene is deserted a few moments, then Katerina enters from the opposite side and slowly crosses the stage. She speaks her soliloquy in a pensive manner, drawing out her words and repeating them, as if in a trance.

KATERINA: Nowhere. Not a sign of him. I wonder what he's doing now, the poor man? If I could only just say goodbye to him, and then... well, I don't care if I die. Why did I cause him so much trouble? I mean, it hasn't done me any good. I should've perished alone. And now I've ruined myself, and him too, brought dishonour on myself, and eternal disgrace to him. Yes! I've dishonoured myself, and disgraced him. If I could only remember what he said to me. How he took pity on me. The words he spoke. No, I can't remember, I've forgotten everything. The nights, the nights are so terrible. Everyone goes to bed, and I go too – it's nothing to them, but to me it's like going to my grave. The darkness is so terrifying. I hear noises, and singing, as if someone was being buried, only so quietly that I can barely make it out, in the distance, so far away... And when the morning light comes, you're so glad, but you don't want to get up, to the same people, the same talk, the same agony. Why do they keep looking at me like that? Why don't they kill people nowadays? Why did they stop? They used to kill people like me, they say. They would've seized me and flung me into the Volga and I'd have been happy. But now they say, "If we execute you, your sin will be taken away, so you must live on and suffer for it." Oh, and how much I've suffered! How much longer can I go on like this? What have I got to live for now, what reason have I to live? There's nothing I want, nothing I care for, not even God's light of day. But still death won't come. I cry out for death, but it doesn't come. No matter what I see, no matter what I hear, I'm sick to my very heart. If I could live with him, maybe I would see some happiness. Well, why not? I've damned my eternal soul, what does it matter? Oh, God, how I miss him. How I long for him! Oh, darling, if I can't see you, at least you can hear me from afar. Oh, you wild winds, carry my sorrow and yearning to him! Blessed saints, how I long for him! *(she walks up to the river and cries out at the top of her voice)* Oh, my joy, my life, my soul, I love you! Answer me!

Enter Boris.

BORIS: Good God! That's her voice, surely! Where is she?

Katerina runs to him and flings herself into his arms.

KATERINA: Yes, yes, I've seen you!

BORIS: At least God has allowed us to cry together.

KATERINA: You haven't forgotten me?

BORIS: Katya, how could you say that?

KATERINA: No, no, of course not. You're not angry with me?

BORIS: Why should I be angry?

KATERINA: Please forgive me. I didn't want to cause you harm – I scarcely knew what I was doing. I can't even remember now what I said or did.

BORIS: Don't, please, that's enough.

KATERINA: Anyway, how are you? What's happening now?

BORIS: I'm going away.

KATERINA: Going away where?

BORIS: Far away, Katya, to Siberia.

KATERINA: Take me with you, away from this place!

BORIS: Katya, I can't. I'm not going of my own free will. My uncle's sending me away, the horses are already waiting. I managed to get my uncle to release me for a few minutes, so I could at least say goodbye to those places where you and I were together.

KATERINA: Then go, and God be with you. Don't grieve for me. You'll be lonely for a while, of course, my poor darling, but you'll soon forget.

BORIS: Don't worry about me. I'm a free agent. What about you? What about your mother-in-law?

KATERINA: She torments me, keeps me locked up. She tells everyone, she even tells my husband: "Don't trust her, she's a cunning woman." They follow me around the whole day and laugh in my face. Every word they speak is a reproach about you.

BORIS: What about your husband?

KATERINA: Sometimes he's affectionate, other times angry, and he drinks all the time. He disgusts me, he really does – his caresses are worse than beatings.

BORIS: Is it difficult for you, Katya?

KATERINA: Terribly. Yes. it's very hard. Dying would be easier.

BORIS: Who could've known that we'd have to suffer so much for our love? I should've run away, long ago.

KATERINA: Just seeing you was the cause of my ruin. I've known little enough joy, but oh, so much grief. And how much more to come! Well, why think of what's to come? I've seen you again, and they can't take that away from me. I don't need anything else. That's all I wanted, to see you again. That's made me feel much better, as if a great burden has been lifted from my shoulders. I kept thinking you were angry with me, that you were cursing me...

BORIS: Katya, what are you saying?

KATERINA: No, that's not what I meant, I didn't mean to say that. It's just that I've missed you so much, and now I've seen you again...

BORIS: Katya, they mustn't find us together here!

KATERINA: No, wait! Stay! There's something I wanted to tell you. Oh, God, I've forgotten. There's something I've got to tell you, but it's flown right out of my head, I can't remember anything.

BORIS: Katya, I've got to go.

KATERINA: Wait! Wait!

BORIS: What was it you wanted to say?

KATERINA: I'll tell you in a minute. Oh, yes – when you're on your travels, don't pass by a single beggar, give something to them all, and ask them to pray for my sinful soul.

BORIS: Oh, Katya, if only these people knew what it's like for me having to part with you. My God, I hope they'll one day feel what I feel now, I hope they enjoy it. Goodbye, Katya. *(embraces her and makes to leave)* Villains! Beasts! Oh, if only I had the strength!

KATERINA: Stay, don't go! Let me look at you one last time. Well, it's all over. Now go, and may God go with you. Go quickly, now.

BORIS: Katya, something's wrong. You're not thinking of doing anything, are you? I'll be worried sick about you on the road.

KATERINA: No, no, it's nothing. Go with God. No, don't come back. It's over...

BORIS: God bless you, Katya. There's only one thing I pray for and that's that she'll die soon, so you won't be tormented any longer. Goodbye!

KATERINA: Goodbye!

Boris exits. Katerina watches him go, and stands a few moments deep in thought.

What now? Do I go home? No, whether I go home or to my grave, it doesn't matter. They're all the same. The grave? The grave's better. A last resting-place under a little tree – that would be good. With the dear sun to warm it, and a little rain to water it... In the spring the grass'll grow over it, so sweet... The birds'll come to the tree, and sing, and raise their little ones, the flowers'll grow all around – yellow, red, blue... All kinds of flowers. *(after a pause)* All kinds... How quiet it is, how lovely. I feel much better. I don't even want to think of life. Go on living? No, no, I can't... It's too awful... I hate these people, I hate that house, the very walls are hateful to me. I can't go back there. No, no, I won't go back. If I go back, they'll carry on the same way, talk the same way, and I don't want that. Ah, it's so dark now. And there's that singing again! What are they singing? I can't make it out... If I could only die now... What are they singing? I don't care if death comes to me, I can't go on living. But that's a sin. No-one will pray for me. Whoever loves me, they'll pray for me... They cross your hands, one over the other... in the coffin. Yes, that's how they do it, I remember now. What if they catch me and force me to go back home? No, no, I must hurry, hurry! *(goes up to the edge of the river and cries out)* Oh, my love! My joy! Farewell! *(exits)*

Enter Kabanova, Tikhon, Kuligin and a Workman with a lantern.

KULIGIN: This is where she was last seen, apparently.

TIKHON: Are you sure?

KULIGIN: They say it was her for certain.

TIKHON: Well, thank God, at least somebody saw her alive.

KABANOVA: Huh, and you're scared stiff already, weeping and wailing. Well, you've got good reason. Don't you worry, we'll have plenty of trouble with that one yet.

TIKHON: Who'd have believed she'd come here, to such a busy place? Who'd even think of trying to hide here?

KABANOVA: You see what she's like? Nothing but a pest. That's just another one of her tricks.

People with lanterns begin to assemble from all sides.

1ST MAN: Has she been found?

KULIGIN: Not a sign of her. It's as if she's vanished from the face of the earth.

SEVERAL VOICES: We've got a real mystery here. Strange on-goings, and no mistake. Where can she have got to?

1ST MAN: She'll turn up all right.

2ND MAN: We'll find her.

3RD MAN: You wait and see, she'll come back of her own accord.

A voice off-stage: "Hey, let's get a boat!"

KULIGIN: Who's that shouting? What is it?

The voice is heard again off-stage: "It's a woman – she's thrown herself into the river!" Kuligin and several others run out. Tikhon makes to go too, but Kabanova catches him by the arm.

TIKHON: Oh, my God, it must be her! Mama, let me go, for God's sake! I'll either pull her out, or else I'll... I'll... Mama, I can't live without her!

KABANOVA: No, I won't let you go, don't even think of it! Destroy yourself for her sake? No, she's not worth it. As if she hadn't brought enough shame on us all, now she's dreamed this up!

TIKHON: Mama, let me go!

KABANOVA: There's enough people there without you. I'll curse you if you go.

TIKHON: *(falls to his knees)* Just to have one last look at her, please!

KABANOVA: They'll drag her out, you can have a look at her then.

TIKHON: *(stands up and calls to the men)* Oh, God, sirs, tell me, can't you see anything?

1ST MAN: It's pitch dark down there, you can't see a thing.

2ND MAN: I think they're shouting something, but I can't make it out.

1ST MAN: That's Kuligin's voice.

2ND MAN: Look, they're running up the river-bank with lanterns.

1ST MAN: They're coming this way. Look, they're carrying her!

Several people return from the river.

3RD MAN: Well done, Kuligin! She was quite close in, in one of those pot-holes by the shore. You could see a fair way down with the lantern. Kuligin spotted her dress and dragged her out.

TIKHON: Is she alive?

2ND MAN: Not a chance. She jumped in off the cliff, and she must've hit an anchor and killed herself, the poor creature. But I tell you, lads, she looks just the way she did when she was alive. Not much more than a scratch on her temple, and one solitary little drop of blood.

Tikhon rushes off, is suddenly confronted by Kuligin and the others carrying the dead Katerina.

KULIGIN: Here she is, here's your Katerina. Do what you will with her. Her body's here, you can take it, but her soul's no longer yours. She stands now before the judgment of one more merciful than you!

He lays the body on the ground and hurries off.

TIKHON: Katya! Katya!

KABANOVA: That's enough! It's sinful to cry over someone like her.

TIKHON: It was you that killed her, mama! You did it! You! You!

KABANOVA: I'll speak to you later at home. *(bows low to the crowd)*
Thank you, thank you, good people, for all your help. *(they all bow)*

TIKHON: You're happy now, Katerina. But why must I go on living
and suffering? *(falls upon his wife's body)*

THE END

(Groza, 1859)

TOO CLEVER BY HALF

CHARACTERS

GLUMOV (Yegor Dmitrich, a young man)

GLAFIRA (Klimovna, his mother)

MAMAEV (Nil Fedoseyich, a wealthy gentleman, distantly related to Glumov)

KLEOPATRA (Lvovna, Mamaev's wife)

KRUTITSKY (An old man, a very important personage)

GORODULIN (Ivan Ivanovich, a young man, likewise very important)

KURCHAEV (Yegor Vasilich, a hussar)

GOLUTVIN (A young man with no occupation)

MANEFA (A fortune-teller)

TURUSINA (Sofya Ignatyevna, a wealthy widow, originally of the merchant class)

MASHA (Turusina's niece)

TWO HANGERS-ON (Lady companions of Turusina)

ANDREI (Mamaev's servant)

GRIGORY (Turusina's servant)

FOOTMAN (Krutitsky's servant)

ACT ONE

The scene is a clean, well-furnished room, with a writing desk and a mirror: one door leads to an inner room: another, at stage right, is the street entrance. Glumov and Glafira are heard off-stage.

GLUMOV: Oh, for God's sake – of course, it's necessary! We've got to press on, and finish the job. *(he emerges from the side door)* Do as you're told, and don't argue!

GLAFIRA: *(also emerges from the side door)* Why are you making me write all these letters? Honestly, it's too much.

GLUMOV: Just get on with it and write!

GLAFIRA: But what's the point? I mean, they won't let her marry you. The Turusina girl has a dowry of two hundred thousand, she's well bred, good connections – she'll make a bride for some prince or general. And they won't let her marry Kurchaev either, so why am I laying all these various slanders and fantastic stories on him, the poor wretch?

GLUMOV: Listen, who are you more sorry for – me, or Kurchaev? Why should he get the money? He'll only lose it all at cards. And you're forever whining: "Oh, and I brought you into this world..."

GLAFIRA: Let's just hope it'll work!

GLUMOV: You leave that to me.

GLAFIRA: D'you think you really have a chance?

GLUMOV: Yes, I have. Mother dear, you know me: I'm smart, envious and bloody-minded, just like yourself. And what have I been doing till now? Writing spiteful little epigrams on everybody in Moscow – twiddling my thumbs, in other words. No, I've had enough of that. You shouldn't laugh at stupid people, you should exploit their weaknesses. Of course, this is no place to make a career, St. Petersburg's the place for that, for a career in business – here they do nothing but talk. Still, you can find a cushy billet and a rich wife even in this place, and that'll do for me. And how do you get into society? Not by deeds, that's for sure – talk's the thing. Yes, that's what we all love in Moscow – talk! So why shouldn't I be a success in this vast talking-shop? Eh? I'll ingratiate myself with the top people, and find a patron, you'll see. It's stupid trying to annoy them, you've got to flatter them, you've got to be absolutely shameless. That's the secret of success, yes. I'll start out with the minor players, the people around Turusina, squeeze all I need out of them, and then move up the ladder. Now go on, get busy writing! We'll talk about this later.

GLAFIRA: God help you! *(exits)*

GLUMOV: *(sits down at the desk)* To hell with epigrams! That kind of poetry brings its author nothing but trouble. We'll take up panegyrics. *(takes a notebook out of his pocket)* I'll unload all my bile here, in this little diary, leaving nothing but honey on my lips. And when I'm alone, at the dead of night, I'll draw up a chronicle of human nastiness. This manuscript isn't meant for public consumption, I alone shall be both author, and reader. Although later, when I've consolidated my position, I might publish the odd extract...

> *Enter Kurchaev and Golutvin: Glumov stands up and conceals the notebook in his pocket.*

KURCHAEV: Bonjour!

GLUMOV: Delighted. To what do I owe the honour?

KURCHAEV: *(sits down at Glumov's writing-table)* We're here on business. I want to put in a good word for Golutvin here...

GLUMOV: Him? I've known him for ages. What are you recommending him for?

GOLUTVIN: I'm not sure I like your tone, sir – no, indeed.

GLUMOV: Suit yourself. I presume you've had a decent breakfast, gentlemen?

KURCHAEV: That's of no importance. *(he picks up a pencil and paper and starts drawing something)*

GLUMOV: Obviously not. Well, sirs, I haven't much time to spare. What is it you want?

KURCHAEV: Haven't you any verses?

GLUMOV: What verses? You must've come to the wrong place.

GOLUTVIN: No, this is the place.

GLUMOV: *(to Kurchaev)* Look, don't spoil that paper!

KURCHAEV: We need an epigram. I know you've got some.

GLUMOV: I've got nothing of the sort.

KURCHAEV: Oh, come on! Everybody knows it. You've written stuff about the whole town! My friend here simply wants to contribute to the comic papers.

GLUMOV: *(to Golutvin)* Ah, I see. And have you written anything before?

GOLUTVIN: Yes, I have.

GLUMOV: What?

GOLUTVIN: Everything, you name it: novels, short stories, tragedies, comedies...

GLUMOV: Have you indeed?

GOLUTVIN: Yes, but they won't publish them, not for love nor money. No matter how I beg, they won't even accept them in a gift. So I'm taking up scandal.

GLUMOV: They won't publish that either.

GOLUTVIN: I can try.

GLUMOV: Besides which it's dangerous.

GOLUTVIN: Dangerous? What, you mean I'll get beaten up?

GLUMOV: Possibly.

GOLUTVIN: No, I've heard of people getting beaten up in other places, but not here – that's unheard of.

GLUMOV: Well, go on and write, then!

GOLUTVIN: But who can I write about? I don't know anybody.

KURCHAEV: You're supposed to have some sort of diary, where you've picked everybody to pieces.

GOLUTVIN: So, come on then, give us it, hand it over!

GLUMOV: Oh, of course, by all means – why not?

GOLUTVIN: And we'll publish it and be damned!

GLUMOV: I haven't got any such diary.

KURCHAEV: That's rubbish – you've been seen with it.

GOLUTVIN: See, look at him play-acting. He's one of us all right.

GLUMOV: I'm not one of either of you.

GOLUTVIN: Just think how much money we could get for it...

KURCHAEV: Actually, the fact is, Golutvin really needs the money. "I've finished sponging off other people," he says, "I want to work." And this is his idea of work. Well, go on, tell him!

GLUMOV: I'm listening, I'm listening.

GOLUTVIN: I haven't any material.

KURCHAEV: There you are, you see? He hasn't any material. Give him some material, and let him work.

GLUMOV: Look, don't spoil that paper!

KURCHAEV: Oh, come on – what's all the fuss about?

GLUMOV: You're drawing some sort of cockerel on it.

KURCHAEV: No, you're wrong. That's not a cockerel, that's my dear uncle Mamaev. There, you see? It's just like him, right down to the top-knot.

GOLUTVIN: Is he an interesting person? For my purposes, I mean?

KURCHAEV: Extremely interesting. For a start, he thinks he's terribly clever, and keeps lecturing everybody. If you want to make him happy, just ask his advice, that's meat and drink to him.

GOLUTVIN: Well, then – just write a caption under that cockerel: "The Latest Instruction Manual"!

Kurchaev does so.

Right, we'll go and get it published.

KURCHAEV: No, we can't – good God, man, he's my uncle, and
I'm his sole heir. *(puts the paper aside. Glumov picks it up and puts it
in his pocket)*

GOLUTVIN: So what other tricks does he get up to?

KURCHAEV: Oh, lots. He's been looking for an apartment the past
three years. He doesn't even need one, he just goes around for the
gossip, as if he was on serious business. He drives out in the morning,
inspects a dozen or so flats, and has a chat with the owners and
caretakers. Then he trots round all the shops sampling the caviar and
sturgeon, plonks himself down and launches into a discussion. The
shopkeepers can't get rid of him, and meanwhile he's delighted with
himself that he hasn't wasted the morning. *(to Glumov)* Oh yes, and
there's something else I forgot. His wife's absolutely wild about you.

GLUMOV: What do you mean?

KURCHAEV: Yes, my aunt spotted you at the theatre, couldn't take
her eyes off you, craning round to see. She kept asking me about
you: who is he? Who is he? You won't make a joke about this?

GLUMOV: Not me – you're the joker.

KURCHAEV: Well, it's up to you. But if I were in your place...
Anyway, are you going to give us some verses?

GLUMOV: No.

GOLUTVIN: Oh, come on, there's no point in arguing with him,
let's go for dinner!

KURCHAEV: All right then. Goodbye, sir! *(bows and makes to leave)*

GLUMOV: *(stops Kurchaev)* Look, why did you bring him with you?

KURCHAEV: Because I like clever people.

GLUMOV: You call him clever?

KURCHAEV: Beggars can't be choosers. I mean, what would really
clever people want with the likes of us? *(exits)*

GLUMOV: *(calling after him)* Huh, just you wait! Mother!

Enter Glafira.

GLUMOV: *(shows her the caricature of Mamaev)* Have a look at this.
  This one'll do to start off with.

GLAFIRA: Who is it?

GLUMOV: It's our distant relative, my dear uncle Mamaev.

GLAFIRA: Who drew that?

GLUMOV: His nephew Kurchaev, the hussar, no less. We'll put this
  drawing aside, on the off-chance. Trouble is, Mamaev can't abide
  his relatives. He's got about thirty nephews, and he picks out one
  of them, makes him his sole heir, and the others can go whistle.
  Then when he gets fed up with his favourite nephew he slings him
  out, chooses another one, and instantly rewrites his will. At the
  moment it's Kurchaev that's in his good books.

GLAFIRA: Oh, if you could only...

GLUMOV: It'll be hard work, but I'll give it a try. I mean, he doesn't
  even know I exist.

GLAFIRA: Oh, if you could just meet him – first the inheritance,
  then a beautiful house, lots of friends, all the right connections...

GLUMOV: Indeed! But there's more to come – my aunt Kleopatra's
  taken a fancy to me, she's seen me somewhere or other. Now you
  just think about that! Anyway, my first task is to get close to uncle
  Mamaev – that's the first rung on the ladder. He'll introduce me
  to Krutitsky and Gorodulin: they've got real influence, for a start,
  and for another thing, they're close friends of Turusina. All I need
  is an entrée, and I'll marry her niece for sure!

GLAFIRA: Yes, dear, but it's the first step that's the hardest.

GLUMOV: Don't worry, mother, it's as good as done. Mamaev's
  coming here.

GLAFIRA: Eh? How did you manage that?

GLUMOV: Couldn't have been easier – it's all fixed up already.
  Mamaev loves looking at apartments, and that's the hook we've
  caught him on!

Mamaev's footman Andrei enters.

ANDREI: Mr Mamaev is here, sir.

GLUMOV: Splendid! Here you are... *(gives him some money)* Ask
   him to come in, please.

ANDREI: Hm... he's not going to be pleased. I told him this was a
   nice flat.

GLUMOV: I'll take the blame for that. Now, trot off to your room,
   mother – I'll call you when I need you...

   *Andrei exits. Glumov sits down at the table and pretends to be
   busy. Mamaev enters, followed by Andrei. Without taking his hat
   off, Mamaev looks round the room.*

MAMAEV: This is a bachelor flat.

GLUMOV: *(bows, and carries on writing)* That's correct.

MAMAEV: It's not bad, but it's a bachelor apartment. *(to Andrei)*
   What did you bring me here for?

GLUMOV: *(pulls out a chair and continues writing)* Won't you sit down?

MAMAEV: *(sits)* Thank you. Why did you bring me here? Eh?

ANDREI: I'm sorry, sir...

MAMAEV: Good heavens, man, don't you know what kind of apartment
   I need? I'm a State Councillor, for God's sake, and my wife – your
   mistress, sir – likes to entertain. We need a proper drawing-room, and
   not just the one, either. Now where's the drawing-room, eh?

ANDREI: Sir, I'm sorry...

MAMAEV: Where is it? *(to Glumov)* My apologies, sir...

GLUMOV: That's all right, you're not disturbing me.

MAMAEV: *(to Andrei)* Don't you see there's a gentleman sitting here
   writing? And we're very likely disturbing him. Of course, he's too
   well-mannered to say, but it's all your fault, you stupid creature!

GLUMOV: That's all right, don't shout at him, please, it's my fault.

He asked me about an apartment on the stairs, and I pointed out this one, told him it was very nice – I didn't realise you were a family man.

MAMAEV: You occupy this apartment?

GLUMOV: I do.

MAMAEV: Why are you renting it out?

GLUMOV: I can't afford it.

MAMAEV: So why did you take it in the first place, if you can't afford it? Did somebody force you? I mean, did somebody grab you by the collar and shove it down your throat – here, take it, take it! Eh? And now of course you've got yourself into debt. Up to your eyes in it, are you? Well, yes, of course you are. And now you've got to move out of this big apartment into a single room – how will you like that, eh?

GLUMOV: Actually, I'm looking for a bigger one.

MAMAEV: What d'you mean bigger? You can't afford to stay here, but you're renting a bigger place? Where's the sense in that?

GLUMOV: There's no sense in it. It's stupid.

MAMAEV: Stupid? What sort of nonsense is this?

GLUMOV: It's not nonsense. I'm an idiot.

MAMAEV: An idiot? That's bizarre. What d'you mean, an idiot?

GLUMOV: It's quite simple, I've no brains. What's so surprising about that? It's not unusual, is it. Happens all the time.

MAMAEV: Now, hold on, this is most interesting! A man who calls himself an idiot...

GLUMOV: Well, what would you like me to do? Wait till other people tell me? It makes no odds, surely. It's not something you can hide.

MAMAEV: That's true – it's quite hard to conceal that particular deficiency.

GLUMOV: So, I don't even try.

MAMAEV: Well, I'm sorry for you.

GLUMOV: I thank you most humbly.

MAMAEV: Look, don't you have anybody to advise you?

GLUMOV: No, I haven't.

MAMAEV: I mean, there are advisers, you know – really sound teachers, only nobody listens to them these days. Well, I suppose you can't expect much from the older generation – they think they're clever, just *because* they're old. But if young people won't listen, what can you expect from them later on in life? I'll tell you a story – just the other day there was a young lad running out of the school gates – practically flying – and well, naturally, I stopped him, and started to read him a lecture, by way of a joke, you understand... 'Well, well', I said, 'Creep like snail unwillingly to school, eh? Fly like the wind home to play... it ought to be the other way round, you know...' Anyone else would've been grateful, don't you think, if a respectable person had stopped in the street for them, they'd have kissed my hand, even, but not that young whelp!

GLUMOV: You know, these days, sound instruction is so...

MAMAEV: 'We get enough of this in school', he says, 'I'm fed up with lectures. If you want to lecture, why don't you get a job as a headmaster? Anyway, I'm starving, so just let go of me!' I mean, a lad like that, saying that to me!

GLUMOV: Yes, he's on the slippery path, that boy. I feel sorry for him.

MAMAEV: Hm, and you know where that slippery path leads to.

GLUMOV: I do indeed.

MAMAEV: And why are all the servants useless nowadays? It's because they're free, they're no longer obliged to listen to instructions. In the old days, I used to go into every detail with our serfs. I instructed them all, from the youngest to the oldest. I'd give two-hour lectures to each and every one of them, and sometimes I'd reach the very highest plane of thought, and a serf would be standing before me, and he'd be gradually overcome by emotion, to the point that he'd faint clean away at my feet. That was beneficial to him, and an honorable calling for me. But nowadays, after all this... you understand what I'm driving at?

GLUMOV: I understand.

MAMAEV: You try that nowadays with your servant, yes, just you
  try! Read him some metaphysics a couple of times, and he's
  handing in his notice! "What sort of punishment's this?" he says.
  Yes, that's what he says, "What sort of punishment's this?"

GLUMOV: It's immoral, that's what it is!

MAMAEV: I mean, I'm not a hard master, I'd rather talk things out.
  The merchants here have a really stupid habit of grabbing them by
  the hair, and tugging it at every word. It makes the point more
  forcibly, they get the message, they'll say. Well, that's just
  wonderful! But I'd rather give them a good talking-to, except that
  nobody wants that nowadays.

GLUMOV: Yes, indeed, sir – I should think you find all that very
  unpleasant.

MAMAEV: *(sternly)* Please, let's say no more about it. It was as if
  something pierced clean through me, right here... *(points to his
  chest)* Even now, I still feel a kind of...

GLUMOV: Here, do you mean?

MAMAEV: No, a bit higher.

GLUMOV: What, here?

MAMAEV: *(testily)* No, higher, I'm telling you!

GLUMOV: Please forgive me, sir, and don't be angry. I told you I
  was stupid.

MAMAEV: You certainly are stupid. That's bad. Actually, it's not that
  bad, if you have an older, more experienced relative or acquaintance.

GLUMOV: That's just the trouble, sir, I haven't. Well, there's my
  mother, but she's even stupider than me.

MAMAEV: Mm, you're in a bad situation altogether. I'm sorry for
  you, young man.

GLUMOV: I'm told I have an uncle, but it doesn't make any difference.

MAMAEV: Why not?

GLUMOV: Well, he doesn't know me, and I've no desire to see him.

MAMAEV: That does you no credit, young man, none whatsoever.

GLUMOV: Well, for goodness' sake! If he was poor, I'd probably go and kiss his hand, but he's a rich man. If I were to go to him for advice, he'd think I was after his money. I mean, how can I convince him that I don't want a single kopeck from him, that all I want is advice, that I hunger after instruction, like manna from heaven? I'm told he's a man of remarkable intelligence, and I'm prepared to listen to him day and night.

MAMAEV: You're not quite as stupid as you say.

GLUMOV: Oh, now and again enlightenment dawns, and things suddenly become clear, but only now and again. Most of the time I haven't a clue what I'm doing. And it's then I need advice.

MAMAEV: So who's this uncle of yours?

GLUMOV: D'you know, I've almost forgotten his name. Mamaev, I think.

MAMAEV: And what's yours?

GLUMOV: Glumov.

MAMAEV: The son of Dmitri Glumov?

GLUMOV: The very same.

MAMAEV: Well, this is Mamaev, yes, it's me.

GLUMOV: Oh, my God! Really? No, it can't be! Oh, give me your hand, sir! *(almost in tears)* But, dearest uncle, I've heard you can't abide relatives – you needn't worry, we can be just as distant as before. I wouldn't dream of visiting you unless you said so. It's enough for me even just to have seen you, and enjoyed the conversation of such a brilliant man.

MAMAEV: No, no, please call on me whenever you need advice about anything.

GLUMOV: Whenever I need advice? I need it constantly, every minute of the day! I feel as if I'll perish without direction.

MAMAEV: Then call on me this very evening!

GLUMOV: I thank you most humbly, sir. Please, allow me to present my aged parent – she's none too bright, but she's a decent, kindly soul.

MAMAEV: Why, yes, of course.

GLUMOV: *(loudly)* Mother!

     Glafira enters.

GLUMOV: Mother, dearest! Look! Only please don't cry! A happy accident has brought us dear uncle Mamaev, whom we've longed so much to see.

GLAFIRA: Oh, that's true, dear cousin, I've been dying to meet you for ages. But you didn't even want to know your relatives.

GLUMOV: Mother, that's enough. I'm sure uncle has his reasons.

MAMAEV: Ah well, there are relatives and relatives.

GLAFIRA: Let me have a look at you. Well, really, there's no resemblance at all, is there, Georges dear?

GLUMOV: *(tugging at her dress)* That'll do, mother. Stop it!

GLAFIRA: What do you mean, stop it? There isn't the slightest resemblance, absolutely none...

MAMAEV: *(sternly)* What are you whispering about? Who is it I don't resemble? I resemble myself.

GLUMOV: *(to Glafira)* That's all we need, this nonsense of yours.

MAMAEV: Go on, you've started now, you might as well say your piece.

GLAFIRA: I'm saying you don't look at all like the portrait.

MAMAEV: What portrait? Where did you get a portrait?

GLAFIRA: Well, you see, cousin, there's a certain Kurchaev who visits us now and again – I believe he's also a relative of yours?

GLUMOV: He's a splendid chap, very witty...

MAMAEV: Yes, yes, what about him?

GLAFIRA: Anyway, he draws portraits of you all the time. Show him, Georges dear...

GLUMOV: Now would you believe, I don't know where I put it?

GLAFIRA: Well, have a good look! He did one quite recently, I'm sure you remember. He had that fellow with him, one of those... oh, what d'you call 'em? You know, those people that write verses – satirists, isn't it? And Kurchaev says, "I'll draw you a picture of my uncle," he says, "And you can write a caption." That's what they said, I heard them myself.

MAMAEV: Let me see that portrait! Show it to me this instant!

GLUMOV: *(hands over the portrait)* You know, you shouldn't say things like that, mother – people's feelings can get hurt.

MAMAEV: That's right, teach your mother to be a hypocrite. Don't listen to him, cousin, come straight out with it. That's the best way. *(peers at the portrait)* Good God! Well, really, my own nephew, who'd have believed it!

GLUMOV: Oh, throw it away, uncle – it's not in the least like you, and the caption doesn't fit either: "The Latest Instruction Manual"

MAMAEV: Indeed it does look like me, and the caption fits only too well! Anyway, it doesn't concern you, I'll deal with it myself. You won't draw caricatures of me, I hope?

GLUMOV: Good heavens no, uncle, what do you take me for? The very idea!

MAMAEV: Well, anyway, you'll come and visit me, without fail, this evening – and you're welcome too, of course.

GLAFIRA: Oh, you know me – I'd just get on your nerves with my silly chatter.

Mamaev exits, Glumov sees him out.

Well, well – things are looking up. But Georges still has his work cut out. Oh dear, it's such a palaver trying to make your way in this world!

Glumov re-enters.

GLUMOV: Listen, mother, Manefa's coming up. Now be civil to her, do you hear? In fact, don't just be civil, butter her up for all you're worth.

GLAFIRA: What, you want me to lower myself to that old bag?

GLUMOV: Well, you want to play the grand lady, but where's the money coming from? If it wasn't for my neat footwork, you'd be out on the streets by now. So you'd better help me, I'm telling you, I need your help.

> *Hearing footsteps, he rushes into the hallway and re-enters with Manefa.*

MANEFA: Flee, flee this vain world, I say!

GLUMOV: *(with a pious expression, sighing)* Oh, I shall, I shall!

MANEFA: And selfish greed, shun that also.

GLUMOV: Verily, I know not that sin.

> *Manefa sits down, without paying any attention to Glafira, who curtseys to her repeatedly.*

MANEFA: I took wing, I flew, and did come unto you!

GLUMOV: We are truly grateful, truly.

MANEFA: Indeed, I was in a certain god-fearing house, where they did give me ten roubles out of Christian charity. Through my hands, they perform God's charitable work. These blessed hands are more receptive than those of a sinner.

GLUMOV: Please, accept these fifteen roubles from thy servant Yegor.

MANEFA: Blessed are they that give!

GLUMOV: Remember me in your prayers.

MANEFA: And in that same god-fearing house verily I did imbibe tea and coffee.

GLAFIRA: Oh, come with me, dear lady, it's just ready now...

> *Manefa rises, they take her arm and accompany her to the door.*

Glumov re-enters and sits down at the table.

GLUMOV: Now, some notes! *(takes out his diary)* 'To Mamaev's footman, three roubles... to Manefa, fifteen roubles. And the entire conversation with my uncle, herewith...' *(begins writing)*

Kurchaev enters.

KURCHAEV: Right, now listen to me – was my uncle here just now?

GLUMOV: He was.

KURCHAEV: He didn't say anything about me, did he?

GLUMOV: No, why on earth should he? He scarcely knew where he was. He'd dropped in, following his usual custom, to have a look at the apartment.

KURCHAEV: It's a conspiracy, that's what it is, some sort of hellish conspiracy!

GLUMOV: Go on, I'm all ears.

KURCHAEV: I mean, would you believe it, my uncle stopped me in the street, and... and... and...

GLUMOV: Yes?

KURCHAEV: He told me never to darken his door again! Can you imagine it?

GLUMOV: I'm trying to.

KURCHAEV: So I drive over to Turusina's – they won't even let me in! They send out one of their menials, some scruffy old woman, to tell me they're not receiving! Do you hear what I'm saying?

GLUMOV: I do.

KURCHAEV: Then kindly explain to me what all this means.

GLUMOV: What makes you think I know?

KURCHAEV: Well, you're a clever chap – at least, you know more than I do about these things.

GLUMOV: All right, if you insist... Just take a good look at yourself, the kind of life you lead.

KURCHAEV: What do you mean? It's the same as everybody else's, why pick on me? So for that they deprive a chap of his inheritance, take away his fiancée, treat him like dirt?

GLUMOV: But look at the company you keep! Golutvin, for instance.

KURCHAEV: What's the matter with Golutvin?

GLUMOV: He's a parasite! People like that are capable of anything. Now, there's your explanation! And why did you bring him here the other day? I'm choosy about my friends – I've got to look after myself. Don't ever come here again, please.

KURCHAEV: What is this, have you gone mad?

GLUMOV: Your uncle has thrown you out, and I intend to follow that worthy gentleman's lead in all things, including my acquaintance!

KURCHAEV: Aha! I think I'm beginning to understand...

GLUMOV: Well, thank God for that!

KURCHAEV: So, my fine fellow, it's you, isn't it? If my suspicions turn out to be correct, then just watch out! You won't get away with it, you'd better take care, sir!

GLUMOV: Oh, I'll take care, when I need to, but for the present I see no particular danger. Goodbye, sir!

KURCHAEV: Goodbye! *(exits)*

GLUMOV: So, uncle's thrown him out. That's the first step...

END OF ACT ONE

ACT TWO

The scene is Mamaev's house , a large drawing-room with one door leading out to the hall, and two side doors. Mamaev and Krutitsky enter fhrough a side door.

MAMAEV: Well, we're going somewhere, we're being led somewhere, but we don't know where, and nor do the people who are leading us. And how will it all end, eh?

KRUTITSKY: Quite frankly, I look on all this as a frivolous experiment, and I don't see any particular harm in it. We live in frivolous times, for the most part. It's all youth and inexperience, let's try this, let's have a shot at that, let's change this, let's alter that. Change is easy enough. I mean, I could take all my furniture and stand it upside-down, and there's change, if you like. But what's happened to that age-old wisdom, all those centuries of experience, that tell us furniture should stand on legs, eh? Look, there's a table standing on four legs, and doing quite well. Firm enough, isn't it?

MAMAEV: Indeed.

KRUTITSKY: And solid?

MAMAEV: Yes, solid.

KRUTITSKY: And suppose I stand it upside-down? I mean, that's what they've done.

MAMAEV: *(waves his hand dismissively)* Indeed.

KRUTITSKY: Well, they'll see, won't they?

MAMAEV: Ah, but will they see?

KRUTITSKY: Of course they will! What a strange thing to say. And if they don't see, well, there are people who'll point it out.

MAMAEV: That's true. Yes, that's for sure. There are plenty of them, I can tell you, but nobody's listening. That's the whole trouble, there are plenty of clever people, but no-one's listening to us.

KRUTITSKY: It's our own fault. We don't know how to speak, we don't know how to express our opinions. Who's doing all the writing and shouting? Snotty-nosed brats. And we say nothing, then complain that they don't listen to us. We've got to write, we've got to write more.

MAMAEV: That's easily said – write! It takes practice, you need to have some sort of knack. It's all nonsense, of course, but you need it just the same. I mean, look at me – I could talk all night, but if I took up writing, God only knows what would come out. And it's not as if I'm a fool. Anyway, what about you? What's your writing like?

KRUTITSKY: No, don't bring me into it. I can write – I write plenty.

MAMAEV: Really? You write? I didn't know that. Still, I mean, you can't expect that of everybody.

KRUTITSKY: Well, time passes, my dear Mamaev, time passes. And if you want to make yourself useful these days, you have to take up the pen.

MAMAEV: It's not everyone's forte.

KRUTITSKY: True enough. Incidentally, you haven't come across some young man, some unassuming and well-educated chap, of course, who might be able to set down various ideas and projects on paper, and so forth?

MAMAEV: Indeed I have. I know just the man.

KRUTITSKY: He's not a loudmouth, one of these modern scoffers?

MAMAEV: No no no! Just say the word, and he'll be as silent as the grave.

KRUTITSKY: Hm. You see, I've got this very serious plan drawn up, or memorandum, whatever you want to call it, but as you well know, I'm a man of the old school...

MAMAEV: Yes, a sound education.

KRUTITSKY: Oh yes, I agree, I agree. But I write in the old style – how can I put it? You know, something along the lines of the great Lomonosov.

MAMAEV: The old style was more powerful. Today's is nowhere near.

KRUTITSKY: I agree, but all the same, to write nowadays in the manner of Lomonosov or Sumarokov, well, I mean, people might laugh at me. Anyway, d'you think he might give my work a what-d'you-call-it... yes, a literary polish?

MAMAEV: He might, he might indeed.

KRUTITSKY: I'll pay him, of course.

MAMAEV: No, you'll insult him, he'll be honoured to do it.

KRUTITSKY: Will he indeed? And why should I be indebted to him?
Who is he, exactly?

MAMAEV: He's my nephew – yes, my nephew.

KRUTITSKY: Well, tell him to look in on me – quite early, say,
around eight o'clock.

MAMAEV: Fine, good – rest assured, sir.

KRUTITSKY: Oh, and tell him not a word, mind. I don't want it
going the rounds before the proper time, it'll weaken the effect.

MAMAEV: Good Lord, no, I quite understand. I'll make that point, yes.

KRUTITSKY: Goodbye, sir.

MAMAEV: I'll bring him over myself tomorrow.

KRUTITSKY: You'll be very welcome, sir.

Exits, accompanied by Mamaev. Enter Kleopatra and Glafira.

KLEOPATRA: And he's so young, and handsome – and educated,
too, a darling boy. Oh, indeed!

GLAFIRA: Yes, and despite all that, he might have perished in
obscurity, my dear Kleopatra.

KLEOPATRA: And who kept him languishing in obscurity, eh? I
mean, isn't it enough that he's young and goodlooking?

GLAFIRA: But if you've no family connections, or decent
acquaintance, how are you going to see anybody? Where are you
going to find a patron?

KLEOPATRA: Yes, but he didn't need to avoid society – we'd have
spotted him, we'd have picked him out without fail.

GLAFIRA: Well, you have to be extremely clever if you want to be noticed. It's hard for ordinary people – oh yes, it's terribly hard!

KLEOPATRA: You do your son an injustice – he's really quite clever. Anyway, he doesn't need a great intellect, not if he's goodlooking. What's he need brains for? He's not going to be a professor. No, believe me, people will always help out a handsome young man, and give him the means to get on in the world, just out of compassion. I mean, if you see a clever man poorly dressed, living in some nasty apartment, taking hired cabs, it doesn't strike you as odd, or give you a pang – it actually rather suits them, there's no obvious contradiction. But if you see a handsome young man poorly dressed – well, that's painful to behold, that shouldn't happen, and it won't happen, no, never!

GLAFIRA: Oh, you have the heart of an angel!

KLEOPATRA: No, it's impossible! We women won't permit it. We shall rouse up our husbands, and all our friends, all the top people – we'll set him up in life. We can't allow anything to stop us admiring him. Poverty! Fie! We shall spare nothing, so that... No, it's impossible, truly! Beautiful young men are so rare.

GLAFIRA: Oh, if only everyone thought like that.

KLEOPATRA: Everyone does. I mean, in general, we're bound to sympathise with poor people, it's our duty, we're obliged to, there's no disputing that. But surely anyone's heart would go out at the sight of a handsome man in poverty, and so young. His coat sleeves frayed, or too short, his collar grubby... oh God, that's awful, absolutely awful! Apart from that, poverty is so humiliating, it soon kills any joie-de-vivre, and removes that triumphant look, that boldness which is so pardonable, and indeed so becoming in a handsome young man.

GLAFIRA: That's true, that's absolutely true, my dear Kleopatra!

Mamaev enters.

MAMAEV: Ah, good morning!

GLAFIRA: I think I'm going to lodge a complaint against you, my dear sir.

MAMAEV: What d'you mean?

GLAFIRA: You've won my son over completely. He's quite given up loving me, and dreams of no-one but you. He keeps on about your brilliant mind, and your conversation – all he can do is gasp in astonishment.

MAMAEV: He's a fine boy, yes indeed.

GLAFIRA: As a baby he was quite amazing.

MAMAEV: Well, even now he's practically a child.

GLAFIRA: He was so quiet, it was really a marvel. And he never once forgot to kiss his father's hand, or his mother's. And he used to kiss all his grandmothers' and aunties' hands, too. We even had to forbid him, in case they'd think we'd trained him to do it deliberately. And then he'd do it on the quiet, so no-one would see him, he'd sneak up and kiss them. And then there was one time, when he was just five, and he really astonished us all! He came in one morning and said, "What a dream I've had! Angels flew down to me in my little bed, and told me: love your mama and papa, and obey them in all things! And when you grow up, love your superiors. And I said to them, "Oh yes, angels, I'll obey everybody!" He really surprised us, he made us so happy, I can't tell you how much. And that dream's stayed in my mind, always.

MAMAEV: Well, I must say goodbye, I have some business to see to, a little more important than yours. I'm very pleased with your son. And you can tell him I said so. *(puts on his hat)* Oh yes, I almost forgot – I'm aware that you're not wealthy, and you're having trouble getting by. Why don't you look in on me tomorrow morning, and I'll give you some...

GLAFIRA: Oh, thank you, thank you most humbly...

MAMAEV: No, not money – better than money. I'll give you some advice on how to manage your budget. *(exits)*

GLAFIRA: Well, he's pleased – praise the Lord for that! And there's no-one better at showing gratitude than my Georges.

KLEOPATRA: I'm glad to hear it.

GLAFIRA: Not only is he grateful, he absolutely adores his benefactors.

KLEOPATRA: Adores? That's going a bit far.

GLAFIRA: No, not at all. It's just his character, the way he feels. Of course, it's not right for a mother to brag about her son, and he doesn't like me talking about him...

KLEOPATRA: No, go on, feel free – I won't tell him a thing.

GLAFIRA: Well, he's simply dazzled by his benefactors – as far as he's concerned, there's no-one better in the whole world. In all of Moscow, he says, there's no-one to match your dear husband for intelligence. And what he says about your beauty, well, it ought to be published in a book, honestly.

KLEOPATRA: You don't say!

GLAFIRA: Oh, the things he compares you to!

KLEOPATRA: Really?

GLAFIRA: I mean, hasn't he seen you somewhere before?

KLEOPATRA: I don't know. I've seen him, at the theatre.

GLAFIRA: No, he must've seen you.

KLEOPATRA: What makes you say that?

GLAFIRA: Are you asking me? Well, really, he's known you such a short time, and yet suddenly he feels...

KLEOPATRA: Yes? Yes? Feels what?

GLAFIRA: He feels – oh, I don't know – so warmly disposed towards you.

KLEOPATRA: Oh, the darling boy!

GLAFIRA: I can't understand it. My dear uncle, he says, is so clever, quite brilliant, and my dear aunt is an angel, yes, a perfect angel...

KLEOPATRA: Go on, please, please! I'm dying to know.

GLAFIRA: You won't be angry with me for being silly? For being so frank?

KLEOPATRA: No, of course not.

GLAFIRA: She's an angel, he says, a heavenly angel. And then he falls on my breast, in tears, yes...

KLEOPATRA: Well, now... You don't say? How strange.

GLAFIRA: *(a change of tone)* He's just overjoyed at your kindness to him, a poor orphan. He cries out of gratitude.

KLEOPATRA: Oh, the boy's all heart, truly!

GLAFIRA: You can say that again. Boiling over, it's just his nature.

KLEOPATRA: Well, that's understandable at his age... one can forgive...

GLAFIRA: Oh, please forgive him, do. He's still so young.

KLEOPATRA: What on earth should I forgive him for? What has he done?

GLAFIRA: Oh, dear – I mean, you realise this is perhaps the first time in his life that he's seen such a beautiful woman – where would he get the chance? And she's so kind to him, so indulgent... as a member of the family, of course... Well, he's such a hothead, you'll drive him crazy...

KLEOPATRA: *(thoughtfully)* Mm... he really is a sweet boy.

GLAFIRA: Of course, these warm feelings of his are family feelings, but... well, as you know, the proximity of such a fascinating woman, and his young years... I mean, he's not sleeping at nights. When he comes home from your house, he tosses and turns...

KLEOPATRA: He confides in you? He doesn't hide his feelings from you?

GLAFIRA: No, no fear of that. His feelings are still those of a child.

KLEOPATRA: Yes, of course – a child. He still needs someone to guide him in such matters. And in time, under the direction of a clever woman... yes, he might just...

GLAFIRA: Oh please, direct him! That's just what he needs in life. You're so kind...

KLEOPATRA: *(laughs)* Oh yes, I'm kind all right. But I mean, you do know, it could be dangerous. I might even... I might even get carried away myself.

GLAFIRA: Really, you're such a kind person.

KLEOPATRA: I can see you love him very much.

GLAFIRA: He's my only child – why shouldn't I love him?

KLEOPATRA: *(languidly)* Well then, let's love him together.

GLAFIRA: You're making me envious of my own son. Yes, he has indeed found happiness in your family. However, it's time I was going. Don't be angry with me for jabbering on like that. If my son finds out, there'll be trouble, so please don't give me away. He gets embarrassed sometimes, because I'm so brainless, and I'm sure he'd like to say, "Oh, come on, mama, don't be so silly!" but he won't say it. He avoids things like that out of respect for his dear mother. But I'd willingly forgive him, if it'd only keep me from being silly in the future. Anyway, goodbye, dear Kleopatra.

KLEOPATRA: *(hugs her)* Goodbye, my dear Glafira. I'll look in on you one of these days, and we can have another talk about Georges.

Sees her to the door. Glafira exits.

What a chatterbox! If her son heard that, he'd scarcely thank her her for it. He's so proud, he behaves so respectfully, and so coldly with me, and yet he's like that at home? So, it seems I can still inspire real passion in a young man. And that's as it should be. Of course, this while back I've been feeling a distinct shortage of admirers. But that's obviously because all the people in our circle are so jaded and worn-out. So – here we are at last. Oh, my darling boy, I'm going to look after you now. No matter how shy he is, true passion must break out. And it's so terribly interesting to observe, when you know in advance that a person's in love with you.

Glumov enters, bows, and waits respectfully.

Come here, please.

Glumov shyly approaches.

KLEOPATRA: Why are you standing like that? Really, is that how nephews behave?

GLUMOV: *(kisses her hand)* Good morning, dear lady.

KLEOPATRA: Bravo! I'm surprised you've finally plucked up the courage.

GLUMOV: I'm really rather shy.

KLEOPATRA: Well, be a little more forward. What on earth are you afraid of? I'm human, the same as everyone else. You really ought to be more trusting, more open with me, entrust all the little secrets of your heart to me. After all, I am your aunt, don't forget.

GLUMOV: Well, I wouldn't mind being more open with you, if you were...

KLEOPATRA: If I were what?

GLUMOV: If you were an old woman.

KLEOPATRA: Oh, stuff and nonsense! I've absolutely no wish to be an old woman.

GLUMOV: No, no, I don't wish that either. God grant that you keep your full bloom of youth as long as possible. All I'm saying is that I wouldn't be so shy then, I'd feel more at ease.

KLEOPATRA: But in heaven's name why? Here, come and sit down beside me, and tell me the truth – why would you feel more at ease, if I were an old woman?

GLUMOV: *(picks up a chair and sits beside her)* Well, young women have their own interests, their own concerns – why on earth should they be bothered about poor relations! But that's all an old woman has.

KLEOPATRA: And why can't a young woman concern herself with her relatives?

GLUMOV: Well, she might, but it's embarrassing to ask her, one wouldn't want to pester her. All she's got on her mind is fun, entertainment, amusement, and then suddenly there's the dreary face of her nephew, asking more favours, constantly whingeing. But for an old woman, that would even be a pleasure. She'd drive around Moscow, making a fuss. She'd find it a relief from boredom, as well as a good deed, which she could brag about afterwards.

KLEOPATRA: All right, supposing I were an old woman, what would you ask of me?

GLUMOV: Oh, if only you were. The trouble is you're not – on the contrary, you're a very young woman. You're trying to trap me.

KLEOPATRA: It doesn't matter, honestly – go ahead and ask.

GLUMOV: Ah, but it does matter. I mean, for example, I know you'd only have to speak one word to Mr Gorodulin, and I'd have a very good position.

KLEOPATRA: Well, yes, I suppose a word from me would be enough.

GLUMOV: Nevertheless, I wouldn't dream of bothering with such a request.

KLEOPATRA: Why on earth not?

GLUMOV: Because that would be coercion. He's absolutely enchanted by you.

KLEOPATRA: You think so?

GLUMOV: I know so.

KLEOPATRA: You really are extremely perceptive. But what about my side of it?

GLUMOV: Well, that's your own business.

KLEOPATRA: *(aside)* He isn't jealous – that's strange.

GLUMOV: There's nothing he wouldn't do for you. Then again, a request from you would delight him. Making you ask him – well, it's like offering him a bribe.

KLEOPATRA: Oh, this is all nonsense, sheer imaginings. You really don't want me to ask him for you?

GLUMOV: Absolutely not. Besides which, I don't want to be in your debt. I mean, how on earth could I repay you?

KLEOPATRA: Well, how would you repay an old woman?

GLUMOV: By constantly humouring her. I'd carry her lapdog around, put her footstool under her, kiss her hand non-stop, congratulate her on birthdays and so on, every possible occasion. Old women particularly appreciate these things, of course.

KLEOPATRA: Of course.

GLUMOV: Then, if the old woman was really good to me, I'd become quite attached to her, even come to love her.

KLEOPATRA: And you couldn't come to love a young woman?

GLUMOV: I could, but I wouldn't dare.

KLEOPATRA: *(aside)* At last!

GLUMOV: I mean, what would it lead to? Nothing but unnecessary suffering.

A servant enters.

SERVANT: Mr Gorodulin, ma'am.

GLUMOV: I'll go into my uncle's study, I've left some work there. *(bows very respectfully and exits)*

KLEOPATRA: *(to the servant)* Send him in.

The servant exits. Enter Gorodulin.

GORODULIN: Madame, may I have the honour to present myself.

KLEOPATRA: *(reproachfully)* Well, you're a fine one. Sit down. What wind has blown you in my direction, what storm, eh?

GORODULIN: *(sits)* The wind that blows through my head, and the storm of passion that rages in my heart.

KLEOPATRA: Why, thank you. It's very sweet of you not to have forgotten me, cast aside and abandoned as I am.

GORODULIN: What! Where is he, where's the unhappy wretch who has abandoned you? Show me the man! I'm in a particularly warlike frame of mind at the moment.

KLEOPATRA: Well, it's you first – it's yourself you need to kill, or deal with in some other way.

GORODULIN: Oh, I'd rather some other way, please.

KLEOPATRA: And I've thought up a punishment for you.

GORODULIN: Do tell me. Announce your verdict – you can't have an execution without one. If you've decided to smother me in your embraces, well, I won't lodge an appeal.

KLEOPATRA: No, I wish to appear before you as a petitioner.

GORODULIN: Doesn't that mean switching roles?

KLEOPATRA: Are you really a petitioner? Aren't you practically a judge or something?

GORODULIN: Yes indeed, ma'am. But among the ladies I always...

KLEOPATRA: Oh, anyway, enough of this nonsense. I have a serious matter to discuss.

GORODULIN: I'm all ears.

KLEOPATRA: My nephew needs...

GORODULIN: Yes, what does your dear nephew need? A nice new jacket? A little pair of trousers?

KLEOPATRA: Now don't annoy me. Listen, please, and don't interrupt! My nephew isn't a child, he's a very sweet young man, extremely good-looking, clever, well educated...

GORODULIN: Hm – so much the better for him, and the worse for me.

KLEOPATRA: He needs a position.

GORODULIN: Well, what sort would you like?

KLEOPATRA: A good one, of course! He's exceptionally talented.

GORODULIN: Exceptionally talented? Oh dear. Exceptional talents'll get you nowhere these days – they're a drug on the market. All the suitable posts are already filled – one by Beist, I believe, the other by Bismarck.

KLEOPATRA: Now listen, you'll make me lose my patience, and we'll start quarrelling. Just tell me, do you have a place available?

GORODULIN: Well, I suppose we can find something for an ordinary mortal.

KLEOPATRA: Excellent.

GORODULIN: *(tenderly)* We need people. Perhaps you'll allow me to cast an eye over this marvel, then I'll be able to tell you precisely what he's suited to, and what position I can recommend him for.

KLEOPATRA: Yegor Dmitrich! Georges! Come here. *(to Gorodulin)* I'll leave you with him for a little while. You can come and see me afterwards. I'll be waiting in the drawing-room.

Glumov enters.

Allow me to introduce my nephew – Yegor Dmitrich Glumov. *(to Glumov)* Mr Gorodulin wishes to make your acquaintance. *(exits)*

GORODULIN: *(offers Glumov his hand)* So, are you a civil servant?

GLUMOV: *(casually)* I was, but no longer, and I've no particular wish to be.

GORODULIN: Why not?

GLUMOV: Well, I haven't the knack. You need a great many different qualities and I haven't any of them.

GORODULIN: It seems to me all you need is brains and the willingness to work.

GLUMOV: Well, let's say I have no problem on that score, but what's the use of having those things? No matter how hard you work, you still end up a dogsbody in some office. If you want any sort of promotion, and you haven't a patron, you need other skills.

GORODULIN: And what would those be exactly?

GLUMOV: Well, don't use your brains unless you're told to. Laugh, whenever the management fancies it's come up with a joke. Do all the thinking and hard work for your bosses, while at the same time assuring them, with as much humility as you can muster, that it's all theirs – oh yes, indeed, sir, silly me, I've only done what you yourself were pleased to command. And apart from that, you need a few other slavish attributes – conjoined, of course, to a certain tincture of grace. For instance, you have to know how to leap up and strain to attention, in a manner both servile, and not servile, at one and the same time. You have to grovel, but with a straight back, in an honourable and graceful fashion. And when the boss sends you out on some errand, you must know how to produce a gentle sort of flutter, about midway between a gallop, march-time, and your normal gait. Anyway, I haven't covered even half of the things you need to know, if you're going to get anywhere in the service.

GORODULIN: Excellent. Or rather, it's all very nasty, but you speak extremely well, and that's the main thing. In any case, that's how it used to be, it's all quite different now.

GLUMOV: Well, I haven't seen much that's different. It's still all paperwork and red tape. Entire walls, whole fortresses of red tape. And out of these fortresses fly all sorts of dreary circulars and memos, like bombs.

GORODULIN: Oh, that's very good! Splendid, absolutely splendid! Such a talent!

GLUMOV: I'm very pleased that you sympathise with my ideas. However, there aren't many who do.

GORODULIN: Who cares about ideas? Everybody has them, we all share them. It's the words, the phrases that are so fine. You know, you might be able to do me a very great favour.

GLUMOV: Whatever you wish.

GORODULIN: Write all that down on a piece of paper.

GLUMOV: With pleasure, sir. What do you want it for?

GORODULIN: Well, I'll be frank with you. We're decent chaps, you and I, and we ought to speak freely. Anyway, here's the thing – I've got to make an after-dinner speech tomorrow, and I've no simply no time to think.

GLUMOV: Yes, of course, certainly.

GORODULIN: *(squeezes his hand)* And you'll do this for me, as a friend?

GLUMOV: Don't mention it, sir, please. No, just give me any sort of position, where I might come face to face with the meanest of my fellow-men. Give me the opportunity to see for myself his most urgent needs, and to satisfy them speedily and with compassion.

GORODULIN: Excellent! First rate! Write that down as well! So, as I understand it, in keeping with your honest outlook on life, you want the post of inspector or supervisor in some kind of government or charitable organisation?

GLUMOV: Yes, whatever you think. I'm not averse to work, and I'll do so assiduously, to the best of my abilities, but on one condition – that my work should be of genuine value, that it should improve the quality of life, something essential to the well-being of the people. To sit twiddling my thumbs all day, and call that service, even get a decoration for it – I wouldn't have it.

GORODULIN: That's absolutely spot on – "improve the quality of life" – wonderful!

GLUMOV: So, would you like me to write the whole speech?

GORODULIN: Would you really? Well now, you see? It doesn't take long for honest men to agree. They exchange a few words, and they're friends. And you speak so well! Yes, we need men like that, good heavens, we certainly do! *(glances at his watch)* Look, drop in and see me around noon tomorrow. *(offers Glumov his hand)* I'm delighted to have met you, sir.

Exits to the drawing-room. Enter Mamaev.

MAMAEV: Oh, you're still here. Come over here. *(mysteriously)* Krutitsky looked in on me recently to ask my advice about a certain matter. He's a decent old stick. He's written something, and it needs polishing, a few syllables smoothed out. So I've pointed him in your direction. Among our circle he doesn't exactly pass for an intellectual, and no doubt he'll have written some foolishness or other, but when you meet him, make sure you butter him up a bit.

GLUMOV: Good heavens, uncle, what sort of lesson are you teaching me?

MAMAEV: Oh, flattery's a bad thing, of course, but it's permissible now and again. Find something to praise here and there and that'll please the old man. He might come in handy later on. We'll put him in his place, he won't escape our censure, but you're still young, you ought to praise him. We'll pay him a call tomorrow. Yes, and there's another rather delicate situation. Tell me, how have you been getting along with your aunt?

GLUMOV: Sir, I've been properly brought up, you don't have to teach me respect.

MAMAEV: No, no, don't be silly. She's still quite young, you know, and rather pretty – it's not your respect she needs. I mean, do you want to make an enemy of her?

GLUMOV: Uncle, I don't understand.

MAMAEV: Well, if you don't understand, listen, and learn! And thank God you've got someone to teach you. You know, women won't easily forgive a man who doesn't notice their beauty.

GLUMOV: Yes, yes, of course! I hadn't given it a thought.

MAMAEV: Indeed! Well, sir – even though the connection's rather distant, you're a relative nonetheless, so you have more freedom than a mere acquaintance. For instance, you can kiss her hand a bit more, as if absent-mindedly, and you can make eyes, if you know what I mean.

GLUMOV: Make eyes?

MAMAEV: Oh, good God, sir – look, like this. *(rolls his eyes upwards)*

GLUMOV: Oh, surely not! How can I do that?

MAMAEV: Well, you can practise in front of a mirror, you'll soon learn. And you should sigh now and again, with a sort of languid expression. These things all tickle their vanity.

GLUMOV: Sir, I'm most humbly grateful to you.

MAMAEV: And I'll feel more at ease too, if you take my meaning. D'you follow?

GLUMOV: Well, no, sir, not really.

MAMAEV: My wife's a passionate woman, you see, rather headstrong, and she could quite easily fall for some young fop, or God knows, take up with some wretched labourer, some jailbird. These sort of parasites have absolutely no conscience. There's no telling what might happen. But here you are, you see, and you'd be on hand to serve, tried and tested, as it were. If the wolves are fed, the lambs are safe. Ha-ha! D'you see what I mean?

GLUMOV: Oh, uncle, what a mind you have!

MAMAEV: Well, I hope so.

GLUMOV: Ah, yes, but there's another problem. To make sure that people don't think there's anything sinister going on – I mean, you know how spiteful they can be – you'll have to introduce me to Madame Turusina. I can openly pay court to her niece, then, and perhaps even get engaged to her, if you approve. That way the wolves really will be fed, and the lambs'll be as safe as houses.

MAMAEV: Yes, yes, absolutely. That's the stuff!

GLUMOV: Of course, we won't say a word about Madame Turusina to my aunt. It's not a question of jealousy, but you know how sensitive women are.

MAMAEV: You don't have to tell me, I know full well. No no no, there's no need to mention it.

GLUMOV: So, when shall we call on Madame Turusina?

MAMAEV: Tomorrow evening. Anyway, you now know what to do.

GLUMOV: What to do? Yes, to be amazed at your cleverness.

Enter Kleopatra and Gorodulin.

GORODULIN: *(to Kleopatra, sotto voce)* He'll be appointed in two weeks' time.

KLEOPATRA: And in two weeks' time I shall kiss you.

MAMAEV: Ah, Gorodulin. I was coming to see you today, to give you some advice on that business at the club.

GORODULIN: I'm sorry, my dear chap, I've no time. *(offers his hand to Glumov)* Goodbye, sir.

MAMAEV: Let's go together, then, I can tell you on the way. I'm wanted at the Senate.

They exit.

KLEOPATRA: *(sits in an armchair)* You may kiss my hand, your affair is settled.

GLUMOV: I didn't ask you.

KLEOPATRA: There was no need, I could guess what you wanted.

GLUMOV: *(kisses her hand)* Thank you. *(picks up his hat)*

KLEOPATRA: Where are you going?

GLUMOV: Home. I'm just so happy. I'm rushing off home to share my joy with my mother.

KLEOPATRA: You're happy? I don't believe it.

GLUMOV: I am indeed, as much as I can be.

KLEOPATRA: Ah, that means not quite. That means you still haven't gained everything you want.

GLUMOV: I've gained as much as I dared hope for.

KLEOPATRA: Oh come, tell me the truth. Have you got everything you wanted?

GLUMOV: What more could I ask? I'm being given a position.

KLEOPATRA: No, I don't believe you. You're simply trying to present yourself as a materialist – at your young age. You would have me believe all you think about is work, and money.

GLUMOV: My dear lady...

KLEOPATRA: You would have me believe that your heart never beats faster, that you never dream, never weep, that you've never loved anyone.

GLUMOV: No, I didn't say that.

KLEOPATRA: And if you are in love, can you possibly not want her to love you too?

GLUMOV: That's not what I'm saying.

KLEOPATRA: But you're saying you've got everything you want.

GLUMOV: I've got everything possible, everything I can allow myself to hope for.

KLEOPATRA: In other words, you can't allow yourself to hope for love in return? In that case, why do you waste your feelings? I mean, these are the pearls of your soul. Tell me, who is this cruel mistress?

GLUMOV: Dear lady, this is torture.

KLEOPATRA: Tell me, you wretch, tell me this instant! I know it, I can see it in your eyes, you're in love. Oh, you poor boy! Are you suffering terribly?

GLUMOV: You have no right to resort to such measures. You know I can hide nothing from you.

KLEOPATRA: Who is she?

GLUMOV: Please, have pity on me!

KLEOPATRA: Is she worthy of you?

GLUMOV: Oh God, what are you doing to me?

KLEOPATRA: Is she able to appreciate your passion, your loving heart?

GLUMOV: Kill me if you must, I dare not tell.

KLEOPATRA: *(in a whisper)* Yes, dare! Courage, mon ami!

GLUMOV: Whom do I love?

KLEOPATRA: Yes.

GLUMOV: *(kneels before her)* You.

KLEOPATRA: *(shrieks softly)* Ah!

GLUMOV: I am your slave for life. Punish me for my audacity, but I love you. Force me to silence, forbid me to look upon you, to admire your beauty, or even worse, make me keep a respectful distance, only please don't be angry with me! You yourself are to blame. If you hadn't been so charming, so condescending to me, I might have restrained my passion within the bounds of decency, however much it cost me. But you, my angel of goodness – you, my vision of loveliness – you have changed me from a sensible young man to a raving lunatic! Yes, I've gone mad! It seemed as if bliss was luring me on, and I threw myself fearlessly into that abyss, wherein I may perish, never to return. Forgive me. *(bows his head)*

KLEOPATRA: *(kisses his forehead)* I forgive you.

Glumov rises, bows respectfully and exits. Kleopatra watches him go.

END OF ACT TWO

ACT THREE

The scene is an opulent drawing-room in Madame Turusina's country house at Sokolniki; a door at centre, another at the side. Turusina and her niece Masha enter upstage centre.

MASHA: Come on, auntie, let's go! Please, let's go out now!

TURUSINA: No, no, my dear, absolutely not. Not for anything. I've already had the horses unharnessed.

MASHA: Oh, auntie, honestly, it's ridiculous. Once in a blue moon we decide to go somewhere, and then we're hardly ten paces outside the gate and we have to turn back.

TURUSINA: *(sits down)* My dear child, I know perfectly well what I'm doing. Why should we expose ourselves to danger when we can avoid it?

MASHA: But what on earth makes you think we were in danger?

TURUSINA: Really, I don't know how you can even ask that question. You saw yourself – that woman walked past us right outside our gate. I'd have ordered the coachman to stop immediately, but I forced myself to go on, and then suddenly, the very next person we see...

MASHA: What next person? What are you talking about?

TURUSINA: I mean, if they'd appeared from the left, but it was from the right...

MASHA: What difference does it make, left or right?

TURUSINA: Don't speak like that, I don't like it. I won't tolerate free-thinking in my own home. I have to listen to quite enough blasphemy from visitors. I can't stop them, they're guests, but I can stop you. We need to live right, and look after ourselves. Of course, it's sinful to be overly concerned with oneself, but we're obliged to take care. Now, don't be so obstinate! Good heavens, we see accidents enough – horses bolting, carriages breaking down, coachmen getting drunk and driving into the ditch. Divine providence watches over us. And if you're told in no uncertain terms – don't go there, you're exposing yourself to danger – then whose fault is it if you ignore that good advice, and wind up breaking your neck!

MASHA: But no-one said anything of the sort – don't go there!

TURUSINA: Does it need to be spelt out? An evil omen is far more
eloquent than any words. If it had been urgent necessity, well, that
couldn't be helped. But going out for no particular reason, to
spend the whole evening in idle chit-chat, gossiping about the
neighbours! And for that we should ignore the clearest signs from
on high, and expose ourselves to obvious danger! No, no, thank
you very much. I'm well aware why you want to go to that place.
You think you'll meet Kurchaev there, that unrepentant atheist, a
man I won't even allow in the house. That's why you're trying to
drag your poor aunt there, for your own selfish pleasure, without
even thinking I might break my leg or an arm.

MASHA: Auntie, I just don't understand why you're so dead set
against Kurchaev.

TURUSINA: Why shouldn't I be? He laughs in my face at everything
I hold most sacred.

MASHA: When, auntie? When does he do this?

TURUSINA: All the time, he never stops – he laughs at my pilgrims,
the holy beggars I take in.

MASHA: I thought you said sacred?

TURUSINA: Well, of course they are. And when I said to him, "Just look
at dear Matryosha – her face is beginning to shine with holiness!" all he
said was, "That's not holiness shining – that's goose-grease!" I'll never
forgive him for that, as long as I live. And that's where all that free-
thinking leads to, young people simply don't know their place these
days! No, I'm very rarely wrong about people, and I know just what
sort he is. I received two letters yesterday. Here, read them if you wish.

MASHA: You surely don't believe anonymous letters?

TURUSINA: If there had been only one, I might've had my doubts,
but suddenly to receive two, and by different hands.

A servant enters and hands Madame Turusina a letter.

GRIGORY: That's some more tramps turned up, ma'am.

TURUSINA: I can't make out what he says. Well, anyway, it's most
likely some holy pilgrims. See that they get something to eat.

The servant exits. Turusina reads the letter.

Hm, another letter... Obviously written by a respectable lady. *(reads aloud)* "My dear Madame Turusina, although I have not had the honour to..." Well, now, just listen to this! "Your choice of a man like Yegor Kurchaev compels me to shed tears in advance for the fate of poor dear Masha..." Yes, and there's more.

MASHA: That's astonishing! I don't know what to think.

TURUSINA: Surely you're not going to argue with me now? Well, my dear, if you're absolutely set on it, go ahead and marry him. *(sniffs at her smelling-salts)* I don't want you calling me a tyrant. Only you should be aware that you'll upset me if you do, and you'll have very little cause to complain, if I decide...

MASHA: If you decide not to give me any money.

TURUSINA: No, no – my blessing, that's the main thing.

MASHA: Well, have no fear, auntie. I'm a typical Moscow miss, I won't marry without money, or my family's permission. I'm rather fond of Kurchaev, but if you don't like him, I won't marry him, and I won't die of consumption on his account either. But do take pity on me, auntie. Thanks to you, I've got some money, and I would like to enjoy life!

TURUSINA: Of course, my dear child, I understand.

MASHA: Find me any young man you like, as long as he's decent, and I'll marry him without a murmur. I want to shine in society, I want to show off a bit. I mean, the kind of life we lead, I'm sure you can imagine, bores me absolutely rigid.

TURUSINA: Hm, I can see your point. A little vanity at your age is excusable.

MASHA: Anyway, it's entirely probable that when I'm a bit older, I'll live just as we do now, auntie – it's in the blood.

TURUSINA: I do hope so – indeed, I wish it with all my heart. It's the strait and narrow way, the true path.

MASHA: Yes, but I've got to get married first, auntie.

TURUSINA: Well, I shan't try and conceal the fact that I'm having some difficulty. Young men are so corrupt nowadays, and it's extremely hard to find one I might like. And you know my requirements.

MASHA: Oh, auntie, if we can't find one in Moscow! Really, we've got everything here – everything you could wish. And you know so many people. You can ask anybody – Krutitsky, say, or Mamaev, or Gorodulin – they'll help, surely. They'll either know, or else they'll be able to find exactly the right sort of young man you want. I'm certain of it.

TURUSINA: Krutitsky, or Gorodulin! They're only men, Masha my dear, they might deceive us, or even be deceived themselves.

MASHA: Well, what can we do?

TURUSINA: We must wait for a sign. Without a special sign, I can make no decision.

MASHA: But where's this sign going to appear from?

TURUSINA: You'll know soon enough. It'll appear today, for sure.

MASHA: Auntie, please don't turn Kurchaev away, let him call on us.

TURUSINA: Only if you acknowledge that you can't marry him.

MASHA: I am completely at your disposal, auntie. I am your most frightfully obedient niece.

TURUSINA: *(kisses her)* You're my darling child!

MASHA: Oh yes, when I'm rich, I shall have such fun! You used to have a good time, didn't you, auntie?

TURUSINA: Who told you that?

MASHA: Oh, I know – you had lots of fun.

TURUSINA: Well, you may know a few things, but you can't, and you shouldn't know everything.

MASHA: I don't care. You're the finest woman I know, and I'll happily take you as my example. *(hugs her aunt)* Yes, I want to have a good time, too, and if I sin, well, I can always repent. I shall sin and repent, just like you.

TURUSINA: Masha, what a shocking thing to say!

MASHA: *(folding her hands)* Sorry.

TURUSINA: Honestly, you've never stopped talking. Now – I'm very
tired, and I need some rest, to gather my thoughts. *(kisses Masha, who
exits)* She's such a dear child. I can't be angry with her. I don't think
she understands what she's saying. Indeed, how could she, she
prattles on so. Anyway, I shall do everything in my power to make her
happy, she thoroughly deserves it. She's such a sensible girl, and so
obedient! Her childish devotion almost moves me to tears. Oh dear,
I'm really quite shaken... *(takes another sniff at her smelling-salts)*

    Enter Grigory.

GRIGORY: Mr Krutitsky, ma'am.

TURUSINA: Show him in.

    Grigory exits. Enter Krutitsky.

KRUTITSKY: *(takes her hands in his)* Good heavens, is it nerves?

TURUSINA: Yes.

KRUTITSKY: That's too bad. Dear me, your hands are freezing.
You must be...

TURUSINA: Must be what?

KRUTITSKY: Well, you must be working too hard... you're
overtaxing yourself... you shouldn't get so...

TURUSINA: I've told you not to mention that.

KRUTITSKY: No no, of course, I shan't.

TURUSINA: Sit down, please.

KRUTITSKY: No, thanks, I'm not tired. I just came out for a stroll,
and I thought, well, why not look in an old acquaintance... an old
friend, eh? Heh, heh, heh! I mean, you remember how we used to...

TURUSINA: Please, don't remind me! No no, these days I'm...

KRUTITSKY: What do you mean? Why shouldn't I remind you?

You had some good times in the old days. And if there were the
odd thing you might regard as naughty, well, you've no doubt
repented long since. Frankly, I must confess I look back on it all
with immense pleasure, I haven't the slightest regret that we...

TURUSINA: *(with a pleading look)* That's enough, please!

> *Grigory enters.*

GRIGORY: That's one of them monkeys arrived, ma'am.

KRUTITSKY: What?

TURUSINA: Shame on you, Grigory! Monks, not monkeys – some
holy pilgrim. See that he gets something to eat.

> *Grigory exits.*

These servants are so stupid, they can't get the most common
names right.

KRUTITSKY: I wouldn't have said pilgrims were that common
nowadays. You scarcely ever encounter one, except here. Anyway,
to resume our earlier conversation – you'll forgive me, but I simply
wanted to point out that you were healthier in those days, when
you led a very different sort of life.

TURUSINA: Healthier in body, not in soul.

KRUTITSKY: Well, I don't know about that, that's not my affair.
But you certainly looked better. I mean, you're quite young... you
could still have a decent life.

TURUSINA: I have a decent life.

KRUTITSKY: It's a bit early to go all sanctimonious.

TURUSINA: I've already asked you not to...

KRUTITSKY: I'm sorry, I'm sorry, I won't say a word.

TURUSINA: You really are a strange person.

> *Grigory enters.*

GRIGORY: Ma'am, there's a strange person arrived.

TURUSINA: Didn't you ask him where he was from?

GRIGORY: He says he's from a strange land.

TURUSINA: Well, bring him in and sit him down with the others.

GRIGORY: Ma'am, if you put him with the others...

TURUSINA: Go on, go on!

Grigory exits.

KRUTITSKY: You know, with all these people turning up from 'strange lands', you might at least ask them for their passports.

TURUSINA: Why?

KRUTITSKY: Well, you could easily find yourself in trouble. For instance, I know somebody who took in three strangers off the street.

TURUSINA: And?

KRUTITSKY: And they turned out to be first-rate engravers.

TURUSINA: What's wrong with that?

KRUTITSKY: Oh, it's an evil trade.

TURUSINA: Engraving? What's evil about it?

KRUTITSKY: Well, it isn't portraits they engrave, in their little hidey-holes.

TURUSINA: *(in a whisper)* Not icons?

KRUTITSKY: Icons, my foot! Banknotes!

TURUSINA: *(alarmed)* What are you saying!

KRUTITSKY: *(sits down)* Exactly that! Charity's all very well, but it does no harm to be careful, you especially. It's a well-known fact, that once a lady gets a reputation for good deeds, she's an easy mark for swindlers. They'll pull the wool over your eyes very easily.

TURUSINA: I do good for its own sake, I don't discriminate. Anyway, I'd like your advice on a very important matter.

KRUTITSKY: *(drawing closer)* Go on, ask me. I'll be delighted to serve you in any way I can.

TURUSINA: Well, you know my dear Masha is now at that age, when...

KRUTITSKY: Yes, yes, I know.

TURUSINA: You wouldn't have a young man in mind, perhaps? You know the sort I require.

KRUTITSKY: The sort you require? Ah, well, there's the snag... There are so few young men nowadays that... No, wait a minute! There is one, exactly what you're looking for.

TURUSINA: Really?

KRUTITSKY: What am I saying? He's discreet beyond his years, intelligent, noble birth and all that, he'll make an outstanding career. He really is a splendid young man, quite... splendid, yes. He was recommended to me for a certain job of work, and I tried him out, as you might say – let's see what sort of bird we've got here! And he's a first-rate lad. He'll go far, you mark my words.

TURUSINA: So who is he?

KRUTITSKY: Who is he? Oh, God, what a memory! Ah, wait a minute – he gave me his address. I don't need it now, the servants know it. *(takes out a piece of paper)* Here we are... *(reads)* 'Yegor Dmitrich Glumov...' See, look how he writes – neat and precise, a beautiful hand. You can tell a person's character instantly from their handwriting. It's precise – that means he's accurate... decent round letters with no flourishes – that means he isn't one of those freethinkers. Anyway, there you are, you might find that useful.

TURUSINA: *(takes the address)* Thank you.

KRUTITSKY: What are you thanking me for? It's our duty. *(stands up)* Well, goodbye. I may call again, yes? Or are you still angry with me?

TURUSINA: Oh, don't be absurd – I'm always pleased to see you.

KRUTITSKY: Well, then... I'm an affectionate chap... It's such a pity...

TURUSINA: Do come again.

KRUTITSKY: For old times' sake? Heh, heh, heh! Ah, well... au
revoir! *(exits)*

TURUSINA: What a silly man he is, and at his age. How can one
trust him? *(puts the address in her pocket)* Still, I must make
enquiries about this Glumov.

Grigory enters.

GRIGORY: Mr Gorodulin, ma'am.

TURUSINA: Show him in.

Grigory exits. Enter Gorodulin.

I'm pleased to see you. Aren't you ashamed of yourself? Where
have you been all these weeks?

GORODULIN: Oh, business, business. One minute it's an official
dinner, next minute they're opening a railroad.

TURUSINA: I'm not sure I believe you. You're simply bored with
us. Well, at any rate, thank you for dropping in, even once in a
while. So, what's happening with that business of ours?

GORODULIN: What business?

TURUSINA: Don't tell me you've forgotten. That's marvellous! I'm
most humbly grateful to you. I was a fool to ask you in the first
place. I mean, you're a busy man, occupied with all manner of
important affairs – when would you have time to remember the
poor, unhappy, downtrodden wretches of this world? They're
beneath your notice.

GORODULIN: Downtrodden, you say? I don't recall anything about
downtrodden wretches. Ah, now I remember – you asked me to
find out about some fortune-teller.

TURUSINA: Not a fortune-teller, a true medium, a psychic – there's
a big difference. I wouldn't dream of going to a fortune-teller.

GORDODULIN: Oh, I'm sorry – I'm not up on the finer points of
these things. Anyway, you're talking about Ulita Shmygaeva, the
collegiate registrar's widow.

TURUSINA: I don't care what her rank was, she's a most respectable lady, of blameless life, and I confess myself proud to have enjoyed her special favour.

GORODULIN: Yes, well, according to the evidence, it seems her special favour was also enjoyed by a retired soldier.

TURUSINA: What are you saying! That's absolute nonsense, malicious gossip! She was successful, yes, she had friends in the very best circles, and people simply envied her, that's why they slandered her. I sincerely hope she's been acquitted, innocence must triumph.

GORODULIN: I'm afraid not – she's been exiled to Siberia.

TURUSINA: *(stands up)* What! Well, where's your much-vaunted justice now, eh? Sending an innocent woman into exile! And for what? Because she tried to help people?

GORODULIN: Actually, she wasn't charged with fortune-telling.

TURUSINA: No, I won't hear another word! It was all done to please these fashionable modern unbelievers.

GORODULIN: She was charged with receiving stolen property, harbouring known criminals, and poisoning some merchant or other.

TURUSINA: Oh, my God! I don't believe it.

GORODULIN: It's the gospel truth. The merchant's wife asked her for some sort of potion to give her husband, so he'd love her again, and it seems they brewed up the potion in Madeira, observed all the rules, and so on, except one – they failed to clear it with the Health Board.

TURUSINA: What happened to him?

GORODULIN: Oh, it had an effect. He almost died, but not from love.

TURUSINA: I can see you think all this is funny. Lawyers and dcotors have no feeling. Couldn't even one person be found to speak up for this poor woman?

GORODULIN: I beg your pardon, she was defended by one of our finest advocates. A positive river of eloquence gushed forth, swirled round the court, burst its banks, and finally subsided to a mere trickle. There was nothing anyone could do – they themselves made a full confession. First the soldier, the one who'd enjoyed her special favour, then the woman.

TURUSINA: Well, I wouldn't have believed it. How easily one can
be mistaken. It's quite impossible to live in this world.

GORODULIN: No, not impossible, but very difficult if your head's in
a permanent stew. Actually, the study of mental disorder has
advanced quite far these days, and hallucinations...

TURUSINA: I've told you never to speak to me about these things.

GORODULIN: Sorry, I forgot.

TURUSINA: Well, I may be mistaken about some people, I may be
deceived, but helping people, caring for those less fortunate, is the
only blessing I enjoy.

GORODULIN: And blessing's not to be sneezed at. A truly blessed
person is a rare bird these days.

> *Grigory enters.*

GRIGORY: That's another blessed person arrived, ma'am.

GORODULIN: Really?

TURUSINA: Who is he?

GRIGORY: I'd say he's one of them Asiatics, ma'am.

TURUSINA: What makes you think that?

GRIGORY: He's fearsome, ma'am – scare you half to death just
looking at him. If he's still here at night, ma'am, God help us all.

TURUSINA: What do you mean, fearsome? What nonsense is this?

GRIGORY: He's got an uncommon fierce look to him, ma'am. He's
all covered in hair, you can just about see his eyes.

TURUSINA: He's Greek, most likely.

GRIGORY: No, not Greek, ma'am, the colour's not ripe enough. I
reckon he's one of them Hungarians.

TURUSINA: Hungarians? Honestly, what rubbish you talk. What
Hungarians?

GRIGORY: The ones that sells mouse-traps.

TURUSINA: Anyway, invite him in, give him something to eat, and ask him if he needs anything.

GRIGORY: Ma'am, I think he's a bit...

TURUSINA: Don't argue, just go!

GRIGORY: Yes, ma'am. *(exits)*

TURUSINA: Now, Ivan Ivanych... I have a favour to ask.

GORODULIN: I'm all ears.

TURUSINA: It's about my niece Masha. You wouldn't happen to have anyone in mind for her?

GORODULIN: A fiancé? Oh, spare me that! What on earth possessed you to ask me? Tell me, do I look like a Moscow matchmaker? It's my job to unravel knots, not tie them. No, no, I'm opposed to any sort of bond, even the matrimonial kind.

TURUSINA: But you wear a ring yourself.

GORODULIN: Yes, and that's why I wouldn't wish it on a dog.

TURUSINA: Anyway, joking apart, do you know anyone?

GORODULIN: Now, wait a minute... yes, I did see someone the other day, he had it practically written on his forehead, in big letters – "GOOD CATCH". You only had to look at him to see he was poised to marry some rich heiress.

TURUSINA: What was his name? Try and remember.

GORODULIN: Yes... yes... Ah, Glumov.

TURUSINA: And is he a good man?

GORODULIN: Well, he's an honest man, that's as much as I know. No, seriously – he's a very fine young man.

TURUSINA: Just a moment – what did you say his name was again? *(takes the paper out of her pocket)*

GORODULIN: Glumov.

TURUSINA: Yegor Dmitrich?

GORODULIN: That's right.

TURUSINA: He's the one Krutitsky told me about.

GORODULIN: Well, there you are, then – written on his forehead, as I said. Or rather, in his destiny. Goodbye... *(bows and exits)*

TURUSINA: Now, just who is this Glumov? That's the second time today I've heard his name. And although I don't really trust either Krutitsky or Gorodulin, still, there must be something in it, when two people of such opposite views recommend him. *(rings the bell)*

Grigory enters.

Call the young mistress, and tell her they can all come in.

Grigory exits.

Oh, what a tragic loss it was to Moscow, when dear Ivan Yakovlich died. Life here was so simple and straightforward when he was still with us. Now I can't sleep at nights for wondering what I'm going to do with Masha. I mean, I could make a dreadful mistake, and it'd be on my conscience. But if dear Ivan were alive, I wouldn't even have to think about it. I'd just pay him a call, ask his advice, and I'd be able to relax. Yes, that's when we really appreciate the true value of a person, when they're no longer with us. I don't know if Manefa can take his place, but there's a great deal of the supernatural about her too.

Masha enters, accompanied by 1st Hanger-on, who is holding a pack of cards in front of her like a book, and 2nd Hanger-on, who is cradling a lap-dog in her arms.

1ST HANGER-ON: Shall I lay out the cards?

TURUSINA: No, wait a moment. Masha dear, I've been speaking about you to Krutitsky and Gorodulin.

MASHA: *(excitedly)* So? What did they say? Tell me. I've promised to obey you, and now I can't wait to hear your decision.

TURUSINA: They both recommended the same young man, almost as if they'd agreed beforehand.

MASHA: That's wonderful – he must be ideal. Who is he?

TURUSINA: Yes, but I don't really trust them.

1ST HANGER-ON: Shall I begin now?

TURUSINA: Yes, yes – ask the cards. Let's see if they're telling the truth. *(to Masha)* No, I don't trust them, they could be mistaken.

MASHA: But why, auntie?

TURUSINA: Because they're human. *(to 2nd Hanger-on)* Don't drop that dog!

MASHA: Well, who can you trust, auntie? The oracle? That frightens me.

TURUSINA: That's only natural. It is frightening, and so it should be. We can't, we mustn't lift the veil of the future without fear. For behind that veil lies happiness, and misery, your very life and death, Masha.

MASHA: And who's going to lift the veil for us?

TURUSINA: The one who has the power.

    Enter Grigory.

GRIGORY: Manefa's here, ma'am.

TURUSINA: That's the one. *(stands up, goes to greet Manefa, followed by the others)*

    Manefa enters.

Do come in, please.

MANEFA: And so I come. The great ladle went, and the great ladle came.

1ST HANGER-ON: *(emotionally)* Oh, saints above!

TURUSINA: *(menacingly)* Be quiet!

MANEFA: *(sits down)* Came and sat low, like a lump of dough.

2ND HANGER-ON: Oh! Oh! Oh! Oh, what wise words!

1ST HANGER-ON: It is the Lord's doing, and we've lived to see it!

TURUSINA: Ssshhh!

MANEFA: What are you goggling at?

TURUSINA: We're just overjoyed that we've been granted a sight of you.

1ST HANGER-ON: Oh, that we've been granted a sight!

2ND HANGER-ON: Yes, yes, all of us!

TURUSINA: We're waiting, mother Manefa – what do you say?

MANEFA: Yes, you're waiting – you wait for her in boots, behold she comes barefoot.

1ST HANGER-ON: Oh, my saints! Drink in every word, drink it in!

TURUSINA: Madame Manefa, I wanted to ask you...

MANEFA: Don't ask, I know already. Know-it-all runs ahead, Know-not lies abed! One maid less, one wife more.

2ND HANGER-ON: Yes, yes, it's so true!

TURUSINA: We'd like to know about a certain young man. Won't you speak to your devoted slave Maria? Perhaps you've seen him in a dream, or a vision...

MANEFA: A vision, yes. Cometh one Yegor from the high hills...

2ND HANGER-ON: Yegor! D'you hear that?

MASHA: *(aside to Turusina)* Kurchaev's also called Yegor.

TURUSINA: Wait a minute – what's he like, exactly?

MANEFA: How should I know? You'll know him when you see him.

TURUSINA: But when shall we see him?

MANEFA: The welcome guest needs no behest!

1ST HANGER-ON: Oh, did you hear that!

TURUSINA: If you could just give us some detail...

2ND HANGER-ON: You should ask what colour his hair is, that's the first thing. People always ask that, you surely know that much!

TURUSINA: Will you shut up! What colour is his hair?

MANEFA: To some I say, "Beware!" – to you I say, "He's fair."

MASHA: He's fair-haired. Kurchaev's fair-haired, actually. Maybe it's him.

TURUSINA: Now really, you've just heard her say it was a vision. D'you think decent God-fearing people would have a vision about a hussar? Honestly, Masha, you're so silly.

1ST HANGER-ON: Oh, my God, it's astonishing! Even the cards say it's Yegor!

TURUSINA: What are you talking about? How could you see his name in the cards?

1ST HANGER-ON: No, no, I tell a lie – a slip of the tongue. I mean the cards say 'fair-haired'!

TURUSINA: *(to Manefa)* It's all so clear to you, but we are sinful people, we live in doubt. There are many Yegors, and quite a few of them are fair-haired.

MANEFA: A far-off land the stranger's fate – the chosen one stands by the gate!

ALL: At the gate?

MANEFA: Array thyself, display thyself, the bridegroom cometh sure!

TURUSINA: When? When?

MANEFA: This very hour, this very instant.

    They all turn to the door. Grigory enters.

  Trumpets and drums, he comes, he comes! *(stands up)*

GRIGORY: Mr Mamaev, ma'am.

TURUSINA: Is he alone?

GRIGORY: There's a young gentleman with him – a fair-haired chap.

1ST HANGER-ON: Oh, are we really alive!

2ND HANGER-ON: Surely this is all a dream!

TURUSINA: Show them in. *(hugs Masha)* Oh, Masha, my dear, my prayers have been answered! *(sits down, sniffs at her smelling-salts)*

MASHA: This is extraordinary, auntie – I'm trembling all over.

TURUSINA: Go and calm yourself, my dear. You can come out later.

Masha exits.

MANEFA: All's well that ends well. *(goes to the door)*

TURUSINA: *(to the Hangers-on)* Take her by the arm, and give her some tea – some tea, please.

MANEFA: Tea? Tea is for teetotallers.

TURUSINA: Well, give her whatever she wants.

The Hangers-on lead Manefa towards the door, and pause.

1ST HANGER-ON: Oh, if we could only just get a glimpse of him!

2ND HANGER-ON: I'll just die if we don't see this wonder!

Enter Mamaev and Glumov.

MAMAEV: My dear Madame Turusina, allow me to present my nephew, Yegor Dmitrich Glumov.

1ST HANGER-ON: *(in the doorway)* Oh! His name's Yegor! Oh! He's fair-haired!

MAMAEV: I trust you'll be kind to him.

TURUSINA: *(stands up)* Thank you! I shall love him like my own son.

Glumov respectfully kisses her hand.

END OF ACT THREE

ACT FOUR

SCENE ONE

A reception room in Krutitsky's house; an entrance door, another door at right, leading to his study, and at left to the drawing-room; a table and one chair. Glumov enters, a footman is standing by the door.

GLUMOV: Announce me, please.

FOOTMAN: *(glances into the study)* He's coming out now, sir.

    Krutitsky enters. Footman exits.

KRUTISTSKY: *(nodding)* Is it ready?

GLUMOV: Ready, your Excellency. *(hands him a notebook)*

KRUTITSKY: *(takes the notebook)* Hm... Legible, beautifully written, outstanding. Bravo! Well done, sir. You say 'treatise'? Why not 'project'?

GLUMOV: Well, a project, your Excellency, is when you propose something new. What your Excellency does, on the contrary, is to reject everything new... *(with an ingratiating smile)* .. and quite properly, your Excellency.

KRUTITSKY: So, you think a 'treatise', then?

GLUMOV: Treatise is better, sir.

KRUTITSKY: Really? Yes, I suppose so. "Treatise on the Damage Caused by Reform in General" You don't think "In General" is a bit much?

GLUMOV: Well, that's your Excellency's main contention – that reforms are generally harmful.

KRUTITSKY: Oh, certainly, if they're fundamental, or radical. But if it means making some minor improvements, well, I've nothing against that.

GLUMOV: In that case, they're not reforms, but adjustments. Repairs, so to speak.

KRUTITSKY: *(tapping his forehead with a pencil)* Yes, yes, that's true. Hm... very clever. You've hit the nail on the head, young man. Yes, I'm delighted – keep up the good work!

GLUMOV: I'm most humbly grateful to your Excellency.

KRUTITSKY: *(puts on his spectacles)* Now then, let's go on... I'm curious to know how you begin the exposition of my leading idea... "Article 1: Any reform is harmful by its very nature. For what does reform comprise? Reform comprises two actions: firstly, the removal of the old; and secondly, its replacement by something new. Which of these two actions is harmful? Both are equally harmful. By sweeping away the old, we offer scope to dangerously inquisitive minds, to probe into the reasons why this or that is being abolished, and to draw the following conclusions: since we get rid of whatever we have no use for, then such-and-such an institution, now being abolished, must be useless. But this cannot be allowed, since it gives rise to freethinking, and becomes in effect an invitation to discuss things which are not open to debate..." Well put, sir – sound good sense.

GLUMOV: And absolutely true.

KRUTITSKY: "Secondly, by introducing the new, we make as it were a concession to the so-called 'spirit of the age', which is nothing more than the invention of idle minds..." Yes, very clearly stated. I hope this'll be understood by people – by the general run, I mean.

GLUMOV: Well, it's difficult to expound sophistry, but irrefutable truths...

KRUTITSKY: What, you think these are irrefutable truths?

GLUMOV: I'm absolutely convinced of it, your Excellency.

KRUTITSKY: *(looking round)* Why don't they put another chair out here?

GLUMOV: It doesn't matter, your Excellency, I don't mind standing.

KRUTITSKY: Of course, you can't have everyone sitting – some shopkeeper with his bill, or some tailor, taking his ease...

GLUMOV: Don't let it bother you, your Excellency. Incidentally, I must beg your Excellency's pardon.

KRUTITSKY: Good heavens, what for, my dear fellow?

GLUMOV: Well, I've left certain words and expressions in your treatise completely unaltered.

KRUTITSKY: Why's that?

GLUMOV: Because our language nowadays is simply too feeble to express the grandeur of your Excellency's thoughts.

KRUTITSKY: For example?

GLUMOV: Well, Article 25, for instance, concerning the position of minor civil servants in government posts...

KRUTITSKY: And?

GLUMOV: Your Excellency makes a very strong case, wonderfully expressed, that there should be no salary increase for minor civil servants, or any improvement in their conditions, and that on the contrary, there should be significant salary increases for chairmen and board members.

KRUTITSKY: I don't remember saying that. *(leafs through the notebook)*

GLUMOV: Your Excellency, I know it by heart – and not only that paragraph, but the entire treatise.

KRUTITSKY: No, no, I believe you, I'm just surprised. Why have you done that?

GLUMOV: Well, sir, I have my whole life ahead of me. I need to store up wisdom, and it's not often this sort of opportunity presents itself. When it does, I've got to take advantage of it. You can't train your mind from newspapers.

KRUTITSKY: Absolutely not!

GLUMOV: And young people can be very easily misled.

KRUTITSKY: Well said, sir! Most praiseworthy. I'm pleased to see that sort of thinking in a young man. Say what you like, a decent respect for authority's no bad thing.

GLUMOV: Indeed, it's of the first importance, your Excellency.

KRUTITSKY: So, what exactly have I got in Article 25?

GLUMOV: Article 25: " Salary increases in the civil service, if for some reason these are deemed necessary, should be granted only with extreme caution, and then only to chairmen and board members, and under no circumstances to minor officials. Salary increases to senior ranks should be allowed in order that such persons may maintain an outward splendour commensurate with the great power vested in them. Lower ranks, on the other hand, too well-fed and contented, assume a self-important demeanour which is inappropriate to their position, whereas for the successful and efficient conduct of business, subordinates ought to be kept in a state of fear and trepidation."

KRUTITSKY: Absolutely!

GLUMOV: Yes, it was that word 'trepidation', your Excellency – that bowled me over completely.

KRUTITSKY: *(absorbed in reading, glances at Glumov now and again, as if in passing)* If you want to smoke, please do. There are matches on the mantelpiece.

GLUMOV: I don't smoke, your Excellency. Still, if you'd like me to...

KRUTITSKY: Eh? What's it got to do with me? You haven't shown your uncle this work, have you?

GLUMOV: Good heavens, no! As if I'd dare.

KRUTITSKY: No, exactly. He thinks he's clever, but he's an absolute blockhead.

GLUMOV: I wouldn't presume to argue with your Excellency.

KRUTITSKY: Yes, he's very fond of lecturing people, but just let him try and write something, then we'll see. His wife's remarkably stupid, too.

GLUMOV: Well, I won't defend her either.

KRUTITSKY: I don't understand how you manage to put up with them.

GLUMOV: Sheer necessity, your Excellency.

KRUTITSKY: You're in the service?

GLUMOV: I'm about to enter it, sir. On my aunt's recommendation. Mr Gorodulin has promised to find me a position.

KRUTITSKY: Huh, you've picked one there. He'll find you a position
all right. You want to look for something more solid – all these
Gorodulin posts'll disappear soon enough, you mark my words. He's
regarded as a dangerous character. You should make a note of that.

GLUMOV: Well, I'm not one for these new insitutions...

KRUTITSKY: Good, good. I just thought you might... Anyway, accept
the post. There's nothing worse than hanging about unemployed.
Later on, I'll give you some introductions in St Petersburg, if you
like – you'll be more visible there. I take it you have a clean record,
nothing in your past – I can recommend you to people?

GLUMOV: Well, I was a rather lazy scholar, your Excellency.

KRUTITSKY: Oh, that doesn't matter. Too much learning's worse,
if anything. You're sure there's nothing more significant?

GLUMOV: I'm afraid I do have something to confess to your
Excellency.

KRUTITSKY: *(gravely)* Eh? What is it? You'd better come right out
with it.

GLUMOV: Youthful indiscretions, sir... infatuations...

KRUTITSKY: Speak out, my boy, don't be afraid.

GLUMOV: In my student days, your Excellency... but it was more a
case of keeping up the old customs.

KRUTITSKY: What old customs? You weren't a heretic, were you?

GLUMOV: No, no – I just didn't behave the way students do nowadays.

KRUTITSKY: What do you mean?

GLUMOV: Well, I went on the odd spree, your Excellency – the occasional
adventure after hours, some minor skirmishes with the police.

KRUTITSKY: Nothing else?

GLUMOV: Good heavens, no, your Excellency – God forbid!

KRUTITSKY: Well, that's actually rather a good thing. That's how it
should be. Yes, you need to sow a few wild oats at that age. Why

should you be ashamed of it? I mean, you're not some silly girl, eh? So, I need have no worries on your account. Now then, I'm not one to be ungrateful – you made a good impression on me from the start, and I've already put in a good word for you in a certain house.

GLUMOV: Yes sir, Madame Turusina told me. I can't find words to express my gratitude to your Excellency.

KRUTITSKY: You haven't proposed yet? I mean, there's a tidy sum involved here.

GLUMOV: Oh, I haven't a clue about money, your Excellency, but the young lady is very pretty.

KRUTITSKY: Well, I really couldn't say – they all look the same to me. Her aunt's a sanctimonious hypocrite, I know that much.

GLUMOV: People no longer talk about love these days, your Excellency, but I know in myself what a lofty feeling it is.

KRUTITSKY: Yes, you can deny it all you like, dismiss it out of hand, but once it gets a grip of you, you'll know all about it. Happened to me in Bessarabia, forty years ago, I just about died from love. Why are you staring at me?

GLUMOV: Your Excellency, I can't believe it!

KRUTITSKY: I was in an absolute fever. Dismiss that, if you will! Well, I wish you luck, my boy, all the luck in the world. I'm delighted to have met you. We'll make a capitalist out of you, find you a better position, more visible, as I say, something a bit safer. We need people like you. I mean, you'll be one of us, won't you? We need all the support we can get these days, stop these young upstarts taking over. Anyway, my dear chap, how much do I owe you for your labour?

GLUMOV: Please, your Excellency, don't insult me!

KRUTITSKY: Now now, don't you insult me.

GLUMOV: Excellency, if you wish to reward me for my labour, there is a way...

KRUTITSKY: What do you mean? What way?

GLUMOV: Marriage is such a big step, such an important event in life... Please don't refuse me, sir – the blessing of such an exalted benefactor would be a guarantee of... well, even to be acquainted with a person like your Excellency is happiness itself, a kind of family relationship, albeit in a spiritual sense, and for our future offspring, well...

KRUTITSKY: You wish me to be your sponsor at your wedding? I'm not sure I understand.

GLUMOV: You'd make me very happy, your Excellency.

KRUTITSKY: Yes, of course. Why didn't you say so? That's easy enough.

GLUMOV: I can tell Madame Turusina?

KRUTITSKY: By all means.

GLUMOV: Is there anything else I can do for your Excellency?

KRUTITSKY: No.

GLUMOV: Then if I may be excused?

KRUTITSKY: Don't say a word about my scribbling, mind. It'll be published soon enough, without my name on it, naturally. A certain publisher has requested it – he's quite a decent chap, strange to say, writes to me very respectfully – if your Excellency would do me the kindness, and so forth. By the way, if there's any talk about who wrote it, you don't know a thing.

GLUMOV: Of course not, your Excellency. *(bows and exits)*

KRUTITSKY: Goodbye, dear boy. Well, well – why do we abuse young people, eh? Now there's one of them, and he's got brains, and a good heart to boot. He's a bit of a flatterer, of course – bit of a parvenu – but I daresay that'll pass with time. If he's base metal at the core, that's very bad, but if it's only his manner, then that's no great problem. With a little money and position that'll gradually disappear. His parents were poor, presumably, and his mother's a frightful sponger: "Kiss this one's hand, now kiss that one's." It's got into his blood. Still, it's better than downright rudeness.

Enter Footman.

FOOTMAN: It's Madame Mamaev, sir! She's waiting in the drawing-room. I did say the mistress wasn't at home, sir...

KLEOPATRA: *(behind the door)* I'm not disturbing you, am I?

KRUTITSKY: No, no. *(to the Footman)* Bring in an armchair.

The Footman exits, returns with an armchair. Enter Kleopatra.

KLEOPATRA: Heavens, it's time you took a rest from work, and started chasing us young ladies instead! Locked up in that study of yours – you're a most uncivil old man.

KRUTITSKY: And what could I do, eh? Yes, I was a stallion once, but I'm worn out now – heh, heh, heh! Time to give way to the young colts.

KLEOPATRA: *(sits down)* Huh! These days the young are worse than the old.

KRUTITSKY: Is that a complaint?

KLEOPATRA: Well, isn't it the truth?

KRUTITSKY: It is, it is. They've no poetry, no finer feelings. I think it's because they don't put on tragedies at the theatre any more. If they'd only bring back Ozerov, young people'd soon acquire these so delicatre, subtle feelings. Yes, they ought to put on a tragedy every other day. And Sumarokov, too. I've written a treatise, in fact, on how to improve the morals of the younger generation. For the nobility, the tragedies of Ozerov, and for the common people, legalise home-made booze. I mean, we used to know all those tragedies by heart, and now? Fat chance. They can hardly even read. That's where we got our ideas of chivalry and honour from, and now all they think about is money. *(recites)*

> "And shall I wait till Fate cuts short my days,
> Days that bring only suffering to my soul?
> I shall not!..."

You remember those lines?

KLEOPATRA: Huh, how could I forget them? Good heavens, they're a mere fifty years old, why shouldn't I remember!

KRUTITSKY: I'm sorry, do forgive me. I keep thinking you're my age. Incidentally, before I forget – I'm very pleased with that relative of yours. He's a splendid young man.

KLEOPATRA: He's a darling, isn't he.

KRUTITSKY: Yes, and I think you're spoiling him.

KLEOPATRA: In what way?

KRUTITSKY: Ah, listen – I've remembered some more!

"Oh, gods, it is not eloquence I seek –
Let but my heart in honest feeling speak!"

Magical, eh?

KLEOPATRA: In what way are we spoiling him?

KRUTITSKY: Eh? Marrying him off, of course. And what a bride
you've found for him!

KLEOPATRA: *(alarmed)* A bride? No, you must be mistaken.

KRUTITSKY: "Oh, mother, stem the flow of thy tears,
And sister, put an end to all thy fears..."

KLEOPATRA: Marrying whom? Who is she?

KRUTITSKY: Oh, good heavens, the Turusina girl, of course! As if
you don't know. She'll have a dowry of two hundred thousand.

KLEOPATRA: *(rises)* No, it's impossible. It can't be, I'm telling you.

KRUTITSKY: "Such news doth make thy senses reel,
And inward sighs thou dost conceal,
Though every line proclaims thy grief..."

KLEOPATRA: Oh, for God's sake, I'm sick of your poetry!

KRUTITSKY: He seems a goodhearted lad. Don't think I'm doing
this for money, your Excellency, he says. He's asked me to sponsor
him at his wedding. You'd be doing me a great honour, he says.
Well, why shouldn't I? I'm not marrying her for her money, he
says, I really am fond of her. She's an angel, an absolute angel,
and he speaks with such feeling. Well, anyway, that's splendid.
Good luck to him. Listen to this now, something from Donskoi...

"When a Russian swears a solemn oath,
To break his word he is full loath..."

KLEOPATRA: Oooh!

KRUTITSKY: Eh? What's the matter?

KLEOPATRA: I have a migraine. I feel quite ill.

KRUTITSKY: Oh well, it'll soon pass.

> "For thou dost know, this union will be true,
> Until..."

KLEOPATRA: Oh, stop it! Look, tell your wife I was going to wait
for her, but I can't now, I feel quite dreadful. Oh! Goodbye!

KRUTITSKY: It's nothing, surely? What's the matter? You look
absolutely fine.

> "Fling in her rival's face his Judas kiss,
> Thus jealously to poison all his bliss..."

KLEOPATRA: Goodbye! Goodbye! *(hurriedly exits)*

KRUTITSKY: What on earth's eating her? Honestly, women! Worse than
commanding a regiment. *(takes out his notebook)* Well, now I've a bit of
spare time... And I don't want to see anybody! *(exits to his study)*

SCENE TWO

*Glumov's apartment, the same as in Act One. Glumov emerges from the
side door with his diary.*

GLUMOV: Thank God that's finished. I've noted down the whole of
that fascinating conversation with Krutitsky. A bizarre memorial for
posterity. It took some doing, remembering all that drivel. I
probably laid it on a bit thick with him. Well, I'm still young, I do
get carried away. Anyway, it'll do no harm, you can't have too
much of a good thing. And isn't that uncle of mine just priceless!
Giving me lessons in how to seduce his own wife! I got carried
away there too. I mean, it's no joke. I'd better keep my ear to the
ground – no matter how we try and keep our marriage plans a
secret, she's bound to discover them. And she'll no doubt kick up a
stink, if not out of love, then jealousy. Women are so envious – they
don't all know how to love, but they're past-masters at jealousy.

> *Enter Glafira.*

Mama dear, are you going to visit Madame Turusina?

GLAFIRA: Yes, I am.

GLUMOV: *(looks at his watch, then sternly)* Well, you're rather late. You should go there first thing. And every day, besides. You ought to be practically living there.

GLAFIRA: They might get fed up, you know.

GLUMOV: That can't be helped. Make friends with the servants, all those fortune-tellers, and pilgrims, and hangers-on – give them presents, and don't stint. You want to go into town right now, and buy a couple of modest-sized silver snuff-boxes. All these parasites take snuff like mad, and they just love free gifts.

GLAFIRA: All right, all right!

GLUMOV: The main thing is to keep an eye on all the comings and goings, so that absolutely nothing gets past you into the house. Butter up the servants, they have a good nose for these things. Anyway, off you go! And hurry – the sooner this engagement is announced the better.

GLAFIRA: They're saying it can't be done, it'll take at least a week.

GLUMOV: My God, that long? I'll be exhausted. A fortune swimming right into my hands – I can't let an opportunity like that slip by, it'd be an unforgivable sin. *(sits down at his desk)* There's something I wanted to add to my diary... oh yes, a note of my expenses. *(begins writing)* 'Two snuff-boxes for the hangers-on... '

   A carriage is heard drawing up outside. He crosses to the window.

Who's that? Kleopatra! How very odd. I wonder if she knows? We'll soon find out.

   Enter Kleopatra.

GLUMOV: Madame, what a delightful surprise! If the Olympian gods were to descend from the heavens...

KLEOPATRA: Don't excite yourself, it isn't you I've come to see, it's your mother.

GLUMOV: *(aside)* She doesn't know. *(aloud)* She's just this moment gone out.

KLEOPATRA: That's a pity.

GLUMOV: *(offers her a chair)* Please, sit down. Make me happy –
grace my humble abode with the light of your presence.

KLEOPATRA: *(sits down)* Yes, we bring happiness, but people make
us unhappy.

GLUMOV: Make you unhappy! But that's a serious crime, don't you
know? Why, even just to upset you, a man would need to be a
blackhearted villain, a positive beast!

KLEOPATRA: Blackhearted villain! Beast! Yes, you've never spoken
a truer word.

GLUMOV: Well, since I'm neither blackhearted, nor beastly, in that
case...

KLEOPATRA: What do you mean, 'in that case'?

GLUMOV: In that case, I couldn't make you unhappy.

KLEOPATRA: You expect me to believe you?

GLUMOV: Yes, you must.

KLEOPATRA: All right, I shall.

GLUMOV: *(aside)* No, she doesn't know. *(aloud)* How could I ever
hurt you! I, a passionate, awkward youth, who have so long sought
the warmth of a woman's affection, while my soul languished in
solitude – and with a trembling heart, a fierce yearning, I looked
everywhere for that woman, who would allow me to be her slave!
Yes, I would have called her my goddess, offered up my life to her,
all my dreams and hopes. But I was poor and insignificant, and they
all turned their backs on me. My prayers, my sighs came to nothing,
died away on the wind. And then you suddenly appeared before me,
my heart began to pound even more violently. But you were no cruel
temptress, you did not reject me, you were pleased to condescend to
this suffering wretch, you warmed my poor heart with mutual love,
and I am so happy, so blissfully, eternally happy! *(kisses her hand)*

KLEOPATRA: You're getting married, I hear?

GLUMOV: Eh? What? No, no... well, yes, but...

KLEOPATRA: You are getting married?

GLUMOV: Well, actually, your husband's trying to marry me off, but I haven't given it a thought. Indeed, I have absolutely no inclination to marriage, I don't wish it.

KLEOPATRA: Goodness, he must be very fond of you – wanting to make you happy against your will!

GLUMOV: He wants me to marry for money. I mean, I can't go on as a poor scribbler forever, it's time I became independent, a man of substance. He wants what's best for me, that's only natural, but it's a pity he hasn't taken my feelings into account.

KLEOPATRA: Marrying for money? You mean you don't like your fiancée?

GLUMOV: Of course I don't. How can you even...

KLEOPATRA: You're not in love with her?

GLUMOV: How could I be! Good heavens, who do you think I would deceive, her or you?

KLEOPATRA: Maybe both.

GLUMOV: Kleopatra, why are you tormenting me with these suspicions? No, no, I can see I'll have to put a stop to this.

KLEOPATRA: Put a stop to what?

GLUMOV: I don't care if it angers my uncle, I shall tell him plainly, I don't want to get married.

KLEOPATRA: Really?

GLUMOV: I shall tell him this very day.

KLEOPATRA: Good! After all, what sort of a marriage would it be without love?

GLUMOV: And to think you could believe that of me! Aren't you ashamed?

KLEOPATRA: Yes, now, when I see how unselfish you are, of course I'm ashamed.

GLUMOV: *(ardently)* Kleopatra, I am yours forever, and only yours. I was afraid to tell my uncle outright that I didn't want to get married, I kept putting him off with evasions – we'll see, I'll think about it, there's no hurry. And you see what the outcome is – I've given you grounds to suspect me of baseness.

The bell rings.

Who's that? God, that's all I need! *(goes to the door)*

KLEOPATRA: *(aside)* Yes, he's deceiving me, it's obvious. He's trying to reassure me, so I won't interfere with his plans.

GLUMOV: Kleopatra, go into my mother's room, please. Someone's come to see me.

Kleopatra exits. Enter Golutvin. Glumov glares at him.

Well, sir?

GOLUTVIN: Eh? Well, in the first place, that's no way to receive guests, and in the second, I'm very tired. I've trailed all the way here to see you under my own steam. *(sits down)*

GLUMOV: What is it you want?

GOLUTVIN: Nothing, really. A mere twenty-five roubles – minimum, of course. If you want to make it more, I won't object.

GLUMOV: So that's it, is it. Charity? Who told you I was in a position to give that sort of handout?

GOLUTVIN: It's not a handout I'm after, it's payment for work done.

GLUMOV: What work?

GOLUTVIN: Well, I've been following you around, gathering intelligence, all the little details of your life. I've written your biography, even added your portrait. I've described your most recent activities in particularly vivid style. So, if you're not interested in buying the original, I can always sell it to a magazine. I'm not asking much, as you can see – I don't rate myself that highly.

GLUMOV: You don't frighten me. Go ahead and print it. Who's going to read you anyway?

GOLUTVIN: Oh, come on, it's not as if I was asking a thousand roubles. I know I can't do you really serious damage, but still – a little unpleasantness, a minor scandal... I mean, you'd be better off without that, so why not pay up?

GLUMOV: There's a name for what you're doing.

GOLUTVIN: I know. It's called taking advantage of the situation.

GLUMOV: D'you think it's honest?

GOLUTVIN: I haven't given it a thought. But it's got to be more honest than sending out anonymous letters.

GLUMOV: What letters? You can't prove it.

GOLUTVIN: There's no need to get upset. Just pay up, take my advice.

GLUMOV: No, not a kopeck.

GOLUTVIN: Well, you've got a rich fiancée in tow now. That'll be very nice, when she reads it. "Oh, my God!", she'll say. Come on, don't argue, just pay up! I'll get a dinner out of it, and you'll have peace of mind. Cheap at half the price.

GLUMOV: Pay for what? Who's to say you won't get the taste for it, and come back again?

GOLUTVIN: My word of honour. Really, what do you take me for?

GLUMOV: *(showing him the door)* Goodbye, sir.

GOLUTVIN: Right then, it'll be in the next issue.

GLUMOV: Whatever issue you like!

GOLUTVIN: Look, I'll come down five roubles, that's chickenfeed.

GLUMOV: I wouldn't give you five kopecks.

GOLUTVIN: All right, so be it. You wouldn't happen to have a cigarette?

GLUMOV: No. Do me a a favour and take yourself off.

GOLUTVIN: In a minute. I need a breather.

GLUMOV: Did Kurchaev put you up to this?

GOLUTVIN: No, he and I have fallen out. He's another stiff-necked ass, like yourself.

GLUMOV: Right, that's enough – get out.

GOLUTVIN: *(rises and peers into the other room)* So, who have you got in there?

GLUMOV: What a damnable cheek! Clear off!

GOLUTVIN: Just curious.

GLUMOV: Get out of here, I'm warning you!

GOLUTVIN: *(on his way out)* Huh, you don't appreciate other people's good nature because you've none of your own. *(exits to the hall)*

GLUMOV: That's all I need! Well, who cares – let him print it. *(follows Golutvin out)*

GOLUTVIN: *(from the hall)* Just one more thing...

> *Glumov exits to the hall and closes the door behind him. Kleopatra re-enters.*

KLEOPATRA: Nobody here. Where on earth has he gone? *(crosses to the desk)* What's this? His diary? Oh, my God... oh, my God! This is terrible! And what's this about marriage? Oh! I knew it, I knew it – he's been deceiving me! The stupid, stupid man! Oh, dear God! He says that about me! Oh, I feel ill, I'm going to faint! The wretched, miserable creature! *(she wipes away her tears, thinks for a moment)* I have an idea. He'll never dream it was me... *(pockets the diary and moves away from the desk)* Oh, yes, I'll bring him down a peg or two. How I'll enjoy seeing him humiliated! When everybody turns their back on him, when they fling him aside like an old sock, he'll come crawling back to me as meek as a lamb.

> *Glumov re-enters.*

GLUMOV: Damn nuisance!

KLEOPATRA: Who was that?

GLUMOV: You know, people like that shouldn't be admitted under any pretext. He's written a scurrilous article about me, and came looking for money – otherwise he'll publish it, he says.

KLEOPATRA: That's dreadful! These people are worse than hired assassins. Who is he, I'd like to know?

GLUMOV: What for?

KLEOPATRA: Well, so I can avoid him.

GLUMOV: Golutvin.

KLEOPATRA: Where does he live?

GLUMOV: Here today, gone tomorrow. You could find out his address from his publisher. What do you want it for?

KLEOPATRA: Well, if somebody does me an injury, there's my revenge. Women have no other recourse, we can't fight duels.

GLUMOV: Are you serious?

KLEOPATRA: No, of course not. Did you give him any money?

GLUMOV: Some. He wasn't asking for much. Peace of mind, really. Any sort of scandal's a bad thing.

KLEOPATRA: And what if somebody else offers him more?

GLUMOV: Why on earth should they? I haven't any enemies.

KLEOPATRA: So, your mind's at ease now. Oh, you poor boy! He must really have upset you. And you're absolutely determined to break off your engagement?

GLUMOV: ·Absolutely.

KLEOPATRA: And you do realise what you're giving up?

GLUMOV: Money, that's all. Should I exchange paradise for money?

KLEOPATRA: Actually a great deal of money – two hundred thousand.

GLUMOV: Yes, I know.

KLEOPATRA: Who would do that?

GLUMOV: Someone who truly loves.

KLEOPATRA: No, these things just don't happen.

GLUMOV: Well, here's your proof that they do.

KLEOPATRA: Oh, you're a hero! An absolute hero! Your name will
go down in history! Come to my arms! *(she embraces him)* Now,
goodbye, my darling! I shall wait for you this very evening. *(exits)*

GLUMOV: Whew! That's a load off my mind. Time I saw my fiancée.
(picks up his hat and looks in the mirror) Of course, it's all rather
trivial, but in a risky business like this, you're always on edge. To be
honest, I haven't the least right to that young lady, or her dowry,
more to the point. It's sheer energy that's done it, that's all. An
entire castle floating in mid-air, with no foundations. And it might
well crash to the ground in pieces any second. Small wonder you
feel nervous, and wary. Well, I've nothing to fear now. I've managed
to reassure Kleopatra, I've paid off Golutvin, so everything's settled
for the moment. *(hums softly to himself)* Yes, it's all settled, it's all
fixed. Hm, all this fussing has made me absent-minded. Hat,
gloves... Now, where are my gloves? Gloves, gloves... Ah, there
they are. *(crosses to the desk)* Notebook in this pocket, diary in
this... *(without looking, he feels on the desk with one hand, and in his
hip-pocket with the other)* I've got my handkerchief... *(goes back to
the desk)* Hullo? Where is it? *(opens the drawer)* Where did I put it?
What's happened to it? Don't tell me... No, it can't be. I put it
down right here. I saw it just a moment ago. Good God, where is
it! Oh no, no, it's impossible! *(stands in silence a moment)* It's falling
apart, everything... and I'm ruined, sinking into the abyss. Why in
God's name did I start that diary? My God, what heroic deeds I've
noted in it! Stupid, childish spite, and all just for fun. No no, if you
do those sort of things, don't ever write them down. Well, well,
I've just presented the world with "Diary of a Scoundrel, Written
by Himself"! And what's the point of cursing myself? There'll be
plenty of people ready to save me the bother! Who could've taken
it? Was it him, or her? If it was him, I can buy it back. But if it was
her? I'll have to turn on the charm. Women are softhearted. Yes,
so they say, but once you've hurt their feelings, believe me, hell
hath no fury. I shudder to think. A woman will wreak a terrible
revenge, she'll dream up some frightful trick that would never even
enter a man's head. Well, there's no help for it. Better not stand
around waiting. I'll head straight for Hell-mouth! *(exits)*

END OF ACT FOUR

ACT FIVE

The scene is the spacious terrace of a country house, leading directly into the garden, with doors at each side. Kurchaev and Masha enter from the drawing-room.

KURCHAEV: It's all happened so quickly.

MASHA: I don't understand it. It's either some kind of trick, or else...

KURCHAEV: Or a miracle, you think?

MASHA: I don't think anything – my head's in a whirl.

KURCHAEV: I've known him a long time, and I've never noticed anything special about him. He seems a decent enough chap.

MASHA: Well, it's as if he's quite irresistible. He's got everything in his favour. All my aunt's friends strongly recommend him, those hangers-on of hers dream about him every night, his name comes up in the cards, the fortune-tellers pick him out, and the pilgrims, of course. And finally, Madame Manefa, whom my aunt regards as some kind of saint, described his appearance, even though she'd never seen him, and prophesied to the very second when he would appear! I mean, what possible objection could there be? My fate's in my aunt's hands, and she's totally enchanted with him.

KURCHAEV: So, they'll hand you over to him, along with your money – virtue rewarded, vice sternly punished. Well, if you can't find any objections, I've nothing more to say. I'll have to withdraw, in silence. If it had been somebody else I might've protested, but before such a paragon of virtue, I pass. The other's not my style.

MASHA: Sshhh! Someone's coming.

> *Enter Turusina and Glumov. Turusina sits down in an armchair, Glumov stands to the left of her, with his hand resting familiarly on the back of her chair. Kurchaev stands to her right, looking somewhat dejected, but maintaining a respectful pose. Masha is by the desk, leafing through a book.*

GLUMOV: Yes, when I first felt the call to family life, I gave the matter very serious thought. Marrying someone for money is against my principles – that would be a business transaction, not marriage, which is a sacred institution! Marrying for love, now...

well, love is such a fleeting emotion, a thing of the flesh. Anyway, I
soon realised that there must be something very special about my
choice of a life partner, something fated, if the marriage was to be
a sound one. So, I needed to find a gentle womanly heart, to
which I might bind myself with indissoluble bonds, and I said to
myself: Fate, show me that heart, and I shall submit to thy will! I'll
tell you frankly, I was expecting a miracle! There are miracles all
around us, only we don't want to see them.

TURUSINA: That's just what I say, but not everyone believes it.
(glances at Kurchaev, who clicks his heels and bows)

GLUMOV: Yes, I was expecting a miracle, and that's what I got.

KURCHAEV: Really? You experienced a miracle? That's quite
extraordinary.

GLUMOV: I happpened to visit a certain devout lady.

KURCHAEV: Madame Manefa, perhaps?

GLUMOV: No no, someone else. I don't even know Madame Manefa.
Anyway, the minute I walked in, before I had time to utter a word,
and she hadn't even seen my face – she was sitting with her back to
me – she said: "Thou dost not seek a wife, for thou thyself art sought.
Go forth, with thine eyes closed, and thou shalt find her!" "Go
where?" I said, "Tell me!" And she said, " As soon as thou dost enter
the strange house, where thou hast never before set foot, do thou seek
even there, and they shall know thee!" Well, honestly, I was so taken
aback at first that I didn't quite believe it. She told me all this in the
morning, and that very same evening, your uncle brought me to visit
you. And lo and behold, there's my bride, and everyone knows me!

TURUSINA: Yes, indeed, miracles abound, but few are chosen to...

KURCHAEV: You know, we had a case like that once, when we were
billeted in the Ukraine – there was this Jewish chap...

TURUSINA: I think you should go for a stroll in the garden.

Kurchaev again clicks his heels and bows.

GLUMOV: So, isn't that a clear case of predestination? I haven't
even had time to properly acquaint myself with my fiancée's
feelings... *(to Masha)* I do beg your pardon, my dear Masha – so
far I've had to be satisfied simply with her consent.

TURUSINA: And that's all that's needed.

GLUMOV: And perhaps, if she doesn't quite like me now, she'll do so later. Such a marriage is bound to be happy and prosperous.

KURCHAEV: Oh, undoubtedly.

GLUMOV: It was no human agency that arranged this marriage, so there can be no mistakes.

TURUSINA: How true! Yes, this is someone we should all learn from, how to conduct our lives!

   Grigory enters.

GRIGORY: Mr Gorodulin, ma'am.

TURUSINA: I'll go and put on something warmer, it's getting chilly. *(exits)*

MASHA: *(to Kurchaev)* Let's go into the garden.

   They exit to the garden. Enter Gorodulin.

GORODULIN: Well, good day to you, sir! How much money are you getting?

GLUMOV: Two hundred thousand, I think.

GORODULIN: How on earth did you manage that?

GLUMOV: Well, you yourself recommended me – Madame Turusina told me so.

GORODULIN: When was that? Oh yes, I remember. So how did you contrive to get into Madame Turusina's good graces? I thought you were a freethinker?

GLUMOV: I just don't argue with her.

GORODULIN: What, even when she's talking nonsense?

GLUMOV: She's beyond hope, so why even bother?

GORODULIN: I see, so that's how it goes, eh? Splendid! You'll soon be a man of substance, then. I'll put your name up for my club.

GLUMOV: *(confidentially)* Krutitsky's treatise'll be coming out in a day or two.

GORODULIN: Is it, indeed. Huh, I wouldn't mind giving it a good going-over.

GLUMOV: That wouldn't be difficult.

GORODULIN: No, I should think it wouldn't, for a man of your talent. But it'd be a bit off – you're still a very young man, it might do you some harm. We've got to keep you under wraps. Tell you what – you can write it, and I'll put my head on the block, so to speak, publish it under my name. We'll give these old relics what for.

GLUMOV: Absolutely, that's what's needed. You've only got to look at the rubbish they write!

GORODULIN: Yes, ridicule's the answer. I'd do it myself, but I haven't the time. I'm delighted at your good fortune. I congratulate you. We really do need people like you. Indeed, we do. Frankly, we've been very badly lacking . We've got plenty of activists, but nobody who can talk, and these old fogies catch us on the hop, that's the trouble. We've got some clever chaps among the younger element, but they're very young, we can't let them speak for us, nobody'll take any notice of them. We have a choir, so to speak, but no soloist. You can carry the tune, and we'll join in with the refrain. Where's Masha gone?

GLUMOV: She's out there, in the garden.

GORODULIN: I think I'll go and have a word with her. *(exits to the garden)*

GLUMOV: *(calling after him)* I'll catch you up in a second! I think that's the Mamaevs just arrived. Well, I've certainly talked her round. Not only has she consented to the marriage, she's actually come here in person! That's really quite sweet of her.

    Enter Kleopatra.

KLEOPATRA: Well, have you found it?

GLUMOV: No. Golutvin swears his Bible oath he didn't take it. He'd practically tears in his eyes. I'd sooner starve, he says, than stoop to such a low trick.

KLEOPATRA: So who on earth could have taken it? You must have mislaid it somewhere.

GLUMOV: Well, I can't imagine how.

KLEOPATRA: Someone'll find it, no doubt, and fling it away.

GLUMOV: It'll be a good thing if they do.

KLEOPATRA: But what are you so afraid of? Surely there's nothing in it that shouldn't be?

GLUMOV: No no, there's nothing special in it. Outpourings of the heart, little love notes, passionate declarations, a few verses – eyes, golden curls – in short, all those things you write in private, and which it's embarrassing if other people read.

KLEOPATRA: Really? You write about eyes and curls in your diary? Oh well, why worry? Nobody's going to pay the slightest attention to that. Diaries like that are a drug on the market. Anyway, what are you doing here on your own? Where's your fiancée?

GLUMOV: She's taking a stroll in the garden with some of the young men. That's proof, if you like, that I'm in no hurry to get married. I do need money, I must have a position in society. I don't want to be a darling boy forever, it's high time I was a darling man. And you just watch what a fine figure I'll cut, driving my own horses round town! Nobody takes any notice of me now, but soon they'll all be saying, "Who's that handsome fellow?", as if I'd just arrived from Anerica! And they'll all be so envious of you.

KLEOPATRA: Why me?

GLUMOV: Because I'll be yours.

KLEOPATRA: That's all very fine, if you could get the money without the bride, but you will have a young wife, you know.

GLUMOV: That won't bother me. I shall offer my hand to my bride, and my pocket for her money, but my heart will remain yours.

KLEOPATRA: You're a dangerous young man. If people listen long enough to you, they start believing you.

GLUMOV: You wait and see the beautiful trotting horses I'll be driving up to your house!

KLEOPATRA: Yes, do, drive up by all means! But you'd better go out to your fiancée now, it's not nice to abandon her. Even if you can't stand her, you ought to be polite to her, at least for appearance's sake.

GLUMOV: All right, but remember, it's you who are sending me to her.

KLEOPATRA: Go on, go on.

Glumov exits.

Well, well, the triumphant lover! Just you wait, my friend, we'll wipe the smile off your face!

Kurchaev enters.

KLEOPATRA: Where are you going?

KURCHAEV: Home.

KLEOPATRA: Home, with such a sad face? No, hold on – I can guess why.

Kurchaev bows., makes to exit.

No, wait, please.

Kurchaev continues.

Wait! You're such an obstinate creature. Wait a minute, I want to speak to you.

Kurchaev stops.

You're in love, aren't you.

Kurchaev bows and again makes to leave.

You don't know anything at all?

KURCHAEV: Please, ma'am, let me go.

KLEOPATRA: Look, I've got to leave early, and I'm by myself – you can see me home...

Kurchaev bows.

Why don't you ever speak? Now, listen – be open with me – as your aunt, I command you. You're in love, I know that much. Is she in love with you? Well, come on, tell me!

Kurchaev bows.

I'm certain she loves you. Don't give up hope. There may be a few surprises yet.

KURCHAEV: Well, if the circumstances were different, I might...

KLEOPATRA: What circumstances?

KURCHAEV: Madame Turusina makes impossible demands...

KLEOPATRA: What do you mean?

KURCHAEV: I couldn't have anticipated them. And besides, they're quite incompatible with my profession.

KLEOPATRA: Incompatible? How?

KURCHAEV: I mean, nothing in my upbringing prepared me for this...

KLEOPATRA: I don't understand you.

KURCHAEV: What Madame Turusina wants for her niece...

KLEOPATRA: Well?

KURCHAEV: It's simply not credible. I mean, it's such a rare thing these days.

KLEOPATRA: What? What?

KURCHAEV: I've honestly never heard of it...

KLEOPATRA: For God's sake, will you get to the point!

KURCHAEV: She's looking for a truly virtuous man.

KLEOPATRA: Well? So?

KURCHAEV: But I haven't any virtues.

KLEOPATRA: What do you mean, you've no virtues? You've got nothing but vices?

KURCHAEV: No no, I've no particular vices either, I'm just an
ordinary chap. It's bizarre, searching for a virtuous man. I mean, if
Glumov hadn't turned up, where on earth would she find one?
There's no-one like him in the whole of Moscow. And miracles
happen to him, he even sees visions. Well, if you don't mind my
saying, you can't ask that of just anybody, can you.

KLEOPATRA: Listen, just wait. You might well find it's a good thing
to have no virtues, and no vices either.

Masha enters from the garden.

Congratulations, my dear. You're getting prettier every day. I'm
delighted to hear of your good fortune.

MASHA: Mr Glumov has so many fine qualities, it's quite terrifying.
I'm not sure I'm worthy of such a husband.

KLEOPATRA: Well, where else would one seek virtue, if not in your
aunt's home? And you have the advantage both of her instruction,
and her example.

MASHA: I'm really so grateful to her. Indeed, virtue is a very good
thing, but I'm afraid I can boast of only one – obedience.

Enter Madame Turusina, Mamaev, and Krutitsky.

MAMAEV: *(to Krutitsky)* Well, in broad terms I agree with you, but
not on the details.

KRUTITSKY: Why not?

MAMAEV: Why only tragedy? Why not comedy?

KRUTITSKY: Because comedy represents our baser instincts, and
tragedy deals with higher things. And it's higher things we need.

MAMAEV: Yes, but if you'll permit me... we need to look at this
question from all sides.

They move up-stage.

TURUSINA: *(to Kleopatra)* You know, it's quite the fashion
nowadays to believe in absolutely nothing. People keep saying to
me, "Why do you allow that Manefa woman into your house?
She's a fraud!" Well, for two pins I'd invite all those unbelievers

here today, to see just what kind of fraud she is! I'm so pleased for her, she'll be all the rage now, and have a huge clientèle. Moscow should be grateful to me, for discovering such a woman, and doing the town a genuine service.

KLEOPATRA: So, where is the fiancé? I don't see him.

TURUSINA: Masha, my dear, where's Yegor?

MASHA: He's in the garden with Mr Gorodulin.

TURUSINA: Yes, the recommendation of all my friends, and certain other reasons, led me to expect an exemplary young man. But when I came to know him better, well, I could see that he surpassed all my expectations.

MAMAEV: *(approaching)* Who surpassed all your expectations?

TURUSINA: Why, your nephew.

MAMAEV: I knew you would thank me for him. Yes, I always know just what's needed. And I didn't offer him to anyone else, I sent him straight to you.

TURUSINA: It would've been a sin if you hadn't. I'm all alone in the world, as you know.

KRUTITSKY: Yes, Glumov will go far.

MAMAEV: With our help, naturally.

Enter Grigory.

TURUSINA: I don't what I've done to deserve such good fortune. Unless, of course, my... *(to Grigory)* Yes, yes, what do you want? Unless it's my good works!

Grigory hands her a large envelope.

What's this? *(unseals it)* A newspaper? It can't be for me.

KLEOPATRA: *(picks up the envelope)* No, it's for you all right. Look, there's the address...

TURUSINA: No, it must be a mistake. Who delivered it?

GRIGORY: The postman, ma'am.

TURUSINA: Where is he?

GRIGORY: He's gone, long since, ma'am.

MAMAEV: Let's have a look. I'll see if I can sort this out.

He takes the envelope and removes a printed sheet.

Well, it's a newspaper all right, or rather, not the whole paper, just a single sheet, one article.

TURUSINA: Surely it's not come from the publisher like that?

MAMAEV: No, one of your friends must've sent it.

TURUSINA: What on earth does it say?

MAMAEV: Well, we'll soon see. The article's titled: "How to Get On in the World".

TURUSINA: Oh, that's of no interest to us – throw it away.

MAMAEV: Why? Let's see what it says. Hm... look, there's a portrait with a caption underneath: "A Husband in a Million" Good heavens! It's Yegor Dmitrich!

KLEOPATRA: Give it here – this is interesting.

Mamaev hands over the paper.

TURUSINA: This is some kind of nasty trick – he's bound to have lots of enemies.

Mamaev looks meaningfully at Kurchaev.

KURCHAEV: What, you surely don't suspect me? I'm not exactly an artist – the only person I can draw is you.

MAMAEV: *(sternly)* Yes, I know.

KLEOPATRA: Well, whoever wrote this article obviously knows Yegor Dmitrich rather well. It describes his life in the most minute detail – that is, if it isn't a complete fiction.

MAMAEV: *(takes a notebook out of the envelope)* There's something else in here.

KRUTITSKY: That's his handwriting, I'd know it at a glance. Yes, it's his all right, take my word.

MAMAEV: Yes, the diary's in Yegor's hand, but there's a note in someone else's: "This diary is offered as proof that everything in the enclosed article is justified". Well, which should we read, the article or the diary?

KRUTITSKY: Let's have the original.

MAMAEV: There's a bookmark in one of the pages, we'll start with that. It's a note of an account: "To Madame Manefa – twenty-five roubles, then another twenty-five roubles... A complete idiot, yet she claims to foretell the future! Took me ages to get my idea into her thick skull! One bottle also, sent round to her. Another fifteen roubles handed over in my house... It's really not right that such a lucrative business should be in the hands of morons. Wonder what she's making out of Madame Turusina? Must find out, later. Seven roubles fifty each to Madame Turusina's hangers-on, plus two silver snuffboxes at ten roubles the pair, for fortune-telling from the cards, and for narrating the dreams they're supposed to have about me every night..."

TURUSINA: *(sniffing at her smelling-salts)* I shall fling them out of the house, all of them! Wickedness is sinful, but goodness is downright stupid! How can I live after this!

KLEOPATRA: You needn't complain. You're not the only one who's been deceived.

MAMAEV: "For three anonymous letters to Madame Turusina, fifteen kopecks..."

MASHA: So, that's where those letters came from, auntie!

TURUSINA: Yes, my dear, I can see that now. Forgive me. It was terribly wrong of me, trying to organise your life for you. I can see I had neither the intelligence nor the strength. Do whatever you like, I shan't interfere again.

MASHA: *(softly)* I've already made my choice, auntie.

TURUSINA: Splendid. And you won't be deceived in him, since he has no pretensions anyway.

Kurchaev bows.

Now, I shall drive these parasites out forthwith!

KRUTITSKY: And take on some new ones?

TURUSINA: I don't know about that.

MAMAEV: Do you wish me to continue reading?

TURUSINA: Yes, go on, it makes no difference now.

MAMAEV: "To Mamaev's servant, for delivering his master to me,
taking advantage of his weakness for rented flats... three roubles to
my benefactor here. Seems too little..." Hm, then there's a bit
about his conversation with me, nothing of interest, really. "First
visit to Krutitsky... Come, my Muse! Let us sing the praises of this
valiant knight and his treatises! Truly, my admiration for thee
knows no bounds, venerable sir! Tell us, reveal thy secret to the
world – by what cunning art hast thou attained sixty years, and
contrived to keep intact the mind of a six-year old child!..."

KRUTITSKY: All right, that's enough. Damned libel – who needs it!

Gorodulin re-enters.

MAMAEV: *(without noticing him)* Hold on, there's a few words here
about Gorodulin: "Gorodulin got involved in a ridiculous
squabble over racehorses, and some gentleman called him a
liberal. He was so delighted with the name that he spent three days
driving round Moscow, telling everybody he was a 'liberal'. So
that's how he sees himself now..." Yes, that's just like him.

KRUTITSKY: Just like him? Why don't you read out the bit about
yourself, till we see what you're like!

GORODULIN: You think that's me?

MAMAEV: My dear sir, I didn't see you come in. Take a look at
this, we're all written up in here.

GORODULIN: So who is this modern Juvenal?

MAMAEV: My nephew, Glumov.

TURUSINA: I think you should hand this manuscript back to its author, and ask him to leave quietly.

Glumov enters, and Gorodulin dutifully hands him the diary.

GLUMOV: *(accepting the diary)* And why quietly, may I ask? I have no intention of trying to explain, or justify myself. I'll say only this – you yourselves will swiftly come to regret expelling me from your society.

KRUTITSKY: I beg your pardon, my dear sir, but our society is made up of honest men.

ALL: Yes, that's right!

GLUMOV: *(to Krutitsky)* Oh? And at what point did your Excellency realise that I wasn't an honest man? No doubt, with your piercing intelligence, you figured it out the minute I undertook to re-write that treatise of yours. After all, what decently brought-up person would take on a job like that? Or perhaps you became aware of my dishonesty when I was in your study, drooling over your most wildly absurd phrases, grovelling at your feet like an idiot? No, you were practically ready to kiss me for that. And if that wretched diary hadn't fallen into your hands, you'd have regarded me as an honest man for evermore.

KRUTITSKY: Well, of course, but...

GLUMOV: *(to Mamaev)* And you, dear uncle – you worked it all out for yourself, didn't you. Wasn't it that time you were teaching me how to make love to your wife, so as to distract her from her other admirers – while I hummed and hawed and made excuses, said I couldn't do it, I was too embarrassed? Of course, you could see I was putting on an act, but that pleased you nonetheless, because it gave you an opportunity to instruct me on the facts of life! I'm smarter than you by a long way, and you know it, but when I pretend to be an idiot, and ask your advice, why, you're just thrilled to bits, and ready to swear I'm the most honest man alive!

MAMAEV: That doesn't count – we're family, aren't we.

GLUMOV: As for you, Madame Turusina – yes, I did deceive you, and I'm sorry about that – for Masha's sake, that is, but I don't regret deceiving you. You pick up some half-drunk peasant woman off the street, and on the basis of her word, choose a husband for your niece. I mean, who does this Manefa woman know? Who is she going to recommend? Obviously, whoever gives her the most money. You're lucky it turned out to be me. Manefa might've fixed you up with some escaped convict, and you'd have handed Masha over to him no matter what.

TURUSINA: All I know is that there is no truth in this world, and I'm more convinced of it, with every day that passes.

GLUMOV: So, what about you, Gorodulin?

GORODULIN: I'm not saying a word. I think you're an absolutely splendid chap! Here's my hand on it. And everything you've said about us – well, about me at any rate, I can't speak for the others – is perfectly true.

GLUMOV: Yes, you need me, ladies and gentlemen. You can't live without my sort. If it isn't me, it'll be someone else. He'll be even worse than me, and then you'll say, "My God, he's worse than Glumov, but he's a smart lad, all the same." *(to Krutitsky)* Your Excellency has what passes for a very gracious manner in company, but in your study, face to face with a young man, standing to attention and nodding furiously at everything you say – yes, your Excellency, no, your Excellency – well, you're in an absolute transport of joy. You'll refuse your patronage to a genuinely honest man, but you're prepared to run round town and break your neck for a creature like that.

KRUTITSKY: You've gone too far, sir – you're abusing our patience!

GLUMOV: Forgive me, your Excellency! *(to Mamaev)* And you need me too, uncle. Your servants wouldn't listen to your lectures for love nor money, but I did it for free.

MAMAEV: That's enough! If you can't understand, my dear sir, that your continued presence here is positively indecent, then I'll just have to...

GLUMOV: Oh, I understand all right. And even you need me, Gorodulin.

GORODULIN: Indeed I do.

GLUMOV: To supply you with clever lines for your speeches.

GORODULIN: Clever lines for speeches, yes.

GLUMOV: And to help you write criticism.

GORODULIN: To help me write criticism.

GLUMOV: You need me too, aunt.

KLEOPATRA: I'm not denying it. I haven't accused you of anything.

KRUTITSKY: *(to Mamaev)* You know, there was something about him, right from the outset...

MAMAEV: *(to Krutitsky)* Yes, I spotted it too – something about his eyes...

GLUMOV: You spotted nothing, sirs. It was my diary that got your back up, and I've no idea how it fell into your hands. I suppose you could say I've been too clever for my own good. But I'll tell you this, gentlemen – during all the time I spent in your company, in this society of yours, the only honest moments I had were when I was writing that diary. There's no other way for an honest man to deal with people like you. You really did make my gorge rise. So, what was it that offended you about my diary? That you discovered something new about yourselves? I mean, you say the same things about each other all the time, only not to your faces. If I'd read out to each one of you privately, what was written about the others, you'd have applauded me. Indeed, if anyone should feel offended and upset, then it's me. Yes, I should be raging, kicking up hell. I don't know which, but one of you honest people stole my diary. You've ruined everything for me – you've deprived me of a fortune, and my good name. And now you're going to throw me out, and that'll be that – over and done with. You think I'll forgive you. Well, ladies and gentlemen, I wouldn't bank on it. Goodbye! *(exits)*

    A silence.

KRUTITSKY: Well, you can say what you like, sirs – he has a good head on him. He must be taught a lesson, of course, but give it time, and I think we might bring him back into the fold again.

GORODULIN: Oh, absolutely.

MAMAEV: Yes, I think so.

KLEOPATRA: And you can leave that to me...

THE END
(Na vsyakogo mudretsaa dovol'no prostoty, 1868)

CRAZY MONEY

CHARACTERS

VASILKOV   (Savva Gennadyich, a businessman, aged 35. He speaks
   with a strong regional accent, and his provincial manners extend
   also to his mode of dress)

TELYATEV   (Ivan Petrovich, a gentleman of leisure, aged 40)

KUCHUMOV   (Grigory Borisovich, an imposing gentleman in his
   60s, retired minor civil servant, with a number of titled relatives on
   his mother's side, and through marriage)

GLUMOV   (Yegor Dmitrich)

CHEBOKSAROVA   (Nadezhda Antonovna, an elderly lady with a very
   grand manner)

LIDIYA   (Her daughter, aged 24)

ANDREI   (The Cheboksarovs' manservant)

GRIGORY   (Telyatev's manservant)

NIKOLAI   (Kuchumov's manservant)

VASILY   (Vasilkov's valet)

A MAID

A Boy from the coffee-shop, various passers-by.

------oOo------

ACT ONE

The action takes place in the Saxe Gardens in Petrovsky Park; to the right are the park gates, to the left a coffee-shop. People stroll to and fro, occasionally stopping to read the notice on the park gate. Telyatev and Vasilkov emerge from the coffee-shop.

TELYATEV: *(still chewing)* Yes, yes, of course, absolutely...*(aside)* I wish he'd leave me alone!

VASILKOV: I mean, she's an extremely attractive young woman, in every respect...

TELYATEV: You don't say? Well, that's some discovery you've made there. Oh really, who doesn't know that? *(tips his hat, bows to a passing lady)* Yes, that's perfectly true, my dear sir. Lidiya's a beautiful girl, and two and two make four. Have you any more incontrovertible facts for us?

VASILKOV: I just meant I liked her.

TELYATEV: Better still! So who doesn't like her? Good God, what do I care whether you like her or not? You must be from foreign parts, sir.

VASILKOV: Well, that's true – I'm not from Moscow.

TELYATEV: Now, what would really amaze me is if you'd said you didn't like her. Yes, that would've been a distinct curiosity. But the fact that you fancy her is no surprise. I know about fifteen chaps, all madly in love with her, and that's only the grown men – if you count the schoolboys, there's no end to them. No, what you want is to try and get her to fancy you.

VASILKOV: What, is it really that difficult?

TELYATEV: I'll say it is.

VASILKOV: But what is she looking for? What sort of qualities?

TELYATEV: The sort neither you nor I possess, I'm afraid.

VASILKOV: Like what, for example?

TELYATEV: Oh, let's start with half a million roubles or so...

VASILKOV: That doesn't matter.

TELYATEV: Doesn't matter! Dear God, d'you think that kind of money grows on trees? Of course, if you're Rothschild's nephew that's a different story, and we'll say no more.

VASILKOV: No, I'm not, unfortunately, but at this moment in time any man with a few brains can...

TELYATEV: Ah yes, brains... yes, and a few besides. That means you've got to have them to begin with, and I'm afraid brains are as scarce among our lot as millionaires. No, let's not talk about brains – if any of my friends hear us they'll die laughing. Brainy people are one thing, we're something else, so what the hell? That's what I say. And if God didn't give us any...

VASILKOV: No, sir – I'm not going to deny my abilities that easily. What else do I need to make her like me?

TELYATEV: Oh well, a handsome Guards uniform, and the rank of Colonel, at least, plus an innate sophistication, which of course there's no way you can acquire.

VASILKOV: That's very strange. Are there really no other virtues, no other qualities of heart and mind that can win this young lady over?

TELYATEV: And how's she going to find out about these qualities of yours? Maybe you can write a book on astronomy and read it to her.

VASILKOV: Well, I'm sorry, I really am sorry she's so unapproachable.

TELYATEV: Why's that? What's it to you?

VASILKOV: Well, the fact is... Look, I'll be absolutely open with you. The particular line of business I'm in, I really do need a wife like that, you know, beautiful, with a bit of style.

TELYATEV: Don't we all, my dear sir, don't we all! So, are you disgustingly rich?

VASILKOV: Not yet.

TELYATEV: Meaning, you hope to be.

VASILKOV: Well, at this moment in time...

TELYATEV: Oh, for God's sake, why d'you keep on about this moment in time?

VASILKOV: Because it's precisely at this moment in time that a man can easily enough get rich...

TELYATEV: Ah well, that depends, doesn't it. Miracles do happen. But are you telling me – at this moment in time, that you're onto a sure thing? I mean, you can let me in on it – I won't rob you.

VASILKOV: No, you certainly won't, since I do have a sure thing, absolutely no risk whatever – three woodsman's cottages on my own land, that brings in about fifty thousand roubles.

TELYATEV: That's not bad – fifty thousand roubles. In Moscow you can raise another hundred thousand on that, so there you are – a hundred and fifty thousand. With that kind of money you can live quite decently, a fair while.

VASILKOV: Yes, but you've got to pay it back in the end.

TELYATEV: So who cares? What are you getting all worked up about? Have you got some sort of bee in your bonnet? That's your creditors' business, let them do the worrying. You shouldn't get mixed up in other people's affairs: it's our job to borrow, and it's their job to try and get it back.

VASILKOV: No, I'm afraid I've never been involved in those sort of ongoings We run our business on different principles.

TELYATEV: Well, you're still young, you'll pick up our principles soon enough.

VASILKOV: I'm not going to argue with you. But please get me an introduction to Lidiya and her mother. There's probably no chance of her liking me, but well – where there's life there's hope. Since I first caught sight of her a week ago, I haven't stopped thinking about her. I even found out where they live, and rented an apartment in the same house, just to see her more often. I know it's silly, a businessman carrying on like that, but as far as love's concerned I'm a mere boy. Introduce me to them, please.

TELYATEV: Certainly, it'll be my pleasure.

VASILKOV: *(warmly shakes his hand)* And if I can ever be of service to you, sir...

TELYATEV: Oh, a bottle of champagne, that's all you can bribe me with. Shall we say a bottle?

VASILKOV: Yes, of course, whenever you like, and as many as you like! *(squeezes Telyatev's hand)* I truly am grateful to you, sir...

TELYATEV: Please, please – my hand!

VASILKOV: *(looks round, without releasing Telyatev's hand)* Isn't that them?

TELYATEV: Yes, yes.

VASILKOV: I'll walk a little closer, to get a better look. Honestly, I get so emotional! You must think this is funny...

TELYATEV: My hand, for God's sake!

VASILKOV: Oh, I'm terribly sorry. I hope I'll find you here when I return.

TELYATEV: Not if I can help it.

Vasilkov rushes off. Enter Glumov.

GLUMOV: Who's that clodhopper you were talking to just now?

TELYATEV: He's God's gift, my dear chap, a reward for my simplicity.

GLUMOV: Why, what do you get out of it?

TELYATEV: Well, he stands me champagne.

GLUMOV: Really? That's not bad.

TELYATEV: Yes, I'll keep working on him, and next thing you know, I'll put the bite on him for a loan.

GLUMOV: Even better if he gives you the money, of course.

TELYATEV: Well, I think he will. He needs me, you see.

GLUMOV: Oh, come off it, do me a favour – who could possibly need you for anything?

TELYATEV: Now, you listen...

GLUMOV: I'm listening.

TELYATEV: Right, then – I first spotted him in the park here about a week ago. I'm walking along the path, and in the distance I see a man standing openmouthed, with his eyes popping, his hat perched on the back of his head. Of course, I'm gripped with curiosity, to see what he's goggling at. There's no elephants passing, there's nobody staging a cockfight. Anyway, I have a look, and you'll never guess what he was staring at – go on, have a guess...

GLUMOV: What? I don't know. What's so amazing in a public park?

TELYATEV: Cheboksarova...

GLUMOV: What, Lidiya? Well, there's not much wrong with his eyes.

TELYATEV: Her mother's carriage had stopped, and there was the usual crowd of hangers-on. She and her mother were talking with somebody, I don't know who, and he was standing a little way off, drinking it all in. The carriage moved off then, and he made a dash after it, knocking about half-a-dozen chaps down in the process, myself included. He apologised, of course, and that's when we got acquainted.

GLUMOV: Congratulations.

TELYATEV: And today, would you believe, after he saw me chatting to Lidiya and her mother, he practically seized me by the throat and dragged me into the park here, stood me a bottle of champagne, then another – well, I tell you, we had quite a little party. And he's just this minute confessed to being in love with Lidiya. Yes, he wants to marry her. You see, he's in some sort of business, God only knows what, but whatever it is, it's absolutely imperative he marries a girl like Lidiya. And of course, he's asked me to get him an introduction.

GLUMOV: Cheeky sod! That's priceless! Arrives here from some god-forsaken hole and straight off wants to marry the prize catch in Moscow! Oh yes, it's absolutely imperative, for business reasons! What an idiot! My God, we could all do with a business like that! My business demands I should marry a rich heiress, but I'm damned if I can get hold of one! What sort of a creature is he? What does he do, at least?

TELYATEV: Ah, that's a secret between him and Allah.

GLUMOV: Just tell me how he speaks and acts, and I'll tell you what he does.

TELYATEV: I'll bet you can't. He's a gentleman, obviously, but he talks like a deckhand off a Volga steamer.

GLUMOV: He's a ship-owner, he's got his own shipping line on the Volga.

TELYATEV: When he paid for the drinks, he took out a wallet, like this.. a foot thick, just about. And you should've seen what was in it – share certificates, invoices in different languages, greasy-looking letters on grey paper, written by peasants, obviously...

GLUMOV: So, is he rich?

TELYATEV: Hardly. Says he owns a small estate, and some woods, about fifty thousand roubles.

GLUMOV: It's not much, is it. No, he's not in the steamship business.

TELYATEV: He's either not rich, or else he's a miser. He paid for the champagne, and instantly jotted it down in a little notebook.

GLUMOV: He couldn't be a clerk, I suppose? What's he like?

TELYATEV: Oh, absolutely straightforward – as innocent as a schoolgirl.

GLUMOV: Innocent? D'you think he's a card-sharp?

TELYATEV: I couldn't say. He can certainly knock back the champagne, though: one glass after another, systematically, as if it was soda water. We got through a bottle apiece, and he didn't get flushed, or raise his voice, even.

GLUMOV: Oh well, he's from Siberia, he must be.

TELYATEV: He smokes expensive cigars, and speaks very good French, with some sort of slight accent.

GLUMOV: Ah, now I've got it! He's an agent for some London company, he's a commercial traveller, end of story.

TELYATEV: Well, have it your way. He's a problem for sure.

GLUMOV: Anyway, whoever he is, let's have some fun with him. We haven't had a decent laugh in ages, we're all so damn miserable these days.

TELYATEV: Yes, and we might end up playing chief buffoons, in this comedy of yours.

GLUMOV: Not a chance – we'll play the villains, or at least I shall, and this is what we'll do: you can introduce this creature to Lidiya, and I'll tell her mother that he owns goldmines. Then we'll watch her setting out her stall for him.

TELYATEV: And what happens when they find out it's all a hoax, and all he's got is some godforsaken mudhole?

GLUMOV: So who cares? We'll say we heard about the goldmines from him, that he was bragging about them.

TELYATEV: It's a bit much.

GLUMOV: What, you feeling sorry for him? Don't be such a wimp. We can say we misheard him – it's not nuggets he digs up, it's truffles.

Vasilkov approaches.

TELYATEV: So, have you gazed your fill on your beloved?

VASILKOV: To the very last drop!

TELYATEV: Allow me to introduce you – Savva Vasilkov, Yegor Glumov...

VASILKOV: *(warmly shakes Glumov's hand)* Delighted to meet you, sir.

GLUMOV: And I'm not delighted, the way you're squeezing my hand...

VASILKOV: I'm very sorry – it's a provincial bad habit of mine.

GLUMOV: You're called Savva – is that short for Savatius, or what?

VASILKOV: *(courteously)* No, sir, it's a different name.

GLUMOV: What, Sebastian, then?

VASILKOV: No, no – Sebastian comes from the Greek, it means 'worthy of respect'. Savva's an Arab name.

GLUMOV: What about Savyol?

VASILKOV: No, you're wasting your time, sir – get a church calendar and look it up.

TELYATEV: So, you know Greek?

VASILKOV: A little.

GLUMOV: What about Tartar?

VASILKOV: I can keep up a conversation if it's in the Kazan dialect, but I've just been in the Crimea, and I could hardly make myself understood.

GLUMOV: *(aside)* What the hell's he on about?

TELYATEV: So, did you leave the Crimea some time ago?

VASILKOV: About ten days. I stopped there on the way home from England.

GLUMOV: *(aside)* A likely story!

TELYATEV: So how did you manage to fetch up in the Crimea from England?

VASILKOV: Well, I was interested to see the Suez Canal – have a look at the earthworks, and the engineering equipment.

GLUMOV: *(aside)* All right, so maybe it isn't a story. *(to Vasilkov)* My dear sir, you've caught us at a moment when we were discussing matches – not the kind you light fires with – but what the man in the street calls 'made in heaven'.

VASILKOV: A good subject, sir.

GLUMOV: Yes, I wouldn't mind marrying the Cheboksarova girl, personally.

VASILKOV: With looks like hers, I'm sure a great many people could say the same.

GLUMOV: A great many idiots, yes. They don't even know why they want to marry her. They're dazzled by her beauty, but they want to keep that beauty all to themselves, to bury her away like so much dead stock. No, looks like that aren't frozen assets, they've got to earn interest. Only a fool would marry Lidiya without an ulterior motive. She should marry a card-sharp, or some civil service type on the make. The card-sharp would use her as bait, for giddy youths with more money than sense, and the other sort would dangle her in front of his superiors, and shoot up the career ladder.

VASILKOV: No, sir, I can't agree...

GLUMOV: All that po-faced stuff about virtue's frankly silly, it's just not practical. And we live in a practical age, sir.

VASILKOV: No, no, I really must take issue with you...

GLUMOV: Go ahead, feel free.

VASILKOV: Honesty's still the best policy, sir, even these days. In a practical age like ours, it's not only better to be honest, it's more profitable. I don't think you've got the right idea at all – you seem to regard sharp practice as good business, but on the contrary, it's in a romantic age, when emotions are running high, that fraud and deception do best – they've got more room to breathe, and they're more easily masked. Deceiving some innocent virgin, or some poet with his head in the clouds, swindling some starry-eyed youth, or putting one over on your boss, with his head full of love lyrics – that's far easier than trying to cheat hard-headed businessmen. No, sir, believe me – at this moment in time, sharp practice is very bad business indeed.

TELYATEV: That's Lidiya and her mother now...

VASILKOV: *(hurriedly grasping his hand)* Introduce me to her, please!

TELYATEV: Ouch! *(jerks his hand free)* With the greatest of pleasure, sir!

Lidiya and Madame Cheboksarova approach.

TELYATEV: *(to Cheboksarova)* What would you say to meeting a millionaire?

CHEBOKSAROVA: Huh, some hopes. Talk's cheap, and you'll lie for nothing, you impertinent creature.

TELYATEV: Indeed I shall – I won't even take a percentage.

CHEBOKSAROVA: Oh, go on, introduce me, then! But you're such a scoundrel, I can't believe a word of it.

TELYATEV: Heavens, what a thing to say!... Now, Savva Vasilkov...

CHEBOKSAROVA: Hold on, hold on – what sort of name's that?

TELYATEV: It's a millionaire sort of name, what are you worried about?

Vasilkov approaches.

Madame, allow me to present my good friend, Savva Vasilkov...

CHEBOKSAROVA: Pleased to meet you...

VASILKOV: And I you, ma'am, most sincerely. I'm afraid I don't know anyone in Moscow.

TELYATEV: He's a first-rate chap, speaks Greek. *(walks apart with Lidiya)*

CHEBOKSAROVA: Judging by your name, sir, you'll have been born in Greece?

VASILKOV: No, ma'am, in Russia, near the Volga.

CHEBOKSAROVA: And where do you live now?

VASILKOV: In the country, ma'am, but I travel around mostly.

CHEBOKSAROVA: *(to Glumov)* Yegor, please see if you can find my footman...

Glumov approaches.

VASILKOV: If you'll allow me, ma'am – I'll look for him right now. What's his name?

CHEBOKSAROVA: Andrei.

VASILKOV: I'll track him down this instant.

CHEBOKSAROVA: Fetch my shawl from him, will you? It's getting a little chilly.

As Vasilkov exits, she speaks apart with Glumov.

TELYATEV: *(to Lidiya)* Anyway, I'm well prepared for chills.

LIDIYA: What a shame. You know, you're very sweet, I could easily fall for you, but you're such an immoral person.

TELYATEV: Me? Immoral? Well, really, you won't find a more virtuous person anywhere, and I'll prove it to you, right now.

LIDIYA: Go on!

TELYATEV: Indeed I shall. I'm just about to introduce you to my rival, a man who'll completely usurp my place in your affections.

LIDIYA: That won't be difficult – in fact, a lot easier than you imagine.

> *Vasilkov practically runs up to Madame Cheboksarova, carrying her shawl, and followed by Andrei.*

VASILKOV: I've found him – here he is now! *(gives her the shawl)*

CHEBOKSAROVA: Goodness, you gave me such a start! *(puts on the shawl)* Thank you. Andrei, have my carriage wait outside the theatre.

ANDREI: Very good, ma'am.

TELYATEV: *(to Vasilkov)* Savva, dear friend!

LIDIYA: What a name! Is he foreign?

TELYATEV: He's from the boondocks.

LIDIYA: Where are they? I've never heard of them, they're not on the map, surely?

TELYATEV: Recently discovered.

> *Vasilkov approaches.*

Allow me to introduce my good friend Savva Vasilkov... *(Lidiya bows)* He's been in London, and Constantinople, then Cloud-Cuckooland and Kazan; he says he's seen lots of beautiful women, but none to compare with you.

VASILKOV: Oh, stop it, for heaven's sake! You're making me blush...

LIDIYA: You don't happen to know a Madame Churilo-Plenkov in Kazan?

VASILKOV: Indeed I do.

LIDIYA: I hear she's divorced from her husband now.

VASILKOV: Good heavens, no.

LIDIYA: Do you know someone called Podvorotnikov?

VASILKOV: Why, we're inseparable, ma'am.

> *Lidya exchanges glances with Telyatev. An awkward silence, then*
> *Vasilkov withdraws, covered in confusion.*

LIDIYA: What sort of accent's that?

TELYATEV: He spent a long time in Tashkent, as a prisoner-of-war.

> *They speak apart.*

GLUMOV: *(to Cheboksarova)* Yes, those goldmines of his are
extremely rich – every hundredweight of ore produces at least five
pounds of pure gold.

CHEBOKSAROVA: *(looks intently at Vasilkov)* Really?

GLUMOV: That's what he says. That's why he's so uncouth, you
see, spends all his time in Siberia with the natives.

CHEBOKSAROVA: *(gazing fondly at Vasilkov)* You don't say?
Goodness, you'd never guess from his appearance.

GLUMOV: And how are you supposed to tell a gold prospector from
his looks? I mean, he's not going to wear a gold overcoat, is he.
His pockets are lined with gold, and that's what matters: you
should see the way he tips waiters – absolute fistfuls of the stuff.

CHEBOKSAROVA: What a shame he's wasting his money like that.

GLUMOV: Well, who's he going to save it for? He's all alone in the
world. What he needs is a good wife, and even more so, a smart
mother-in-law.

CHEBOKSAROVA: *(gazing yet more fondly at Vasilkov)* Actually, he's
not bad-looking.

GLUMOV: Yes, among the Siberians, I should think he passes for
handsome.

CHEBOKSAROVA: *(to Lidiya)* Lidiya dear, let's take another little
stroll round the gardens. I have to go for a walk every evening,
gentlemen, it's doctor's orders. Now, who'd like to accompany us?

VASILKOV: Ma'am, if you'll permit me...

CHEBOKSAROVA: *(smiling pleasantly)* Why, thank you, young man, I'd be delighted.

Cheboksarova, Lidiya and Vasilkov exit.

GLUMOV: Well, that's the show on the road!

TELYATEV: Did you shoot her a line?

GLUMOV: Now would I miss a chance like that?

TELYATEV: So that's why she was making sheep's eyes at him.

GLUMOV: Let dear Mama and her darling daughter chase after him, till he's gone completely soft. We'll lead them right up to seventh heaven, then whip the rug from under their feet.

TELYATEV: Just don't botch it up. I wouldn't be surprised if he ended up marrying Lidiya and dragging her off to the back of beyond. He scares me stiff, he's like some force of nature bearing down on you.

Kuchumov approaches haughtily, nose in the air. At intervals throughout, he breaks into song, snatches of "Don Giovanni", etc.

KUCHUMOV: *Ma in Spagna, ma in Spagna... mille e tre...*

TELYATEV: Good morning, my dear Prince...

KUCHUMOV: Dammit, that was a superb veal pie I've just eaten, gentlemen, simply delicious! *Mille e tre...*

GLUMOV: What, at a funeral, or in the sweetshop?

KUCHUMOV: Oh, don't talk rubbish! *Ma in Spagna...* A rich businessman invited me to lunch. I've pulled a few strings for him in the past, and now he wants me to do him another favour. Well, I promised I would – I mean, it's no skin off my nose.

GLUMOV: Oh sure, promises cost nothing.

KUCHUMOV: Honestly, what a wicked tongue you have. *(wagging his finger)* Better watch your step, or you'll get drummed out of Moscow. I've only to say the word, you know.

GLUMOV: You should've said it ages ago. With a bit of luck I might've landed among some intelligent people.

KUCHUMOV: Well, really! *(waving his hand)* There's no agreeing with you, is there.

TELYATEV: If you can't agree with a chap, you'd better not start on him – that's what I always say.

KUCHUMOV: *Mille e tre...* Oh, yes! I nearly forgot – wait till I tell you this – I won eleven thousand roubles last night!

TELYATEV: Are you sure it was you? Wasn't somebody else?

GLUMOV: *(eagerly)* Well, come on, come on – where? How?

KUCHUMOV: It was in the Merchants' Club...

TELYATEV: And you got the money?

KUCHUMOV: I did indeed.

TELYATEV: Well, tell us about it – we're all ears.

GLUMOV: This is amazing stuff, if it's true.

KUCHUMOV: *(testily)* There's nothing amazing about it! D'you think I'm incapable of winning? Anyway, I drove round to the Club yesterday, strolled through the rooms a couple of times, had a squint at the menu, ordered up some oysters...

GLUMOV: Oysters, at this time of year?

KUCHUMOV: No, no , I'm forgetting – it wasn't oysters, it was ravioli. So, as I was saying, this gentleman walks up to me, and he...

TELYATEV: What, a stranger?

KUCHUMOV: Absolutely. And he says to me: "Would your Excellency like a game of baccarat?" "Yes," I said, "Why not?" I'd a fair bit of money on me, so I thought I'd chance, oh, a couple of thousand. So we sit down, start off at a rouble a point, and would you believe, I had the most fantastic luck! The luck of the devil, as they say. He kept calling for a new deck, but it made no odds – it just wasn't his day, and he packed it in eventually. And when we came to tot up my winnings – twelve and a half thousand! So he took out the money...

GLUMOV: You said eleven thousand...

KUCHUMOV: Did I? Well, it was there or thereabouts.

TELYATEV: Ye gods, who can afford to lose twelve thousand in one night? That's somebody worth knowing, eh?

KUCHUMOV: He's just arrived in town, apparently.

GLUMOV: Well, I was at the Club last night, and there wasn't a word about this.

KUCHUMOV: I got there early, you see, there was scarcely anybody around, and we'd finished the business in half an hour.

GLUMOV: So, that's a supper you owe us tonight.

TELYATEV: We're having supper with Vasilkov, but you can stand us a glass of brandy – it's getting a bit chilly.

KUCHUMOV: Yes, and you'll polish off the whole bottle. I mean, even by the glass it'll cost me a bomb.

TELYATEV: Not at all, I'll have one glass – two at most.

KUCHUMOV: Well, all right, if it's just a couple. Tell you what, you can have dinner at my place on Sunday – I'll give you fresh sturgeon, got it sent up live from Nizhny, plus a brace of snipe, and a red Burgundy, such as you've never...

TELYATEV: *(taking him by the arm)* Come on, let's go – my teeth are starting to chatter. I'll be catching a fever in a minute.

They exit. Cheboksarova, Lidiya, Vasilkov and Andrei enter.

CHEBOKSAROVA: *(to Andrei)* Tell them to bring the carriage up now.

ANDREI: Very good, ma'am. *(exits, and swiftly re-enters)*

CHEBOKSAROVA: *(to Vasilkov)* Thank you for your company, sir, it's time we were leaving. Please do come and see us.

VASILKOV: Certainly, ma'am. When would be convenient?

CHEBOKSAROVA: Whenever you like. I receive between the hours of two and four o'clock, but why not simply join us for dinner? We generally go out for a drive in the evenings.

VASILKOV: I shall consider it my great good fortune to call on you at the earliest opportunity, ma'am. Miss Lidiya, I'm a straight-forward person – allow me to express my deep admiration for your matchless beauty!

LIDIYA: Why, thank you, sir.

She moves apart, and observing that her mother is still talking to Vasilkov, expresses some impatience.

CHEBOKSAROVA: So, we shall expect to see you.

VASILKOV: Without fail, ma'am. I shall take advantage of your kind invitation tomorrow, if I may. I'm staying not far from you.

CHEBOKSAROVA: Really?

VASILKOV: In the same house, actually, on a different landing.

Cheboksarova exits, turning back to look at him a few times. Vasilkov stands motionless a long time, hat in hand, watching them leave.

VASILKOV: She's so nice to me... it's wonderful! Either she's extremely kindhearted, or else extremely intelligent, to be able to see through my rough provincial exterior to my essential goodness. But I'm such an easy mark. That's what comes of spending long hours, grinding away at pure and applied mathematics. All these dry-as-dust calculations weary the heart, and at the first opportunity it's out for revenge, to show the mathematician up as a complete ass. Well, my heart's got its revenge now – I've fallen head over heels in love, like a teenager, to the point where I'm ready to make an idiot of myself. It's a good thing I've got a strong will, and no matter how infatuated I might be, I'm not about to go over budget. No, by God I'm not! Strict adherence to sound fiscal principles has been my lifeline more than once. *(falls into a reverie)* Oh, Lidiya, Lidiya... my heart melts at the very thought of you... But what if you have no heart? What if all you care about is money? I mean, with my inexperience I'm just putty in the hands of a beautiful girl like that. She can make me her plaything, her abject slave. Yes indeed, it's just as well I've a good business head, and never go beyond my means...

Kuchumov, Telyatov and Glumov approach.

TELYATEV: Well now, have you been introduced? Feeling a bit better? Congratulations, sir! *(embraces Vasilkov)*

VASILKOV: I'm greatly indebted to you, sir, and believe me, I shan't forget it.

TELYATEV: I'll remind you if you do. You owe me a bottle now, sir
– let's go for supper and you can repay your debt. *(to Kuchumov)*
Prince, this is our new friend, Savva Vasilkov.

KUCHUMOV: You've just arrived in Moscow?

VASILKOV: That's right, your Excellency...

TELYATEV: Oh, he's no Excellency, he's plain Grisha Kuchumov –
we only call him that because we're so fond of him.

KUCHUMOV: That's true. Moscow high society's much too
exclusive – it's really quite difficult for a newcomer to break in –
you need lots and lots of...

TELYATEV: Honestly, what rubbish he talks.

GLUMOV: If Moscow society was all that exclusive, they'd never
have let us in!

TELYATEV: Well, what about it, sirs, shall we have a drink here on
the wing?

VASILKOV: If society so desires. Waiter, bring us a bottle of champagne!

GLUMOV: And four large glasses!

KUCHUMOV: Yes, four, why not? I shall do you the honour of
joining you in a glass.

GLUMOV: And then we'll go straight to the Club, for a game of cards.
(to Kuchumov) We'll count that twelve thousand roubles of yours.

KUCHUMOV: Watch you don't find yourself adding to them.

TELYATEV: *(to his manservant, standing by the gate)* Grigory! Come here!

    Grigory approaches.

  Help me on with my coat, there's a good chap. Is my carriage handy?

GRIGORY: *(helping him on with his coat)* It's here, your honour, by
the gate.

KUCHUMOV: *(to his manservant)* Nikolai!

Nikolai approaches.

Well, don't stand gaping, man! Stay here, you can help me into the carriage.

A Boy from the café brings them a bottle of champagne and glasses.

VASILKOV: Help yourselves, gentlemen, do, please.

They raise their glasses.

TELYATEV: Well, here's to success, my dear chap – even if it's a bit unlikely.

GLUMOV: Here's to the chase anyway, you can forget success.

KUCHUMOV: What success are you talking about?

GLUMOV: He wants to marry Lidiya.

KUCHUMOV: What!? No, that's impossible – I won't permit it!

TELYATEV: Nobody's asking your permission.

VASILKOV: Would you like a bet, gentlemen? Say, three thousand. I'll lay you three to one that I do marry Lidiya.

KUCHUMOV: I never bet.

GLUMOV: I'd bet all right, but I've no money.

TELYATEV: And I'm frightened I'll lose.

VASILKOV: *(laughs)* What's the matter, my fine Moscow gentlemen, lost your nerve? So why were you laughing at me? Come on, let's put our cards on the table – there's my three thousand... *(takes out the money, but they all shake their heads)* This wine's loosened my tongue, I'm afraid. Yes, I'm in love with Lidiya, and I'm going to marry her, no matter what. When I say a thing, I do it – I don't waste words. Now, let's go and have supper...

END OF ACT ONE

ACT TWO

The scene is a richly-furnished drawing-room, with paintings and wall-hangings, rugs, etc. There are doors at each side, and upstage centre. Vasilkov is pacing back and forth. Telyatev enters stage left.

TELYATEV: I thought you'd gone ages ago. Why don't you join the ladies, lost your courage?

VASILKOV: It's the bane of my life, I just don't know how to make small talk.

TELYATEV: What's to know? All you have to remember is not to start any intellectual arguments, especially after dinner. Just say the first thing that comes into your head, as long as it's funny or witty, or slightly scandalous – your trouble is you keep going on about truncated pyramids and cubic feet.

VASILKOV: Actually I've just thought up a funny story, which I wouldn't mind telling.

TELYATEV: Well, go and tell it then, before you forget.

VASILKOV: And where are you rushing off to?

TELYATEV: Lidiya's sent me out to buy a bunch of flowers.

VASILKOV: Oh, I see it all now – you're my most dangerous rival.

TELYATEV: No fear of that, my friend. A man who hasn't missed a single ballet in the last twenty years isn't worth a light as a husband. Don't worry about me, just march boldly in and tell them your funny story.

Vasilkov exits left. Glumov enters by the same door.

GLUMOV: Is that creature still here? What an ass! No, it's time to send him packing. We've had our fun with him. It's just a pity we didn't accept his wager.

TELYATEV: I wouldn't take it on even now.

GLUMOV: Well, he certainly took us to the cleaners the other night at the Club. But what about Kuchumov? Tells us he's won twelve thousand roubles the night before, then can't raise so much as six hundred! Claps eyes on a man for the first time and he owes him money already... Where are you going?

TELYATEV: Petrovka.

GLUMOV: I'll come with you.

They exit. Kuchumov and Cheboksarova enter.

KUCHUMOV: *Muta d'accento e de pensier...*

CHEBOKSAROVA: This while back I've had nothing but bad news.

KUCHUMOV: Hm, yes... it's not very nice... *E de pensier...*

CHEBOKSAROVA: Not a day goes by but I can expect to hear something of that sort.

KUCHUMOV: But what's he actually doing there, that husband of yours? I mean, how could he let things slip like that? I just don't understand. He's a decent chap, got a good head on him...

CHEBOKSAROVA: But what *can* he do? You've read his letter yourself: a bad harvest, drought, all the timber burned in the mill, and that mill's been losing money for years. He says he's got to have thirty thousand immediately, the estate's already been marked up for auction.

KUCHUMOV: Well, what's the matter with him, the silly creature? I mean, hasn't he got plenty of friends? There's myself, for example... You tell him to write to me direct. *Muta d'accento...*

CHEBOKSAROVA: Oh, my dear friend, I knew I could rely on you!

KUCHUMOV: Oh, nonsense, what are friends for? For the sake of our long friendship, I'm delighted to help. It's no trouble to me.

CHEBOKSAROVA: Kuchumov, listen, for God's sake – I've been frank with you, but as far as the rest are concerned, they've got to think we're still a wealthy family. I mean, I have a daughter, just twenty-four – think of that, my dear sir!

KUCHUMOV: Of course, of course.

CHEBOKSAROVA: We have to support ourselves... we can still get credit, but not a great deal, and winter'll soon be upon us, with theatres, balls, concerts. You ask any mother what all *that* costs!

Lidiya doesn't even want to hear about it, as long as she gets what she wants. She has no idea of the value of money, or what anything costs. She'll go round the shops, pointing at things, she doesn't even ask the price, and then I'm left to pay the bills.

KUCHUMOV: Isn't there a husband in the offing?

CHEBOKSAROVA: No, she's so hard to please.

KUCHUMOV: Well, in the old days, a girl like that would've been quietly abducted long ago. Yes, indeed, if I wasn't tied to the old woman...

CHEBOKSAROVA: Well, you can joke, but what's a mother to do? To live happily all these years, and now suddenly... Last winter I went the rounds with her everywhere, no expense spared, I even ran through the money that had been put aside for her trousseau, and all to no purpose. And now, when I'm expecting money from my husband, I get this letter instead. I've no idea how we're going to live. What am I going to tell poor Lidiya? This news'll kill her.

KUCHUMOV: Well, of course, anything you need, don't hesitate to... I mean, you must allow me to be a father to poor Lidiya, in your husband's absence. I've known her since childhood, and believe me, dear lady, I love her more than any daughter. Yes, I love her, truly...

CHEBOKSAROVA: I don't know how much you love her, but as far as I'm concerned, there's no sacrifice I wouldn't make for her.

KUCHUMOV: And the same goes for me, absolutely the same. By the way, what's that Vasilkov doing at your house? You ought to be more choosy.

CHEBOKSAROVA: Why shouldn't he be here?

KUCHUMOV: I don't like him. Nobody knows who he is or what sort of background he comes from.

CHEBOKSAROVA: No, and I don't know either. But I do know he's a gentleman, and he's got decent manners.

KUCHUMOV: Yes, so?

CHEBOKSAROVA: He speaks very good French.

KUCHUMOV: That's not exactly a mark of distinction.

CHEBOKSAROVA: And apparently he's in some sort of business, quite important.

KUCHUMOV: Is that it? You don't know very much about him.

CHEBOKSAROVA: And he's no fool.

KUCHUMOV: Well, I'll make up my own mind about that. How did he happen to fetch up here?

CHEBOKSAROVA: I honestly can't remember. Somebody introduced him, Telyatev, I think it was. We see everybody here.

KUCHUMOV: And is he thinking of marrying Lidiya?

CHEBOKSAROVA: Who knows? It's possible.

KUCHUMOV: So what's his condition?

CHEBOKSAROVA: To tell you the truth, I've scarcely given him a thought, so I haven't taken any interest in his condition.

KUCHUMOV: He keeps wittering on about "this moment in time".

CHEBOKSAROVA: Oh, well, everybody says that these days.

KUCHUMOV: Yes, but it can get very boring. If you must talk, go where people are willing to listen. And anyway, what is "this moment in time"? Is it better than previous ones? Where are the palaces all our counts and princes used to have? Who's got them now? Jumped-up tradesmen, that's who. And what's happened to all the horn-players? Time was, you could hear them at sunset, tootling away down by the ponds, and there'd be bonfires, and even ambassadors'd come to watch. Yes, that was in Russia's glory days. Huh, "this moment in time". We ought to send upstarts like him packing, that's what I say.

CHEBOKSAROVA: Why so? On the contrary, I intend to cherish him. In a situation like ours, all sorts of people might come in handy.

KUCHUMOV: Well, it's not likely he'll come in handy. You'd do better to put your trust in us older chaps. Of course, I can't marry, I've got a wife already. Oh dear, oh dear, oh dear, I have indeed. But we still have our fancies, us old folks, and then nothing's too expensive. I've neither parents nor children, you can do whatever you like with me. You could install me as Lidiya's guardian, or her godfather, say. Yes, there's nothing an old man values more than a spot of affection, and

I can't take all my millions to the grave with me, now can I? Anyway, goodbye, my dear lady, it's time I was at the Club.

CHEBOKSAROVA: *(accompanies him to the door)* So, may we look forward to seeing you again soon?

KUCHUMOV: Why, of course. I've lost a bet with your dear daughter, and I owe her a box of chocolates. I may be an old man, but dammit, I've still got young blood in my veins. *(exits)*

CHEBOKSAROVA: Huh, it's not chocolates we need.

> *Stands deep in thought. Vasilkov enters and picks up his hat.*

Where are you rushing off to?

VASILKOV: Madam, if I may be excused...

CHEBOKSAROVA: Wait a minute. *(sits down on the settee)*

VASILKOV: What can I do for you?

CHEBOKSAROVA: Sit down, please. *(Vasilkov does so)* I'd like a word with you. We've been acquainted for some time now, but I know absolutely nothing about you, we've scarcely spoken two words. Obviously you've no time for old women.

VASILKOV: Not at all, ma'am. What is it you want to know about me?

CHEBOKSAROVA: Well, at the very least, I'd like to know enough so that I can answer, when people ask about you. We have a great many callers, and no-one seems to know you.

VASILKOV: The reason no-one here knows me is that I've been living in the provinces.

CHEBOKSAROVA: So, where were you educated?

VASILKOV: Well, I did go to college, but I've been rather more involved in my own line of business.

CHEBOKSAROVA: Splendid. And your parents – are they still alive?

VASILKOV: Only my mother, and she's lived all her life in the country.

CHEBOKSAROVA: So, you're practically alone in the world. And you're a civil servant...

VASILKOV: No, I deal through private companies, mainly, small stuff – contractors, foremen, and the like.

CHEBOKSAROVA: *(nods condescendingly)* Oh yes, foremen, managers, executives... I read an article somewhere...

VASILKOV: No, I'm afraid it's only foremen we have.

CHEBOKSAROVA: Yes, that's very nice. Yes, yes, I remember now. It's all the rage these days... even quite wealthy people... getting closer to the peasants. And I'm sure you'll wear a lovely silk caftan, or velvet, even. Last winter I saw a millionaire on the train and he had on one of those skin things – what d'you call them?

VASILKOV: Sheepskin?

CHEBOKSAROVA: Yes, yes, a sheepskin. And a beaver hat.

VASILKOV: No, I don't go in for fancy dress.

CHEBOKSAROVA: Still, you must have a substantial fortune, to spend your time doing that.

VASILKOV: Well, in the first place, the business is actually quite profitable.

CHEBOKSAROVA: You mean amusing, surely? Good fun. You know, the way they sing songs, all dance round in a ring – no doubt you've got your own Volga boatmen.

VASILKOV: No, we've nothing of that sort, but you're right – you can't start a business like ours without capital.

CHEBOKSAROVA: Well, of course you can't – that's just what I was thinking. I mean, you can see right away that you're a man of substance. You seem a little out of sorts today. *(a pause)* Tell me, why do you keep arguing with Lidiya? She's a spirited girl, and it does annoy her.

VASILKOV: I'm glad she's got spirit – that's an excellent quality in a woman. It's just a pity that Lidiya has so little understanding of things which really are common knowledge these days.

CHEBOKSAROVA: And tell me, dear friend, why on earth she should understand what's common knowledge? I mean, she's had a higher education. We have a superb French library. And you can ask her anything you like about mythology, you just ask her. Believe me, sir, she's terribly well up on French literature, she knows things other young girls wouldn't even dream of. No, there's nothing the most adept scandalmonger could say to surprise her.

VASILKOV: Hm, that sort of education's like self-defence, it's all very well in its place. Of course, I've no right to instruct anybody, if I'm not asked. I wouldn't even be trying to persuade Miss Lidiya, if I didn't...

CHEBOKSAROVA: If you didn't what?

VASILKOV: If I didn't hope I might be of some service to her. If she were to change her way of thinking, she'd have a different outlook on people. She'd begin to pay more attention to their inner qualities.

CHEBOKSAROVA: Oh indeed, yes, inner qualities... yes, you're absolutely right.

VASILKOV: I might have some hopes, then, of winning her favour. But as it stands now, I can't be witty, and I won't be ridiculous.

CHEBOKSAROVA: Oh no, of course not. Heavens, she's still young, she can change her outlook a dozen times. I must say, though, I could listen to you for hours, and I often repeat what you say to my daughter, when we're alone.

VASILKOV: Thank you. To be honest, I was on the point of giving up. I don't want to make a fool of myself.

CHEBOKSAROVA: Oh, for shame, sir.

VASILKOV: I mean, I'm not all that inclined to grovel. Frankly, she needs me more than I need her.

CHEBOKSAROVA: Young man, you may regard me as your ally, I shall willingly assist you to achieve your intentions. *(mysteriously)* But understand me, only because I consider them to be entirely honorable.

> *Lidiya enters, and stands in the doorway. Vasilkov rises to go, and kisses Cheboksarova's hand.*

VASILKOV: Goodbye, dear lady.

CHEBOKSAROVA: Goodbye, my dear young man.

Vasilkov bows to Lidiya and exits.

LIDIYA: What were you talking to him for? What were you saying? He's a dreadful person, quite mad.

CHEBOKSAROVA: Trust me, Lidiya, I know what I'm doing. We can't afford to be choosy, not in our situation.

LIDIYA: What situation? I wouldn't put up with him in any situation! He hasn't a clue about how we live, or what we need – he's completely alien.

CHEBOKSAROVA: Ah, but he quite often speaks the truth.

LIDIYA: And just who gave him the right to preach at people? What sort of prophet is he, eh? I mean, really, maman, a drawing-room's hardly a lecture-hall. Nor is it some sort of Mechanics' Institute, or engineering college.

CHEBOKSAROVA: Oh, Lidiya, you're absolutely heartless.

LIDIYA: Maman, I can't stand to listen to him! Where did he dream up these economic laws he's always on about? Who needs them? Really, I should hope the only laws that concern us are the laws of fashion and good taste. If everybody's wearing the new style, then that's what I'll wear, or die in the attempt. There's no time to think about laws, you just drive to the shop and buy it. No, no, he's quite mad.

CHEBOKSAROVA: I think he's just trying to be original. Lots of people do that. He isn't very well educated, possibly none too bright, but he's got to say something, so he'll be noticed. And that's why he wants to appear original. Most likely he thinks and behaves like any other decent person.

LIDIYA: Maybe so, but I'm sick to death of him just the same.

CHEBOKSAROVA: He's a man of substance, my dear, and we have to be a little more tolerant of those sort of people. I mean, we put up with the others, don't we? Half the people who call on us are absolute windbags – frightful liars.

LIDIYA: What do I care if they're liars? At least you can have some fun with them, and he's just a bore. That's what I really can't forgive.

CHEBOKSAROVA: I'm afraid there's another reason why you have to be more indulgent, my dear, and I'd advise you to...

LIDIYA: What reason? Tell me.

CHEBOKSAROVA: Lidiya, you're a sensible girl... I hope you'll have the presence of mind to hear me out calmly and reasonably...

LIDIYA: *(alarmed)* What are you talking about? What is this?

CHEBOKSAROVA: I've received a letter from your father.

LIDIYA: What, is he sick? Is he dying?

CHEBOKSAROVA: No.

LIDIYA: For God's sake what? Tell me.

CHEBOKSAROVA: I'm afraid our hopes for this season are in ruins.

LIDIYA: In what way? I don't understand you.

CHEBOKSAROVA: I wrote to your father in the country, asking him to send us some money. We owe such a lot, yes, and we need a very tidy sum for the winter season. I received his reply today...

LIDIYA: Well, go on – what does he say?

CHEBOKSAROVA: *(sniffing smelling-salts)* He says he has no money, that he himself needs thirty thousand, or he'll be forced to sell the estate, and the estate's the last thing we possess.

LIDIYA: Well, that's a great pity, maman, but I'm sure I didn't need to know all this. You might at least have spared me, instead of telling me you're ruined.

CHEBOKSAROVA: But you'd have had to find out eventually, my dear.

LIDIYA: Why on earth should I? *(on the point of tears)* I mean, you'll have to find some way of getting us out of this mess, you'll just have to, we can't stay like this. We absolutely can't leave Moscow, we're not going back to the country. And we can't live in Moscow like paupers! One way or another, you'll just have to fix it so that our life here remains unchanged. And I have to find a husband this winter, get properly set up. Good God, you're a mother, you must know that. Surely you can think of something, if you haven't done so already, to see us through just one winter without dropping our standards. Think, mother, think – it's your job! Why are you telling me all this, when it's really none of my business? I hadn't a care in the world, and now you've deprived me of my peace of mind, which is a young woman's finest ornament. You should've used your head, maman, and cried by yourself, if there was any crying to be done. Does it really make things any easier, if I have to cry along with you? Well, go on, does it?

CHEBOKSAROVA: No, of course it doesn't.

LIDIYA: So why on earth should I have to cry too? Eh? Why have you dumped all your worries onto me? Worry makes people old, it gives you wrinkles. Honestly, I feel as if I've aged ten years. I've never known poverty, and I've no wish to either. I know shops – I know linen, silk, carpets, furs, furniture. I know when you need something, you drive up to the shop, choose what you want, hand over some money, and if you've no money, you simply tell the shop-assistant to have it delivered. But as to where the money comes from, or how much it takes for the year, or the season, I've never known, never felt the need to know. I've never known the meaning of 'dear', or 'cheap' – I've always regarded all that as pathetic and degrading, nasty low-class penny-pinching. Oh God, I can't think of it without a shudder. I remember once on the way home from the shops, the thought came into my mind: I wonder if I haven't paid too much for that dress? Well, I was so ashamed of myself, I went bright red all over, I scarcely knew where to look – and that was driving alone in the carriage! I suddenly remembered seeing some merchant's wife in the shop, haggling over a length of stuff. She couldn't bring herself to pay that much money, but she didn't want to put the cloth down either. And she kept picking it up, and dropping it again, and whispering to two other old women, while the shop-assistants had a jolly good laugh at her. Oh God, maman, why are you torturing me like this?

CHEBOKSAROVA: I know, I know, darling – I should have kept our little dérangement hidden from you, but it's simply not possible. If we're to stay in Moscow we'll have to cut back on our expenses, we'll have to sell the silver, a few of the paintings, some jewellery...

LIDIYA: No, no, God forbid! We can't do that, we can't! The whole of Moscow will know we're ruined, they'll come up to us with long faces, feigning sympathy, offering us stupid advice. They'll shake their heads, and sigh, and all so damned phoney and insincere – no, no, it's outrageous! Believe me, they won't even pretend to conceal their delight. *(hides her face)* No! No!

CHEBOKSAROVA: Well, what are we going to do?

LIDIYA: Do? Not lose our dignity for a start. We'll have the flat done up again, we'll buy a new carriage, order up some new livery for the servants, pick out some new furniture, and the dearer the better.

CHEBOKSAROVA: And where on earth's the money coming from?

LIDIYA: He'll pay for it all.

CHEBOKSAROVA: Who will?

LIDIYA: My husband.

CHEBOKSAROVA: What do you mean, your husband?

LIDIYA: Whoever he is.

CHEBOKSAROVA: What, has somebody proposed to you?

LIDIYA: No, no-one's proposed to me, no-one's dared to. I've treated my suitors with nothing but contempt. I've been waiting for a handsome man with a fortune – now all I want is a rich man, and there's plenty of those.

CHEBOKSAROVA: Mm, I hope you're not mistaken, my dear.

LIDIYA: What, has beauty lost its value? No, maman, you needn't worry. There aren't too many beauties, but there's no shortage of wealthy idiots.

Andrei enters.

ANDREI: Mr Telyatev, ma'am...

LIDIYA: And here's the first of them.

CHEBOKSAROVA: *(to Andrei)* Show him in.

Andrei exits.

LIDIYA: Now leave us, don't interfere. This is the one, he'll pay for the lot.

CHEBOKSAROVA: But supposing he...

LIDIYA: Supposing what? What are you on about? So there's Vasilkov, you told me yourself he has a huge fortune, send for him then. He's got goldmines, and he's a fool – the gold's as good as ours.

CHEBOKSAROVA: I'd better send for him now, make sure he's ready. *(exits)*

Telyatev enters with a bouquet of flowers.

LIDIYA: My, how prompt you are – you really do spoil me. Why do you do these things, tell me?

TELYATEV: What, surely this is nothing new? Since when haven't I done your bidding?

LIDIYA: Yes, but why *do* you spoil me so?

TELYATEV: It's just the way I'm made. It's my vocation, to be serviceable. Besides which, I've nothing else to do.

LIDIYA: So it's just to amuse yourself, is it, to keep from getting bored? You do realise all these attentions of yours could turn a girl's head?

TELYATEV: Guilty as charged!

LIDIYA: Well, it's either no crime at all, or else a very great one, depending on whether or not your actions are sincere.

TELYATEV: Of course they're sincere.

LIDIYA: But your constant attention, constant flattery – isn't that all just a sort of hook, which you're trying to catch me on? You're trying to make me believe you're absolutely devoted, and it's not something a person can remain indifferent to.

TELYATEV: So much the better! It's not right I should be the only one with feelings, you know, it's time your feelings were aroused too.

LIDIYA: That's all very well for you – your feelings have long since been turned into fine words. The sort of life you lead, you've had plenty of practice, you know how to control yourself in any situation. But you just imagine an inexperienced young girl, whose feelings are awakened for the very first time – she's in a very difficult and dangerous position.

TELYATEV: That may well be, but I can't really say, not having ever been a girl.

LIDIYA: All you have to do is reveal your feelings, and you're either some man's plaything, or else you're ridiculous. And that's not very pleasant, either way. It's not nice, is it.

TELYATEV: No, it isn't.

LIDIYA: So don't try and turn my head just for the fun of it, be
sincere with me, please, I beg you. Don't say things you don't feel,
and if you don't like me, don't pay me compliments.

TELYATEV: Who ever gave you that idea? Good heavens, I always
say what I feel.

LIDIYA: Truly?

TELYATEV: Yes, of course. I actually say less than I feel.

LIDIYA: Why's that?

TELYATEV: Well, I don't dare... Lidiya, may I speak freely?

LIDIYA: Please do.

TELYATEV: I can scarcely believe my ears. Am I dreaming? This is
my lucky day, surely – what's today's date?

LIDIYA: What do you mean lucky?

TELYATEV: Well, I couldn't have expected this. You're being nice
to me, you've come down from your unattainable heights, down to
ground level, just for me. Up until now you've been Diana,
despising the entire male sex, with the moon in your hair and a
quiver-full of arrows at your side. And here you are transformed
into a simple peasant-girl, naive, warm-hearted, one of those you
see in the ballet, dancing around flapping their aprons. Like so...
(demonstrates a peasant dance routine)

LIDIYA: And does that really make you happy?

TELYATEV: Well, I'm not a statue, you know – I'm not the "Bronze
Horseman".

LIDIYA: How easy it is to make you happy. I'm so glad I can make
you happy!

TELYATEV: Eh? Make me happy? Lidiya, is this really you?

LIDIYA: Why are you so surprised? Don't you deserve happiness?

TELYATEV: I don't know if I deserve it or not, but I think I'll go mad for joy!

LIDIYA: Then go mad, please!

TELYATEV: I shall do all manner of silly things.

LIDIYA: Do them, do them!

TELYATEV: Look, Lidiya, you're either making a fool of me, out of spite, or else you're...

LIDIYA: Go on, finish it.

TELYATEV: Or else you're in love with me!

LIDIYA: Yes, yes, I am, worse luck. That last bit, of course.

TELYATEV: What on earth do you mean, worse luck? It's wonderful luck, sheer bliss! You couldn't have come up with anything better. *(he embraces her lightly)*

LIDIYA: Oh my dearest Jean, are you mine?

TELYATEV: Your slave, absolutely – yes, your captive Ethiopian!

LIDIYA: *(looking into his eyes)* Truly?

TELYATEV: Yes, yes, for as long as I live. Even longer, if that's possible.

LIDIYA: Oh, darling, I'm so happy!

TELYATEV: No, no, *I'm* the happy one! *(kisses her)*

LIDIYA: Oh God, what absolute bliss! *Maman! Maman!*

TELYATEV: What d'you mean, *maman*? What's *maman* got to do with it? Two's company, you know.

LIDIYA: Oh, I know, *Jean* darling – it's just that I'm so happy.

TELYATEV: So much the better, then.

LIDIYA: I'm just so choked up, I've got to share my joy with her.

TELYATEV: No, we don't want to share anything with anybody.

That leaves all the more for ourselves.

LIDIYA: Yes, yes, you're quite right, we needn't share our joy, God knows, there's little enough of it to go round. Still, we really ought to tell her.

TELYATEV: Tell her what? I don't know what you mean.

LIDIYA: Well, Jean, that we love each other, and that we want to be together the rest of our lives.

TELYATEV: Eh? Oh, I get it. You mean, make it official, till death do us part, and so forth. Well, I'm sorry, but I wasn't expecting that.

LIDIYA: What are you saying? You weren't expecting what? Come on, tell me!

TELYATEV: I mean, being your devoted servant, your slave, whatever you want, that's fine, but marriage? Well, that's just not my style.

LIDIYA: So how dare you take liberties with me?

TELYATEV: I didn't take any liberties – I just didn't try and stop you loving me. I'm not going to stop anybody doing that.

LIDIYA: Huh, and you seriously think you're worthy of my love?

TELYATEV: No, of course I'm not, you're quite right. But people don't always love people worthy of them, do they? Eh? I mean, what sort of idiot would I have been, to turn you down and read you a moral lesson? I'm sorry, my dear Lidiya, but I'm not going to take on the job of teaching you morals, I've no aptitude for it, and no inclination either. As far as I'm concerned, the fewer morals a woman has the better.

LIDIYA: Oh! You're a monster, sir! You're a filthy swine!

TELYATEV: You're absolutely right, and that's why you ought to be grateful to me for not marrying you.

   Lidiya exits.

Phew, that was a close shave. Thank God I'm still in one piece. No, I'd better stop playing around, or if I'm not careful I'll play myself right into the ranks of husbands. The flesh is weak, yes, but you've got to keep the devil at bay.

Crosses to the door. Vasilkov enters.

Pray be seated, sir. *(exits)*

Cheboksarova enters.

CHEBOKSAROVA: Good day to you, sir. I'm very pleased to see you.
  I don't seem to be able to do without your company. Sit down
  here beside me, please.

VASILKOV: You sent for me?

CHEBOKSAROVA: Yes, I do apologise for bothering you, but I need
  advice, I'm such a helpless creature, really, and you're the only
  sensible person I know.

VASILKOV: Why, thank you. How can I be of service?

CHEBOKSAROVA: I've been talking things over with my daughter,
  and we want to change our way of life. We're tired of all this
  socialising, and we've decided not to receive anyone, barring
  yourself, of course. I mean, we have very substantial resources, but
  that doesn't oblige us to run mad from morning till night.

VASILKOV: I suppose not.

CHEBOKSAROVA: Lidiya would like to finish her education, and
  that's quite impossible without good direction. Anyway, we've
  decided to turn to you.

VASILKOV: I'd be delighted to help you, with all my heart. But what
  on earth can I teach Miss Lidiya? Spherical trigonometry?

CHEBOKSAROVA: Yes, exactly. Why not, indeed? I mean, teaching a
  young girl is a very pleasant occupation, wouldn't you agree?

VASILKOV: Well, of course, but what would she want with spherical
  trigonometry?

CHEBOKSAROVA: Oh, she does have some peculiar ideas, I know,
  but she's a good girl, she's so kindhearted. *(mysteriously)* You
  know, she really can't abide those foppish creatures.

VASILKOV: You surprise me, ma'am.

CHEBOKSAROVA: As far as I'm concerned, well, I've given up on them long ago. But any mother could entrust her daughter to you without fear. Forgive me, my dear young man, for being so frank with you, but I really do wish Lidiya liked you.

VASILKOV: Thank you.

CHEBOKSAROVA: If it were possible, I think I'd even force her to like you, just to see her truly happy.

VASILKOV: Surely there's some other way?

CHEBOKSAROVA: I don't know, you'll just have to find out. You do love my daughter, don't you? Wait, let me look into your eyes. No, don't say a word – I can see for myself. But you're so shy – do you want me to speak to her for you? Otherwise you'll just wind up arguing again, God forbid!

VASILKOV: No, I'll do it myself, thanks very much. I just need time to prepare, get my thoughts in order.

CHEBOKSAROVA: What's there to think about? Prepare what?

Lidiya enters.

CHEBOKSAROVA: Now there you are, Lidiya, Mr Vasilkov has just asked me for your hand in marriage, and although personally I'm delighted, I don't want to force you into anything.

LIDIYA: Well, of course, in a matter of this sort, I must have my freedom, and if I fancied somebody, then believe me, *maman*, I'd sooner listen to my own heart, then any advice of yours. However, I'm absolutely indifferent to all my admirers – you're well aware how many suitors I've already turned down – but it's time I was married, and that's why I'm placing myself entirely at your disposal.

VASILKOV: So, that means you don't love me?

LIDIYA: No, I don't. Why should I deceive you? Anyway, we can discuss that later. *Maman*, you've taken it upon yourself to decide my fate, bear in mind that you'll be answerable for my future happiness.

CHEBOKSAROVA: *(to Vasilkov)* Do you hear that, sir?

VASILKOV: Well, I'm very sorry.

LIDIYA: What about? That I don't love you?

VASILKOV: No, that I've been too hasty.

LIDIYA: You can refuse, there's still time. Obviously there isn't much
love on your side either, if you can throw me over so easily. Don't be
angry – you should thank me for being so open with you. Pretending
costs nothing, but I'd rather not. Brides always say they're in love
with their husbands, but nobody believes them – love only comes
later. So, put aside your vanity and let's agree. I mean, why should I
love you? You're not particularly good-looking, you've got a
ridiculous name – Savva, for heaven's sake – and your surname's as
common as muck. All right, these things are trivial, but it'll take time
to get used to. Why should you be angry? You're in love with me,
that's just fine. Now try to earn my love, and we'll be happy.

CHEBOKSAROVA: What you must remember is that her father and I
grudged her nothing – absolutely nothing. So she is making a
sacrifice for you.

VASILKOV: I don't want any sacrifices.

LIDIYA: I don't think you know what you want.

VASILKOV: Oh, I know what I want. Yes, of course you can marry
without love, love comes in time, you're quite right. But I want
you to respect me. Without respect, marriage is impossible.

LIDIYA: That goes without saying, otherwise I wouldn't marry you.

VASILKOV: Well, now it's my turn to be frank. You've told me you
don't love me, whereas I've told you I love you, possibly before
you've deserved it. But you've got to earn my love too, otherwise,
quite frankly, it might well turn to hate.

LIDIYA: Huh, really!

VASILKOV: You can refuse me, there's still time.

LIDIYA: Now why should I do that? Ha-ha! Let's act out this
comedy, and try to earn each other's love.

VASILKOV: I don't want any comedy, I want a bright, happy future.

LIDIYA: No, it's a comedy you want, believe me. You've made me
a proposal, and I've accepted – what more do you want? You love
me, you say – all right, you should be eternally happy, and not
lecture me about my duties. That's something we should know for

ourselves, and the only people who go on about how to live are the poor, who've got nothing to live on anyway.

CHEBOKSAROVA: Oh, I can see it, it's obvious – you really do love each other. All your arguments are just literary, as they say.

VASILKOV: Well, as your fiancé, allow me to present you with these. I bought them quite by chance today, and it seems they've come in handy. *(hands her a little box, containing earrings and a brooch)*

CHEBOKSAROVA: Oh! Those must be worth a good few thousand.

VASILKOV: Just three.

LIDIYA: You know, I think I *could* fall in love with you!

Holds out her hand to Vasilkov, who kisses it respectfully.

END OF ACT TWO

ACT THREE

The scene is the drawing-room as in Act Two, but more richly furnished. At stage left is a door leading to Vasilkov's study, at stage left, to Lidiya's room, with an outer door upstage centre. Vasilkov emerges from his study, carrying a briefcase and some newspapers, which he quickly scans before ringing the bell for Vasily.

VASILKOV: Hm, I see the Cheboksarov estate in Kazan's going to be sold off in a few days, along with their sawmill and forest. That's a pity. That mill of theirs could be very profitable, and they've plenty of good timber. Vasily, run round to Yermolaev and tell him to go to the Stock Exchange immediately, and wait for me there. I'll need him to act on my behalf. Tell him to get ready anyway, I'll be sending him to Kazan.

VASILY: Very good, sir.

VASILKOV: You know, Vasily, you really ought to dress a bit more appropriately.

VASILY: No way, sir. I mean, with these boots now, and this thick jacket and velvet cap, I look just like one of them English railway workers – that suits me fine, sir, I gets respect, and people knows what I am.

VASILKOV: Oh well, please yourself. Now off you go.

Vasily exits.

CHEBOKSAROVA: Honestly, Savva, you're so uncouth. Only just married and your mind's on business again.

VASILKOV: The one thing doesn't prevent the other, now does it, Mum?

CHEBOKSAROVA: Does it *what*?

VASILKOV: Mum – it's a nice word, affectionate, gets to the heart of things.

CHEBOKSAROVA: Oh, all right, all right. *(goes up to him)* Tell me, Savva, are you happy? Are you really happy, dear boy? *(tweaks his ear)*

VASILKOV: *(kisses her hand)* Yes, I am. I'm perfectly happy. I can now say I've had a few days of genuine bliss in my life. Oh, Mum, if you only...

CHEBOKSAROVA: Mum again!

VASILKOV: Sorry.

CHEBOKSAROVA: Yes, I wouldn't have expected anything else,
   otherwise I'd never have let my darling Lidiya marry you.

VASILKOV: And I'd be even happier, if... well, if...

CHEBOKSAROVA: *(sits down)* If what? What more do you want, you
   ungrateful wretch?

VASILKOV: Well, if I had nothing else to do but spend my entire life
   tearing round Moscow, paying calls on people, one minute a
   party, next minute a concert – if I wasn't ashamed to live like that,
   and could afford it, yes, I'd be perfectly happy.

CHEBOKSAROVA: But they all do it, everybody who's anybody, at
   least, so it can't be shameful. And you don't need that much money.

VASILKOV: I beg to differ. By my calculations, I've already run
   through a small fortune. And that's not counting how much Lidiya's
   spent, since I don't even know that. I don't interfere in her business.

CHEBOKSAROVA: Indeed no, quite right.

VASILKOV: She's got her own money, and I've got mine. But I'm
   starting to work out just how much this sort of life's going to cost
   me per year.

CHEBOKSAROVA: Oh, rubbish. Life's for living, isn't it? I mean, it's
   not as if a few odd expenses are likely to embarrass you.

VASILKOV: Not embarrass me? Good God, I could run through
   twenty-five thousand in six months at this rate.

CHEBOKSAROVA: And what's wrong with that? Surely you don't
   begrudge it? Honestly, I can't believe my ears.

VASILKOV: Whether I grudge it or not isn't the point – the point is,
   where am I to get it!

CHEBOKSAROVA: Well, how should I know, my dear? You're the
   best judge of that, obviously.

VASILKOV: You'd need to have a million to live like this.

CHEBOKSAROVA: And nobody's stopping you – you can have two, if you like.

VASILKOV: I haven't got two million, I haven't even got one. I have a modest income, that's all.

CHEBOKSAROVA: Half a million, anyway. That's not bad, is it.

VASILKOV: I've got my property, some ready cash, and my business, yes, but I can't afford to spend more than seven or eight thousand a year.

CHEBOKSAROVA: And what about your goldmines?

VASILKOV: My *what* mines?

CHEBOKSAROVA: Your goldmines.

VASILKOV: I haven't any goldmines. I haven't even a copper mine.

CHEBOKSAROVA: *(stands up)* Oh! Why have you so cruelly deceived us, sir!

VASILKOV: What do you mean, deceived you?

CHEBOKSAROVA: You told us you had a fortune.

VASILKOV: And that's true, I have a decent competence.

CHEBOKSAROVA: I don't believe this! You don't know what you're talking about. You don't seem to understand the simplest things, things every schoolboy knows.

VASILKOV: Well, go on, tell me. Why isn't it a fortune? How would you describe it?

CHEBOKSAROVA: What? It's penury, that's what it is, downright misery. What you're calling a fortune, sir, is perfectly suited to the needs of a bachelor. It'll keep him in glove money. But what in God's name have you let my poor daughter in for?

VASILKOV: I wanted to make her happy, and that's what I'll try to do.

CHEBOKSAROVA: With no money? That's laughable.

VASILKOV: I have a sufficiency, I've told you, and I'm trying to get more.

CHEBOKSAROVA: What do you mean a sufficiency? She needs a decent fortune, and there's no way you can provide that. You haven't any franchises, or railway concessions, and you won't get any. The only way you can acquire a fortune these days is by inheritance, or by winning one at cards, if you're lucky.

VASILKOV: No, you've missed one out – I could always rob somebody. Would you like me to have a go at that?

CHEBOKSAROVA: Is that what you think? How little you know me. No, sir, I can see I'll have to take steps myself to rectify our mistake.

VASILKOV: Rectify what? What mistake? Please don't meddle in our affairs. *(picks up his hat)*

CHEBOKSAROVA: You're leaving?

VASILKOV: Yes, I have to go. Goodbye. *(exits)*

CHEBOKSAROVA: Really, this son-in-law's nothing but trouble! Still, who else would've married Lidiya, knowing she hadn't a bean? We'll just have to keep trying for him, there's nothing else for it.

Andrei enters.

ANDREI: Mister Kuchumov, ma'am.

CHEBOKSAROVA: Just in time! *(to Andrei)* Show him in. *(Andrei exits)* I'll get to work on him right away.

Kuchumov enters, singing an aria from Rossini's "Barber of Seville"

KUCHUMOV: *Pace e gioia son con voi...*

CHEBOKSAROVA: I'm so glad to see you – sit down, please.

KUCHUMOV: *(sits) Pace e gioia...* So, where's our nymph?

CHEBOKSAROVA: She's flown off to make a few calls, but she'll be back soon.

KUCHUMOV: And what about our satyr, the one who stole her away from us?

CHEBOKSAROVA: Oh, he's running around on business somewhere. He's got so much on the go.

KUCHUMOV: Hm, a dry stick of a fellow. What on earth's the matter with him? He's her husband, and all we're all left with is sour grapes, licking our lips, like Aesop's wretched fox.

CHEBOKSAROVA: Really, what a thing to say! At your age, too.

KUCHUMOV: But I'm young at heart, dear lady, with a volcanic temperament.

CHEBOKSAROVA: Yes, of course. By the way, have you received a letter from my husband?

KUCHUMOV: Yes, I have. Now, don't concern yourself – I'll send him the money tomorrow. Really, it's a trifling sum. Put it out of your mind.

CHEBOKSAROVA: I have another favour to ask of you.

KUCHUMOV: What is it, tell me, dear lady. I'll be delighted to oblige.

CHEBOKSAROVA: You couldn't possibly find something for an acquaintance of mine – a better job, basically, some sort of trusteeship, a big one, or a manager's position on a large estate?

KUCHUMOV: Well, I'd have to know who it was for.

CHEBOKSAROVA: *(shrugs)* It's for my son-in-law.

KUCHUMOV: I knew it, I knew it! This is a bad business, ma'am, just as I expected.

CHEBOKSAROVA: Indeed, my dear friend, we seem to have made a slight mistake.

KUCHUMOV: I mean, what earthly right had he to your daughter? Pretending he would shower her with gold, and now it turns out he can't even support himself. He's obviously a dyed-in-the-wool scrounger. Most likely he's got lawyer's blood in him. What's he want a job for? To take bribes, that's all. I mean, how on earth can I recommend him? He'll probably disgrace me, the miserable wretch.

CHEBOKSAROVA: Please, you've got to help me – he is my son-in-law.

KUCHUMOV: Huh, you've just told me you'd made a mistake with him. Well, he didn't fool me, that ugly mug of his...

CHEBOKSAROVA: Oh, stop, stop – surely you wouldn't find it too unpleasant, being the patron of a man with such a pretty wife?

KUCHUMOV: Unpleasant? Who told you that? No, I'd be delighted.

CHEBOKSAROVA: If I know my Lidiya, she won't be ungrateful.

KUCHUMOV: Well, I've got the means, I can put the word round all my friends...

CHEBOKSAROVA: And don't think us women don't know how to show gratitude. No, when we really want to...

KUCHUMOV: I'll take wing this instant... Just tell me how, what and where, and I'm at your command.

Lidiya enters.

KUCHUMOV: Oh! Oh! I'm speechless!

LIDIYA: Hm, that'll be a great pity, if that's the case, since you speak so nicely. Oh, I'm absolutely exhausted. *(slumps into an armchair)* I've been running round the whole of Moscow.

CHEBOKSAROVA: Yes, Lidiya, Mister Kuchumov not only speaks nicely, he does nice things too. Tomorrow he's going to send your Papa the money to buy back the estate, and he's also doing us a great service. We should be grateful to him, extremely grateful. *(looks meaningfully at her daughter)*

Andrei enters.

ANDREI: Mister Glumov, ma'am.

CHEBOKSAROVA: Show him into my room, I'll receive him there. *(exits, followed by Andrei)*

LIDIYA: *(to Kuchumov)* Well, go on, tell me – exactly how have you become my benefactor? Surely helping others means giving something away – what on earth can have inspired you to do that?

KUCHUMOV: You're seriously asking me, you of all people?

LIDIYA: Why shouldn't I ask you?

KUCHUMOV: I mean, here I am, ready to sacrifice not only my
fortune, but even my very life for you, and yet...

LIDIYA: Well, I shouldn't think I'm likely to need *that* much of a
sacrifice, but are you really sending money to my father?

KUCHUMOV: First thing tomorrow.

LIDIYA: That's very noble of you. Friendship like that is beyond price.

KUCHUMOV: It's more than friendship, dearest Lidiya – much
more. And do you know what? For two pins I'd buy your father's
estate and make you a present of it.

LIDIYA: Then do – buy it and give it to me. I love getting presents.

KUCHUMOV: I'm writing to your father tomorrow, to tell him I'm
buying his estate, and I'll send him thirty thousand as a deposit. I
mean, what do I want with money? All I really want is for you to
look kindly on me.

LIDIYA: But how on earth can I do that? Good heavens, you're
already like one of the family.

KUCHUMOV: *(moving closer to her)* Yes, that's it, that's it – one of
the family...

LIDIYA: Yes, but what member of my family can you possibly be? I
mean, you're a bit long in the tooth to be my brother. Maybe you
could be my daddy for a while?

KUCHUMOV: *(drops to his knees and kisses her hand)* Yes, yes, your
daddy, that's it!

LIDIYA: *(pulling her hand away)* Now, don't be naughty, daddikins!

KUCHUMOV: Oh, I'm so naughty, I'm so naughty! *(kisses her hand again)*

   Glumov appears in the doorway and hurriedly withdraws.

LIDIYA: *(stands up)* Then you should be ashamed of yourself,
you're not a little boy.

   Kuchumov gets up off his knees. Andrei enters.

ANDREI: Mister Telyatev, ma'am.

LIDIYA: Show him in, please.

Andrei exits.

KUCHUMOV: *Addio, mia carina!* I must fly, I have things to do.

LIDIYA: What things?

KUCHUMOV: You'll find out. *(exits)*

Telyatev enters.

TELYATEV: Well, you can execute me on the spot, as long as it's quick. And if you're going to sulk, I'll run off into the woods somewhere. But I'd honestly rather you beat me up now, so you can forgive me afterwards. I can't live without you, Lidiya, I'll have an attack of the vapours and wind up shooting myself, like an Englishman.

LIDIYA: Why should I be angry with you?

TELYATEV: Oh, how can you say that! Your words are like daggers!

LIDIYA: In what way are you worse than the rest? There are plenty worse than you.

TELYATEV: Oh God, she's said it again! Do you want to torture me? Tell me straight what a rotter I am!

LIDIYA: Well, we won't argue about that. You're to blame, there's no getting away from it. It's because of you I'm now married to a man I don't love.

TELYATEV: You don't love him? That's excellent.

LIDIYA: Yes, and it seems he doesn't love me, either.

TELYATEV: He doesn't love you? Wonderful!

LIDIYA: What's wonderful about it?

TELYATEV: Well, I don't know about you, my dear girl, but for a dissolute rake like myself, that's a real find. I mean, chaps like me, poor abandoned wretches, spend our entire lives looking for just that sort of thing.

LIDIYA: You know, you haven't a moral bone in your whole body.

TELYATEV: Yes, yes, abuse me some more, do!

LIDIYA: No, that's enough of that. Why should I? Because you love me? Can I really abuse somebody for love? Because you wouldn't marry me, even though you loved me? No, that's all water under the bridge. You can't put that right now.

TELYATEV: I can't marry you, that's true. But I can love you.

LIDIYA: I can hardly prevent you, can I. Anyway, it flatters a woman's vanity. The more admirers she has, the better she likes it.

TELYATEV: What do you want with a crowd? Take one, to be going on with.

LIDIYA: No, you know nothing about life, really. One's a bad idea, people start talking straightaway, but with a crowd, nobody suspects a thing. After all, how can you tell which is the real one?

TELYATEV: Fine – you can take me on as the real one, and have four or five bit players.

LIDIYA: (laughs) You're such an clown, it's impossible to be angry with you.

TELYATEV: Well, the storm's over. May I now whisper sweet nothings in your ear?

LIDIYA: Go ahead, I enjoy listening to you. You really are sweet, you are, aren't you?

TELYATEV: Oh, good heavens, yes. And you've blossomed, my dear Lidiya, you really have. You've changed, do you know that? And a change like that always...

LIDIYA: No, no, please – spare me! I'm not long married, and I still haven't got used to that sort of talk. I'm well aware what sort of things you say to married women.

TELYATEV: Oh dear, what a pity you're not used to it. Well, you'd better get used to it, my dear, life's very boring without it. Let's start over again. Will you be taking a lover soon? What the Italians call a *cavalier servente*?

LIDIYA: What, is that the done thing in Moscow?

TELYATEV: Well, if it isn't, it's high time it was. We shouldn't be ashamed to borrow something good.

LIDIYA: And what will the husbands say?

TELYATEV: Oh, they'll come to terms with it. Well, of course, us cavaliers'll get beaten up pretty savagely at first, especially by the merchant classes. They'll drag a few of us through the courts too, but the whole business'll become routine in time. The first ones'll have to sacrifice themselves, to pave the way for the others. You can't introduce any really decent innovation without making a few sacrifices.

LIDIYA: Hm, it sounds wonderful, but it's not likely to happen overnight, is it.

TELYATEV: It's already under way, my dear girl, there's been a few sacrifices made already. One of them was black-and-blue all over, another was even worse.

LIDIYA: Well, anyway, as soon as this praiseworthy custom takes root...

TELYATEV: You'll take me on, right?

LIDIYA: If you're worth it. You're terribly flighty.

TELYATEV: And why's that, do you think?

LIDIYA: It's because you've no soul.

TELYATEV: Not at all! It's because I've got nobody I can be devoted to. Just say the word, and I'll be as constant as any telegraph pole.

LIDIYA: We'll test that, shall we?

TELYATEV: Really? Oh, dearest Lidiya, for that alone I am ready to fall at your feet.

LIDIYA: No, please don't. You can spare me that little ceremony, thanks very much!

TELYATEV: As you will. However, I do feel a pressing need to declare my affection for you in some sort of tangible way...

LIDIYA: *(holds out her hand to him)* You may kiss my hand!

Glumov enters and remains upstage.

TELYATEV: *(without noticing Glumov)* With a glove on? What sort of kiss is that? The electricity with which my heart is now charged, and which I desire to pass on to you, isn't going to reach you through a glove! Kid is a very poor conductor, don't you know. *(kisses her wrist a little above her glove)*

LIDIYA: That'll do! Give you an inch and you take a mile.

TELYATEV: Hardly – it wasn't even half an inch. Why make such a fuss?

LIDIYA: Yes, today half an inch, tomorrow another half-inch, and before you know it... *(notices Glumov)* Oh! My dear Yegor – we didn't see you come in.

GLUMOV: Go ahead, just carry on, don't mind me.

LIDIYA: What do you mean, carry on? What are you implying? You're surely not attaching any significance to the fact that I've allowed Telyatev to kiss my hand? I mean, he is an old friend. I'm perfectly happy to let you do the same. *(holds out her hand to Glumov)*

GLUMOV: I most humbly thank you, my dear lady, but I don't kiss just anybody's hand. I save that for my mother or my mistress.

LIDIYA: Well, in that case you'll never kiss any hand of mine.

GLUMOV: Perhaps not, who knows? Life's full of surprises. Friends meet, but mountains never.

LIDIYA: Let's go now, dear friend. *(offers her hand to Telyatev)* He's extremely rude. *(to Glumov)* Are you waiting for my husband? He'll be home soon.

GLUMOV: Oh yes, my dear lady, I'm waiting for your husband. I've so many interesting things to tell him.

LIDIYA: Really? Well, you might do me a kindness and make him laugh at something. He's so preoccupied these days. And there's nobody better able to amuse him than you, you're such a funny man.

Telyatev and Lidiya exit.

GLUMOV: Yes, I'll make you laugh all right! Well done, Miss Lidiya, bravo! I'd just taken a notion to pay her a call, try my luck, as it were, and here I find her with two of them, no less! Well, there's nothing for it but to set all three at each others' throats, husband included. Vasily!

Vasily enters.

VASILY: Yes, sir, did you call?

GLUMOV: What time does Kuchumov usually visit?

VASILY: Two o'clock, sir, regular. The master's not at home then.

GLUMOV: Oh, and where is he?

VASILY: At a meeting, sir, in his office – all them rich people gets together and has a chat about business and suchlike.

GLUMOV: What sort of business?

VASILY: Well, how to get on, sir, make more money.

GLUMOV: So your master's rich, is he?

VASILY: Too true.

GLUMOV: Hm, I suppose by your standards, 'rich' is anybody with a hundred-rouble note.

VASILY: Maybe not a hundred, or a thousand, even, but more.

GLUMOV: Not exactly a fortune.

VASILY: Well, sir, if we wants it, we'll find it, and that's for sure. Anyways, I'm not supposed to say nothing, and it's not everybody as'll understand anyhow. There's a real art to it, and it's not lying on your ribs neither, sir. Some nights we don't get no sleep at all, we've seen some sights, sir, I can tell you. I mean, what do you know about me, eh? I got as far as London, I did, except for about ten miles or so, then we had to come back home, on them train things. Well, I don't know, I can't hang around here talking to you, sir. *(exits)*

GLUMOV: What the hell's he on about? Anyway, Kuchumov comes at two o'clock, that's the main thing. I'll make a note of that.

Enter Vasilkov, Lidiya, Telyatev and Cheboksarova.

GLUMOV: *(to Vasilkov)* Good morning, sir.

VASILKOV: Good morning.

GLUMOV: You have something on your mind?

VASILKOV: Of course I have. I've certainly more on my mind than chasing dogs round the streets of Moscow. You gentlemen of leisure must excuse me, but do stay and have a chat with the ladies. I haven't the time, I'm afraid, I've a great deal of business to attend to.

TELYATEV AND GLUMOV: Right then, off you go.

VASILKOV: I'll be free by lunchtime. If you want to stay to lunch, make yourself at home, you're very welcome. If you don't, well, you can just clear off.

CHEBOKSAROVA: That's very civil, I must say.

TELYATEV: Oh, that doesn't bother us, he's a decent chap. So, what shall we do? Shall we clear off?

GLUMOV: Yes, let's. I can't stand lunch in people's houses. They've always got something vulgar on the table, a huge jug of watery beer, or some other sort of nasty home brew, a soup-tureen with no handle, or little pies that smell of candle-grease. Of course, everything's first-class at your place, but I'd really rather lunch at the Club or an hotel.

TELYATEV: Let's go to the English Club, they're doing lunch there now.

GLUMOV: Right, let's go.

They bow to the ladies and exit.

CHEBOKSAROVA: Lidiya dear, that husband of yours is either a miser, or else he's got no money at all.

LIDIYA: *(alarmed)* What are you saying?

CHEBOKSAROVA: He's just now told me that his means won't allow him to live as we do, and he's got to cut down on expenses. I mean, what''s going to happen when he finds out how much debt we got into for the wedding, and that he's got to pay for it all? He doesn't even want to know about your debts.

LIDIYA: But what about the goldmines?

CHEBOKSAROVA: Huh! Glumov invented them.

LIDIYA: Oh God, I'm done for. I'm like a butterfly, you know that – I can't live without gold dust. I'll die, I really shall.

CHEBOKSAROVA: I'm sure he's got money, it's just that he's a miser. If you were to show him a bit more affection... Force yourself, my dear.

LIDIYA: *(thoughtfully)* Affection? Really? Oh, maman, if that's all that's needed, he'll have so much affection he'll die of sheer bliss. I'll make it my study. All I have to do is find out how much my caresses are worth in gold, and I'd better do that right now – I just can't live without money.

CHEBOKSAROVA: Lidiya, my dear, what terrible things you say.

LIDIYA: There's nothing more terrible than poverty, mother.

CHEBOKSAROVA: Yes, there is, Lidiya. Vice.

LIDIYA: Vice? What on earth's that? To be afraid of vice, when everybody's vicious, is both stupid and wasteful. Poverty's the greatest vice. No, no, mother, this will be my first truly womanly act. Up until now I've been modestly reserved, now I'll see what I can do when I fling modesty aside.

CHEBOKSAROVA: Oh, stop, Lidiya, please! This is absolutely frightful!

LIDIYA: Mother, you're an old woman, poverty holds no terrors for you, but I'm young and I want to live. And for me, life's all about glamour, being surrounded by adoring men, mad, reckless luxury.

CHEBOKSAROVA: I'm not listening to this.

LIDIYA: So, who's the richer? Kuchumov or Telyatev? I've got to know, they're both in my power.

CHEBOKSAROVA: They're both rich, my dear, and both extravagant, but Kuchumov is richer and nicer.

LIDIYA: Good, that's all I need. Where are the bills we got from the shops? Give them to me.

CHEBOKSAROVA: *(takes them out of her pocket)* Here they are.

Lidiya takes them and strides purposefully towards her husband's study. Vasilkov emerges to meet her.

LIDIYA: I was just coming to see you.

VASILKOV: And I was coming to see you.

LIDIYA: Excellent. We've met halfway. Where shall we go, your place or mine? My room? What d'you think? Come on, darling, tell me, please. Mm?

VASILKOV: Let's stay where we are for the moment. We can have a little chat before lunch. You must forgive me, Lidiya, for leaving you on your own so often.

LIDIYA: The less I see of you, the dearer you become to me. *(embraces him)*

VASILKOV: What's come over you, Lidiya? You surprise me – why this sudden change?

LIDIYA: Well, I'm flesh and blood, aren't I. I mean, I *am* a woman. What did I marry you for? Why should I be ashamed of my love for you? I'm not a girl any longer, I'm twenty-four... I don't know how it is for other people, but my husband's everything to me – yes, believe me, Savva, everything. I've kept aloof from you so long now, but I can see it's quite pointless.

VASILKOV: Oh, absolutely.

LIDIYA: Now, the minute I take it into my head to smother you with kisses, I'll just go ahead and smother you. You'll have to put up with it, my darling.

VASILKOV: And why shouldn't I?

LIDIYA: I don't know what's come over me. I really didn't like you before, but now I've suddenly become violently attracted to you. Listen, can't you hear my heart pounding? Oh, my darling, I love you so much! *(begins weeping)*

VASILKOV: What on earth are you crying for?

LIDIYA: For sheer joy!

VASILKOV: It's me that ought to be crying. All I looked for in you was a beautiful exterior, and now I've discovered a kind, warm heart. Love me just a little, Lidiya, and you'll find I'm worth it.

LIDIYA: I do love you, I do, my wild darling.

VASILKOV: Oh, I'm wild all right, but I have feelings, and good taste, too. Give me your lovely little hand, my darling. *(takes her hand)* How beautiful it is. What a pity I'm not an artist.

LIDIYA: My hand? There's nothing of me mine, it's all yours, all of me! *(presses close against him)*

VASILKOV: *(kissing her hand)* Let me have both of them!

Lidiya hurriedly conceals something in her pocket.

What's that you're hiding?

LIDIYA: Oh please, darling, don't ask me, I beg you!

VASILKOV: Why should you beg? If you've got some secret, keep it to yourself – I'm not keen to know other people's secrets.

LIDIYA: But can I really have any secrets from you? Aren't we one flesh? I'll tell you my secret – in this pocket I've got all the bills from the shops, which maman should've paid for my trousseau. Anyway, now she's in difficulties and Father can't send us anything, he's got some big business venture under way. I'd pay them out of my own money, but I don't know if I can raise enough at this moment in time. It's nothing of importance, really.

VASILKOV: Let me see these bills.

LIDIYA: *(hands them over)* There! Though I honestly can't imagine why you want them.

VASILKOV: I'll tell you why. For the happiness you've brought me just now, I'll willingly pay for your trousseau. After all, I could have married some poor girl, and I'd have had to find her trousseau out of my own pocket anyway. And I'd still not know whether she loved me or not, but you do love me.

LIDIYA: No, no – I really must pay back mother in some way for all the care she's taken of me.

VASILKOV: Keep your money, my darling child, spend it on

yourself. Vasily!

> *Vasily enters.*

Bring me the bills out of my study table.

> *Vasily brings in the bills, then exits. Cheboksarova enters.*
> *Vasilkov sits down at the table and begins to sort the bills.*

LIDIYA: *(aside to Cheboksarova)* He's going to pay for everything. *(stretches out on the couch and picks up a book. Aloud)* Maman, we mustn't bother Savva, he's very busy. *(aside to Cheboksarova, who now sits down at the head of the settee)* I've got him right where I want him.

VASILKOV: *(totting up the bills)* Lidiya, there's a bill here for wallpaper and hangings, which you can hardly call part of your trousseau.

LIDIYA: Oh, darling we had to freshen up everything for the wedding, I mean, we had absolute crowds of people dropping in, and if it hadn't been for the wedding we shouldn't have bothered.

CHEBOKSAROVA: Oh yes, they'd have lasted another winter, easily.

VASILKOV: Fine, fine. *(carries on counting)*

LIDIYA: *(aside to Cheboksarova)* You see, I told you, he'll pay for the lot, absolutely everything.

> *A Maid enters, very fashionably dressed, and hands Lidiya a bill.*
> *She motions her to give it to her husband. The Maid passes it to*
> *Vasilkov. He looks it over, nods to his wife, and goes on counting.*
> *The Maid hands Lidiya another bill. She accepts it and coolly*
> *flings it onto the table. The Maid exits. Andrei then enters with*
> *two more bills, and the pantomime is repeated. Andrei exits. Vasily*
> *then enters with a huge wad of bills and hands them to Vasilkov.*

VASILY: There's a few more, sir! All them French shops waiting for their money.

VASILKOV: Give them to your mistress, dammit!

> *Vasily hands them to Lidiya, who promptly flings them on the floor.*

VASILY: *(picking them up)* What'd you want to do that for? Bills is documents, you've got to pay good money for 'em.

LIDIYA: Get out of here! I can't bear to look at you!

Vasily smooths out each bill, carefully places them on the table, then exits.

VASILKOV: *(rises and begins pacing up and down the room)* I'm finished. That comes to thirty-two thousand, five hundred and forty-seven roubles, ninety-eight kopecks. I'm afraid that sum's over my limit, but I've already given you my word, so I'm bound to pay it. I'll borrow as much as we need today, but in order to balance our budget, we'll have to cut our expenses significantly for some time to come. There's a little one-storey house just across the street, with three windows. I've already had a look at it, and it'll do us quite nicely. We'll also have to get rid of the servants: I'll keep on Vasily, and you can have one maid, a little less expensive, I think – we can dismiss the chef and hire a cook. And we don't need to keep the horses.

LIDIYA: *(laughs)* And just how are we going to get by without horses? Horses are made to be ridden, that's what they're for, you surely know that much. So how are we going to go out, eh? I mean, nobody's yet ridden on a balloon, have they?

VASILKOV: We can go on foot when it's dry, and take a cab when it's muddy.

LIDIYA: Huh! So much for your love!

VASILKOV: It's because I love you I won't ruin myself!

LIDIYA: Well, you'd better pay the bills now. The shopkeepers are waiting, and they're respectable people. They have to be paid, and this is very uncivil of you.

VASILKOV: Pay them yourself, you have money of your own.

LIDIYA: I'm not paying them.

VASILKOV: They'll take you to court.

LIDIYA: But I've nothing to pay them with! My God! *(covers her face)*

CHEBOKSAROVA: *(upset)* Why are you torturing us like this? We deserve better, surely. We've made a mistake, all right – you're poor – but we've got to try and correct that mistake. Of course, you're too coarse-grained to appreciate delicate sensibilities like ours, but you take my husband, for example. He had a very important and responsible position. A lot of money passed through his hands, and I can tell you, he loved myself and our daughter so much, that whenever any substantial sum of money was needed to keep up our social standing, or even simply to satisfy one of our whims, well... well, he just couldn't tell the difference between his own money, and the government's. Believe me, sir, that man sacrificed himself on the sacred altar of family love. He had to stand trial in the end, and was obliged to leave Moscow.

VASILKOV: Serves him right.

CHEBOKSAROVA: If you can't appreciate him, at least think of us. You're poor, but we won't leave you in poverty, we have connections. We'll find you a decent position, for sure, some sort of lucrative trusteeship. Then all you have to do is follow my husband's example, like a true family man. *(she goes up to Vasilkov, places her hand on his shoulder and whispers something)* And don't be backward – d'you take my meaning? *(points to his pocket)* I'll make it my business to see the authorities turn a blind eye, you leave that to me. You've got to seize the main chance, wherever you can.

VASILKOV: And you can take your damnable advice elsewhere, madam! Neither poverty nor any beautiful woman is going to make a thief out of me! And if you dare mention thieving to me once more, I won't be responsible for my actions. Stop howling, Lidiya! I'll pay all your bills, but for the last time, and on the following condition: that first thing tomorrow we move into the little house with the three windows – there's a room there for you and your dear mother – and we start to live a modest life. And that means no visitors. *(inspects the bills again)*

LIDIYA: *(leans on her mother's shoulder)* We'll have to accept. *(sotto voce)* But we'll get money, you'll see, and we'll live decently again. *(aloud to her husband)* Very well, my dear, I agree. I really ought to be grateful to you, and not oppose you. *(aside to her mother)* I'll lead him by the nose. *(aloud to her husband)* And we won't receive any callers.

VASILKOV: *(still counting)* I know, you're my clever girl.

LIDIYA: But there's old man Kuchumov, he's been so good to us, he's practically a member of the family.

VASILKOV: *(counting)* Well, all right.

Lidiya vigorously squeezes her mother's hand.

CHEBOKSAROVA: *(sotto voce)* Have you got something in mind?

LIDIYA: Yes, I have. Nobody's ever humiliated me like this. I'm no longer a woman, I'm a serpent! And by God, I'll sting him!

VASILKOV: Mm... you really are terribly extravagant.

LIDIYA: *(puts her arm round his neck)* I'm sorry, darling, I truly am – please forgive me. I'm a mad, spoilt woman. But I'll try to reform, honestly. You must teach me a lesson, and don't spare me.

VASILKOV: So, are we friends again?

LIDIYA: Oh yes, yes, darling – forever.

VASILKOV: Excellent! Splendid, my dear Lidiya. At least we now understand each other. You now know that I'm a thrifty person, and I know that you're spoilt, but you love me just the same, and bring me happiness of a kind that a rough hardworking type like myself could never have hoped for – and that's so very precious to me, my dearest, darling Lidiya – my angel! *(he embraces his wife)*

END OF ACT THREE

ACT FOUR

A very modestly furnished drawing-room, which also serves as a study. There are windows at each side, and upstage, doors leading off left to the hall, and right to the inner rooms. Between the doors stands a tiled stove, and the furniture is poor – a writing table and an old piano. Vasilkov is sitting at the table, arranging his papers, and Vasily is standing facing him.

VASILKOV: Well, Vasily, d'you think the mistress is getting used to the new flat, and to you?

VASILY: I can't rightly say as I knows about the flat, sir. Her and her ma can't stop laughing, that's for sure. In French, too. But as for meself, sir – well, I don't know why I'm still in the land of the living, I truly don't.

VASILKOV: Good heavens, what's the matter with you?

VASILY: Oh Gawd, sir, you wouldn't believe it. They wants me to wear them button-boots, sir, but I just can't. I mean, it's not like I'm a butler, sir, I'm supposed to be your man, isn't that so, sort of an assistant, even. I mean, begging your pardon, sir, but we've been through some hard times together – damn near drowned together, too, on the river that time, going about our business.

VASILKOV: Well yes, of course. *(gets up from the table)*

VASILY: Yes, and she practically ate me alive, on account of that fruit.

VASILKOV: What fruit?

VASILY: Well, that's what we call it, sir... and there wasn't no more than about that much of it, too... *(indicates on his finger)*

VASILKOV: Of what?

VASILY: A litle bit of radish, sir – that's how much there was. I was sitting in the hall, finishing it off, like.

VASILKOV: Well, really, Vasily...

VASILY: I couldn't help meself, sir, honest! It's how us working folks is brought up. There's nothing I won't do for a nice bit of radish.

VASILKOV: Anyway – listen to me, Vasily. There are to be no visitors while I'm out, apart from Kuchumov, do you understand?

VASILY: Don't you worry about that, sir!

They exit. Enter Lidiya.

LIDIYA: In God's name what's keeping that disgusting old creature! That's three days now I've been cooped up in this wretched hole. I daren't even go near the window – they're no doubt all driving past on purpose, to catch a glimpse of me. Glumov'll have a satirical poem already written. Oh, dearest daddy Kuchumov, for God's sake get me out of jail, please! *Maman* and I could go back to our old apartment and live better than ever. Right, a bit of music, that's the answer! A waltz is such a consolation. I don't care what they say, nobody knows a woman's heart like Johann Strauss. *(tries to play the piano)* Oh, God, this is junk! He got this deliberately, just to humiliate me. Well, you wait, my fine friend, your turn's coming. *(stops to listen, hears a carriage outside)* I'd love to look out, but how can a society lady appear at this sort of nasty little spy-hole – it's too shameful! Is that Kuchumov? He always comes at two o'clock. It's him, it's him! He's at the door now, I can hear his footsteps. Well, now what?

Kuchumov and Vasily are heard off-stage.

KUCHUMOV: Is your mistress at home?

VASILY: Indeed she is, sir.

Kuchumov enters.

LIDIYA: Oh, daddy dear, at last!

KUCHUMOV: *(kisses her hand, surveys the room angrily)* Well, really! What's going on? Is this where you've ended up? I mean, look at the furniture – it's like some sort of cheap lodging-house! Seriously, I'm asking you, what's the meaning of this? Oh, my angel, don't be angry with me for being so rude. There's no other way to speak in rooms like this. How did this happen? How on earth could you let yourself be brought so low? Good God, Lidiya, you're a disgrace to the family name!

LIDIYA: You should pity me, rather than blame me.

KUCHUMOV: My dear young lady, I can't pity you. You've brought shame on the Cheboksarovs. What would your poor father say if he knew of your humiliation?

LIDIYA: But what am I to do?

KUCHUMOV: Run away, my dear girl – clear off without a backward glance.

LIDIYA: But where to? *Maman* hasn't a penny, and he's paid off all our debts.

KUCHUMOV: Well, that's only his duty. I mean, to possess such a treasure, to enjoy such happiness as you've bestowed on that... that walrus, he's duty bound to carry out your every wish.

LIDIYA: Obviously he doesn't think possessing me is any great happiness.

KUCHUMOV: Well, if he doesn't, so much the better. You've got to appreciate your own value. Why don't you and your *maman* move back to your old flat? It's not that bad. You can't live in this chicken-coop, it's shameful.

LIDIYA: But, daddy dearest, what are we to live on? *Maman* hasn't a bean, nor have I. We can't rely on credit.

KUCHUMOV: Credit? What d'you want credit for? Oh, shame on you, Lidiya, shame! Why didn't you come to me? You're ashamed to ask me for money, but you'e not ashamed to live in a hovel like this? You're our gossamer-winged fairy – have you forgotten your powers? One wave of your magic wand, and you can turn this hovel into a palace!

LIDIYA: Daddy dear, what d'you mean? What wand?

KUCHUMOV: Lidiya, you're a fairy, and a woman, so you should know better than any man. Fairies and women are well-stocked with magic wands, believe me.

LIDIYA: *(flings herself around his neck)* D'you mean like this?

KUCHUMOV: Er... yes, yes... *(screws up his eyes and sinks onto a chair)* Will forty thousand do to begin with?

LIDIYA: I'm not sure, daddy.

KUCHUMOV: You don't need much at present, you can move back into your old flat, it's beautifully decorated, and it's still not taken. And you have a superb wardrobe! Forty thousand's more than enough to be going on with. Lidiya, I swear if you won't take it,

I'll simply throw the money out of the carriage window, or gamble it away at the club. One way or another, I'll get rid of it, if you won't accept it from me.

LIDIYA: Oh, well, in that case, daddy dear, let me have it!

KUCHUMOV: *(searches his pockets)* Oh, damn it! This could only happen to me. I put my wallet out on the table on purpose, and I've left it at home. Oh, my dear child, please forgive me. *(kisses her hand)* I'll bring it to you tomorrow, at the housewarming. And I do hope you'll move right now. I'll have a special cake sent round from Einem's, and I'll buy a gold salt-cellar at Sazikov's – a really big one, five pounds or so – and put the money inside it. It'd be nice to have it all in gold coins for luck, but you can't get that sort of money at the bank. Anyway, I'll top it up with about a hundred half-imperials of my own.

LIDIYA: Oh, *merci, merci,* daddy dearest! *(strokes his head)*

KUCHUMOV: Sheer bliss! Ecstasy! Who cares about money! Even if I had millions, without those eyes, those caresses, I'd be a beggar!

   Cheboksarova enters.

LIDIYA: *Maman,* dear Grigory Borisych says we should move back into our old flat.

KUCHUMOV: Well, of course. I mean, you simply can't stay here, my dear lady, it's impossible.

CHEBOKSAROVA: Oh, don't say another word, dear sir – you've no idea what I've had to put up with, how much I've suffered! You know how I lived when I was young, I go into fits even just thinking about it. I'd have gone back to my husband with Lidiya, but he's written to tell us not to. He doesn't mention the money you sent him either.

KUCHUMOV: Well, it can't have reached him yet. *(counts on his fingers)* That's Tuesday, Wednesday, Thursday, Friday... He'll have got it last night, or else this morning.

LIDIYA: *Maman,* we've got to move right now.

CHEBOKSAROVA: Lidiya, we need to give it some thought. I can't help thinking your husband's only pretending, and he really is rich.

LIDIYA: I don't care whether he's rich or poor, he's humiliated us, and it's all over between us. Grigory Borisych has done a lot for us, and he doesn't want me to stay with my husband. Our life'll be absolutely taken care of, my dear daddy's promised me.

CHEBOKSAROVA: Daddy? Where did you learn that? Oh, Lidiya, how can you speak like that? I can't stand to listen to you, no mother could.

LIDIYA: What! You're ashamed? Well, from now on I've decided to be ashamed of nothing but poverty, there's no shame in anything else. *Maman,* you and I are women, we don't have the means to live decently. You want to live with a bit of style, don't you? How can you expect me to feel ashamed? No, no, whether you like it or not, you'll just have to turn a blind eye. That's the common fate of mothers who bring up their daughters in luxury and then leave them with no money.

KUCHUMOV: *Benissimo!* Such worldly wisdom from one so young, who'd have believed it!

LIDIYA: Listen, maman, dearest daddy has promised us forty thousand roubles as soon as we move.

CHEBOKSAROVA: *(overjoyed)* Really? *(to Kuchumov)* You're a dear, kind man! All the same, we'll have to think about it.

LIDIYA: What's to think about? This is humiliation, and there's happiness!

CHEBOKSAROVA: Look, let's go into my room, we need to consider this from all angles. It's important we keep up appearances.

LIDIYA: Don't worry, I'll take care of that.

KUCHUMOV: I mean, I'm not a schoolboy, I know how to enjoy my good fortune on the quiet, I'm not likely to blab about it.

Vasily and Glumov are heard off-stage.

VASILY: Sir, there's no visitors allowed!

GLUMOV: Oh, don't talk rubbish!

Kuchumov, Lidiya and Cheboksarova exit, leaving Kuchumov's hat on the table. Vasily and Glumov enter.

GLUMOV: So what nonsense is this, you halfwit? I'm not allowed to visit? Impossible!

VASILY: Sir, I'm no halfwit. D'you see me in a dunce's cap? It's not my fault you're not allowed in.

GLUMOV: So who told you not to let me in, your master or your mistress?

VASILY: As far as you're concerned, sir, it makes no odds. It don't matter who gave the order, I'm letting nobody in. But if you really wants to know, it's like this: the master says you're not allowed in, and the mistress don't want to see you at any price.

GLUMOV: My God, your stupidity passes belief, it's the stuff of legend! Surely you know the reason why I've not to be admitted? Eh? I mean, you must've heard *something,* my dear chap, even with the tip of those ass's ears of yours. Come on, out with it – a silver rouble's not to be sneezed at.

VASILY: Oh, thank you kindly, your honour. *(pockets the rouble coin)* Now then – what can I apprise you of, like? I mean, you know how things stand hereabouts. If you come in, next thing there's somebody else, then a third – that's a glass of vodka, and another one, five, ten, it all mounts up, you know. And pickings is pretty lean right now in our line of work, leastways so the master says. I'm sure you'd do the same, sir. Why should he waste good money, feeding all them parasites? I mean, it'd be different if they was respectable business people, but the sort of riff-raff we get here...

GLUMOV: That's enough. Give me a piece of paper and clear off. I'll write your master a note and go.

VASILY: Paper's on the table, sir, right in front of your eyes. Use a bit of scrap, and don't go wasting it, d'you hear. All right, all right, I'm going. *(exits)*

GLUMOV: *(takes up pen and paper)* Now, what shall I say? *(spots Kuchumov's hat)* Well, well – whose is the hat? *(picks it up)* Aha! Kuchumov's, no less! So – His Highness is here, is he? Wonderful! Vasilkov will have got his letter by now, so will Telyatev, that means they'll all be coming here. That'll be fun. I'd better write something to divert their suspicions. *(writes, then reads aloud)* "My dear friend Savva, I just dropped in to ask your advice on a business matter. It's a pity I missed you, but I'll look in again tomorrow, a bit earlier. Yours, Glumov..." Now, couldn't be clearer, I'll put it in the middle of the table, so he'll see it right away.

Telyatev is heard off-stage.

TELYATEV: I don't care, I'm coming in regardless!

Telyatev and Vasily enter.

TELYATEV: *(to Glumov)* Have you seen Lidiya?

GLUMOV: No, why should I? I just dropped in for a word with Savva, but he's out, so I've left him a note. Anyway, I'm off, goodbye. If you're looking for him you might try the Stock Exchange, that's where he spends the day.

TELYATEV: Good, so much the better.

GLUMOV: I hear he's got involved in some new line of work, buying and selling silk.

TELYATEV: Mm, a first-class business.

GLUMOV: Oh yes, on a good day you can make as much as five roubles.

VASILY: Now then, sir, there's no call for that.

GLUMOV: Yes, well, we've had our fill of these provincials, we know the type. Supposed to have goldmines, pots of money, but you just watch. Runs riot for about six weeks, then either winds up in the army, or else gets shipped back home without the option, or his father'll turn up, and yank him by the hair out of some tavern and drag him to the back of beyond. *(looks at his watch)* Anyway, I'd better go. Can't stand here gossiping. *(quickly exits)*

TELYATEV: *(sits down at the table, holding his hat)* Well, then, Vasily, so you've been told not to admit anyone?

VASILY: That's right, sir.

TELYATEV: You're sure this isn't your own daft idea?

VASILY: No, sir, I swear to God. I mean, honestly – as if I'd dare!

TELYATEV: So you won't take pity on me, Vasily?

VASILY: Oh, I do, sir, I do. You're not like them others.

TELYATEV: Better, would you say?

VASILY: Oh, much better, sir.

TELYATEV: Sit down, Vasily, sit down.

> *Vasily sits down, rests his elbows on his knees.*

Yes, let's have a chat, you and I.

VASILY: What, you don't think I can?

TELYATEV: I don't think anything of the kind. You've been in London, from what I hear, but you've never been in Morocco?

VASILY: Morrocky? No, them sort of countries I've not heard tell of, sir. If folks wants to stay in murky dens, then let 'em, but it's not for the likes of us. We got plenty of them back home, for our sins, we got enough murky goin's-on. But does they know the meanin' of cold and hunger, sir, eh?

TELYATEV: I don't know about hunger, but cold no, since it's extremely hot there.

VASILY: Well, let 'em die hungry or hot if they wants, sir, as long as we got our hopes, that's all we needs.

TELYATEV: What sort of hopes?

VASILY: Hopes for a better life, sir. We've seen a few bare feet in our time, sir, and bare arses – of course, that's as it should be, since afore the Flood, but God works unseen, sir.

TELYATEV: Mm... I'm not sure it's a good idea, going off into philosophy like that.

VASILY: I can talk about summat else, if you like.

TELYATEV: No, I'll be off, I think. *(absentmindedly picks up Kuchumov's hat from the table with his free hand and tries to put both on)* Eh? How did I do this?

VASILY: It's a bad habit, sir – we all does it.

TELYATEV: Bad habit? What are you on about?

VASILY: Stealin' people's hats, sir.

TELYATEV: What! Don't talk rubbish!

VASILY: Well, try 'em both on, sir, and the one that fits is yourn.

TELYATEV: That's better. Now you're talking sense, Vasily, it's a
pleasure to listen to you. *(tries on his own hat)* This is mine. Now just
whose is this? Aha – it's the little Prince's. So that means he's here?

VASILY: *(enigmatically)* Oh, he's here, sir.

TELYATEV: And where exactly is he?

Vasily points silently and solemnly to the door leading to the inner rooms.

TELYATEV: So why is he admitted, and I'm not?

VASILY: Well, he's a relative, sir.

TELYATEV: What? He's no more a relative than you are. Anyway,
you'll have to excuse me, but I'm staying here. You can take
yourself back to the hall.

VASILY: Well, fact is, sir, the master's never home this time of day,
but if you was to come another time...

TELYATEV: That's enough, Vasily. Now kindly do me a favour and
go, before I kick you out!

VASILY: And you just might do that, sir, and all! *(exits)*

*Left alone, Telyatev takes a letter out of his pocket and begins
reading.*

TELYATEV: Telyatev, you're a trusting chap,
        But signs and wonders never cease;
        The little prince will spring his trap
        At two o'clock at Lidiya's place...

And that's exactly what he's done. He's a relative, and I'm not even
allowed in! What can I do? I'm damned if I'm just going to give up,
it's hardly the done thing, and besides there's something nagging at
me. I'll wait here, and watch how she sees him to the door. Yes,
that'll give them a turn, their jaws'll drop when I stand in front of
them like the accusing Fates. Yes, like the statue of the *Commendatore*
– some German chap swore to me, with tears in his eyes, no less, that
it represented conscience. They'll be in a terrible predicament.

Maybe I'd better go into them direct? Of course, it's not manners, but still... Where are they hiding? *(goes up and listens at the door)* Nobody. I'll penetrate a little deeper. *(cautiously opens the door, exits, and closes it behind him)*

Vasilkov and Vasily enter.

VASILKOV: Has somebody been here?

VASILY: Yes, sir, Mister Glumov. He's left a note, see.

VASILKOV: *(sternly)* And who else?

VASILY: Mister Kuchumov... but he...

VASILKOV: Right, that's enough – off you go.

Vasily exits.

Kuchumov's too old to be a threat. My wife's a woman of taste.

Vasilkov pauses in front of the table, deep in thought, and sees Glumov's note. He takes a letter out of his pocket and compares it with the note.

Mm... nothing like it. I thought it was him. *(reads the letter)*

The husband blithely quits the house,
The morning's business all his care,
And fancies that his loving spouse
Sits idly waiting for him there...
Poor man!
So he makes merry with his chums
While wife at home has naught to do,
And either must she twiddle her thumbs,
Or find herself a good friend too!
Poor man!

"Be home at two o'clock without fail, and you will learn the meaning of these words". *(a pause)* What is this, a joke, or a disaster? If it's a joke, then it's stupid, and quite unforgiveable to play tricks on a man with no regard for his feelings. And if it *is* a disaster, then why has it befallen me so soon, and so unexpectedly? If I really knew my wife, I'd have no misgivings. I know what ordinary young girls and women feel, how they love, but I haven't a clue about society ladies. I can't see into her heart, I'm a stranger to her, and she's a stranger to me.

She's got no time for a man's heart, all she wants is fine words. And I don't have any. Oh, to hell with fine words! How easily we can pick up other people's manner of speaking, but their minds are a different matter. Everybody's making speeches these days, as if they were in the English Parliament, but they still think like cavemen! And as for doing anything... Well, what do they do? Absolutely nothing. Anyway, what about this letter? I'll go and show it to Lidiya. But what if... what if... oh, my God! What'll I do then? How shall I behave? No, no – it's quite shameful to prepare for something like this, to act a part! Whatever my stupid provincial heart prompts me to, that's what I'll do.

> *Vasilkov opens a box with pistols, inspects them, then replaces them, leaving the box open. He goes up to the door, and just at that point Telyatev emerges, tiptoeing backwards into the room.*

VASILKOV: Real friends don't do that sort of thing, Telyatev.

TELYATEV: Oh, hullo! *(sotto voce)* Just wait, they'll be out in a minute.

VASILKOV: You'd better answer my questions, or I'll shoot you on the spot!

TELYATEV: Not so loud, for heaven's sake! *(listens)* All right, then, fire away.

VASILKOV: You've been visiting my wife, haven't you?

TELYATEV: Yes.

VASILKOV: Why?

TELYATEV: Passing the time of day, that's all, a little mild flirtation. Why are you asking such silly questions?

VASILKOV: Why is it my wife you choose to visit, and not the others?

TELYATEV: Because I've got good taste, why d'you think?

VASILKOV: Right, we'll shoot it out!

TELYATEV: All right, then, fair enough. Only don't make such a row. I can hear voices.

VASILKOV: I don't care whose they are, they won't stop me.

TELYATEV: Honestly, you're quite mad, Savva. Calm down, have a glass of water.

VASILKOV: No, Telyatev. I'm a peaceable man, kindhearted, but there comes a moment in this life... Oh, God, I just can't tell you what's going on in my heart... Look, I'm crying... Here, take the pistols! Choose whichever you like.

TELYATEV: Oh well, if you want to make me a present of them, why not give me both? Why split up the pair? But if it's a shooting-match you want, what are you in such a hurry for, you idiot? I've got a good dinner in prospect today, and after a heavy meal, I always feel a bit sluggish. You can shoot me then if you want.

VASILKOV: No, no – it's got to be right now, here on this spot, with no witnesses.

TELYATEV: Well, I have principles, too, let me tell you. I'm not doing it here, and that's that. I mean, what sort of place is this? You've got to do things properly, Savva, yes! Now just hold on! First of all, you can tell me why on earth you've moved into this wretched hole.

VASILKOV: Because I can't afford to live elsewhere.

TELYATEV: Well, why didn't you say so? *(takes out his wallet)* How much do you need? Go on, take it, take the lot, I can rub along in Moscow without money.

VASILKOV: You think you can buy my compliance with your money? You think you can buy my wife? *(takes out a pistol)*

TELYATEV: No, no, listen, my dear friend! Kill me if you like, but don't insult me. I respect you far more than you think – more than you deserve, even.

VASILKOV: I'm sorry, forgive me. I think I'm going mad.

TELYATEV: I'm simply offering you some money, out of the goodness of my heart, or rather, out of our basic couldn't-care-less outlook on these things. If you've got money, you give it away to the first person you meet; if you haven't, you borrow it from the first person you meet.

VASILKOV: All right, fine, give me the money. How much is there?

TELYATEV: You can check it afterwards – about five thousand, I think.

VASILKOV: No no, I'll count it now, and give you a receipt.

TELYATEV: Oh, don't bother, old chap, forget it. People take receipts from me, but I can't be bothered. Anyway, if I did ask for a receipt I'd only lose it.

VASILKOV: Thank you. I'll pay you a decent rate of interest.

TELYATEV: You can pay me in champagne, that's the only interest I charge.

VASILKOV: Well, anyway... you've been making love to my wife, so we'll still have to fight a duel.

TELYATEV: Oh, it's not worth it, my dear sir, believe me. If she's an honest woman, nothing's going to come of my attentions, and I've had some entertainment, so where's the harm? And if she's a loose woman, she's not worth fighting over.

VASILKOV: And if that's the case, then in God's name what am I going to do? *(in despair)* What can I do?

TELYATEV: Get rid of her, and there's an end to it.

VASILKOV: I was so happy, and all the time she was only pretending she loved me! I mean, just imagine what the affections of such a beautiful woman meant to an awkward cuss like me, a provincial businessman – it was Paradise on earth! And now she's deceiving me. My heart's been ripped apart, I can scarcely stand up, my whole life's gone sour, and all because she's betrayed me.

TELYATEV: So why kill me, old chap? Why not kill her?

VASILKOV: Because you've corrupted her. She's a decent creature at heart, but a woman can drown in that cesspool of yours, she can lose everything – her honour, her conscience, any kind of shame. And you're the most corrupt of the lot. No, no, take the pistol, or I'll beat you to death with this chair!

TELYATEV: Oh, the hell with it! I'm fed up with you – let's fight a duel! *(goes to take a pistol, stops to listen at the door)* Look, I'll tell you what – before we die, let's just hide behind the stove for a second.

VASILKOV: No! No! We'll have it out now!

TELYATEV: *(grips him by the shoulders)* For God's sake be quiet! *(forcibly leads him behind the stove)*

> *Kuchumov and Lidiya enter, Kuchumov singing as usual.*

KUCHUMOV: *In mia mano al fin tu sei!*

LIDIYA: Goodbye, daddy darling!

KUCHUMOV: Kiss me, my love! Oh, your kisses... *Addio, mia carina!*

LIDIYA: With pleasure! *(kisses him)*

> *Telyatev and Vasilkov emerge from behind the stove.*

Oh my God! *(runs out of the way)*

KUCHUMOV: *(wagging his finger)* It's not what you think, sirs! I'm an old friend of the family. *Honi soit qui mal y pense,* and all that.

VASILKOV: *(pointing to the door)* Get out! I'll send my seconds to you tomorrow.

KUCHUMOV: Now just hold on, young man – I'm not going to fight with you. My life's much too precious to this town, to set it against yours, which is of no use to anybody, frankly.

VASILKOV: I'll kill you for this! *(goes to the table)*

KUCHUMOV: No, wait, wait! This isn't funny, young sir, this isn't funny at all! *(exits hurriedly)*

> *Cheboksarova enters.*

CHEBOKSAROVA: What's all the racket?

VASILKOV: Just take your daughter and go! We're quits now. I'm handing her back exactly as I got her, the same depraved wretch I took from you. She complained about having to change her exalted family name to my commonplace one. Well, it's my turn now to complain that she's disgraced my name – it may have been common, but at least it was honest. She told me she didn't love me when she married me. Well, after barely a week with her, I now despise her. She married me for free – I had to pay for her trousseau, and all her outfits – so she can count that as payment for one week's affection, which I seem to have shared, besides!

LIDIYA: *(laughs)* Oh, that's tragic!

CHEBOKSAROVA: Savva, for goodness' sake! There's some sort of misunderstanding, surely. I mean, these things happen, people split up, but they do it quietly, with a bit of decorum.

VASILKOV: *(to Telyatev)* No, don't leave me, dear friend. We've a few things to settle. Here's your money, take it. I only wanted it to earn you some good interest, for your kindness. Take it!

> *Gives the money to Telyatev, who casually stuffs it into his pocket. Lidiya stares fixedly at the money.*

I've a few other matters to arrange, write to my dear mother... then I'll shoot myself. *(lowers his head to his chest)*

TELYATEV: No, no, don't! Good God, Savva, you're an idiot. A friend of mine had two wives run out on him, and d'you think he should've shot himself twice? Savva, come on, look at me. Listen – I'm a sensible chap, and I'm going to give you some seriously good advice. Firstly, don't even think of shooting yourself in the house, it's just not done. It's Petrovsky Park, if you want to shoot yourself. Secondly, let's you and I have a decent dinner first, things'll be clearer then.

VASILKOV: *(to Cheboksarova)* Get your daughter out of my sight! Go on, take her away!

LIDIYA: Oh, I'll go, and sooner than you think. We were going to move out today anyhow. We've rented our old apartment again, and we'll try not even to look out of its splendid windows at this pitiful hovel, with its equally pitiful owner! You were playing a part, and so were we. We've got more money than you, but we're women, and women don't like paying for things. I had to pretend I was in love with you, but it made me sick – I had to do it, so you would pay our debts. And now that I've succeeded, that's it, finished. Were you impressed with my acting ability? With talent like that, no woman need ever starve. Go ahead, shoot yourself, the sooner the better. Don't try and talk him out of it, Telyatev. You'll untie my hands, and I won't make the same mistake twice with a husband, or a... well, you know what I mean. Goodbye, sir! All I want is never to see you again. *(to her mother)* Have you sent for a carriage?

CHEBOKSAROVA: Yes, it's waiting. *(exits, followed by Lidiya)*

VASILKOV: That's it, it's all over, I'm finished now.

TELYATEV: What d'you mean finished? You've surely got
something left to live for?

VASILKOV: No, it's all over. If I were as evil a creature as she, I'd
bite through my own arms right now, I'd bash my head off the
wall. If I'd betrayed her in any way, I could've forgiven her. But
I'm too kindhearted, I trusted her, and she made a complete
mockery of my good nature. She can mock my appearance, or my
name, but to jeer at my kindness!.. To jeer at the fact that I loved
her, that after every embrace I would sit for a whole hour in my
study, crying from sheer happiness! No, no, dear friend, it's not
my vanity she's offended, but my very soul! She's killed my spirit,
all that's left is to kill my body. *(weeps)*

TELYATEV: For heaven's sake, stop, listen – you'll have me crying
next, and that'll look just wonderful! Stop it, Savva, please! Put
yourself in my hands for a couple of hours, that's all I ask. We'll
have a spot of dinner for a start, and I'll see you're decently fed
and watered, all right?

VASILKOV: *(picks up a pistol and puts it in his pocket)* What's that?
(rushes to the window) It's a carriage! They're leaving! *(completely
crushed)* You can take my corpse wherever you like, until it's lying
under a bush somewhere. *(exits)*.

END OF ACT FOUR

ACT FIVE

The scene is the boudoir of the Cheboksarovs' former apartment. At stage left, a door leading to the drawing-room; at centre, the outer door, and a large picture window stage right. Lidiya is stretched out on the settee in a day-gown. Cheboksarova enters.

CHEBOKSAROVA: Hasn't he been yet?

LIDIYA: No.

CHEBOKSAROVA: I'm losing my mind completely – what are we going to do? It's a week since Kuchumov came to the housewarming, and instead of what he promised, all he gave us was six hundred and thirteen roubles, and with such a long face, you'd think he was doing us some sort of favour! We've started piling up a mountain of debts again. Don't forget this is all new furniture, the old stuff was sold by that villainous husband of yours.

LIDIYA: Kuchumov promised to bring it today without fail. It's not right to mistrust him, after he's done father such a big favour.

CHEBOKSAROVA: Ah, but has he? I have my doubts. I've just had a letter from your father, and he says he's received no money of any kind, he's had to sell the estate, and he's now living with a friend. He says that after the sale, to clear off his debt, he's been left with a piddling amount of money, and he intends to start up some sort of dairy business, to go into partnership with some Bashkiri or Tartar.

LIDIYA: Now I understand. Do you know who's bought the estate?

CHEBOKSAROVA: No, who?

LIDIYA: Kuchumov. He promised to buy it and make me a present of it.

CHEBOKSAROVA: Huh, a likely story. According to your father, the biggest bid at the auction came from one Yermolaev, acting on behalf of your husband. Isn't that him now? *(points out of the window)*

LIDIYA: That's ridiculous – where would he get the money? You've seen him yourself, borrowing money off Telyatev, and promising to pay him a good rate of interest. People only pay high interest if they're desperate. Anyway, he's too stupid for that sort of business. And I'll feel a good deal easier if his name isn't mentioned, thank you very much.

CHEBOKSAROVA: As you wish.

LIDIYA: I feel ashamed to have married him, and I want to erase all memory of him from my mind. If they weren't so valuable, I'd fling his presents back in his face. Anyway, I'll have all the jewels reset, to change their appearance.

CHEBOKSAROVA: I'll go and find out if the carriage has arrived. I managed to get one on credit from a coachmaker, and I've told him to put our coat-of-arms on it. We can always hire horses, but we've simply got to have our own carriage. You can tell a hired carriage a mile off. *(exits)*

LIDIYA: Yes, experience, that's the thing. I'm still much too gullible, and that's how you make mistakes that can't be corrected.

Andrei enters.

ANDREI: Mister Kuchumov, ma'am.

LIDIYA: Show him in!

Andrei exits. Enter Kuchumov. He kneels and kisses Lidiya's hand, singing.

KUCHUMOV: *Il segretto per esser felice...*

LIDIYA: Oh, stop your nonsense! Sit down, I want to have a talk with you.

KUCHUMOV: Oh, how cold we are! What sort of tone is that, sweet child?

LIDIYA: Ooh! That's enough! The joke's over, now listen to me! You made me move out of my husband's flat, we're in debt now, and I'm ashamed to have to remind you about the money, as if I was some sort of kept woman, but you yourself promised it.

KUCHUMOV: *(sits down)* Well, you'll either have to kill me, dear Lidiya, or else excuse my absentmindedness. I was counting the money into my wallet a second ago, to bring it here, when my wife walked in and I had to stuff it into the desk drawer. I started talking with her and it went clean out of my mind. I'll bring you the money in half an hour.

LIDIYA: So who bought my father's estate?

KUCHUMOV: Well, I did, of course.

LIDIYA: According to my father, it was Vasilkov's agent.

KUCHUMOV: That's absolutely right, I asked someone called Vasilkov
to bid for me, an old business acquaintance. I stood godfather at his
son's christening. He doesn't know the ropes, so he must've
entrusted somebody else with it. Ha! He wrote me such an amusing
letter. Anyway, I'll bring it round in about ten minutes. *(stands up
and looks round the room. Sings) Io son ricco! Tu sei bella!* Well, this is
quite nice, not bad at all. You have such good taste, my dear, but
you want some greenery here. I'll send you a potted palm and some
tropical plants. This'll make a good place for our intimate little tête-
à-têtes, under the palm-tree. I'll send it round today without fail. *(sits
down beside Lidiya)*

LIDIYA: *(moves away)* Well, when you bring us the money, I'll start
calling you daddy again, and maybe even love you a little.

KUCHUMOV: *(sings) Io son ricco! Tu sei bella!* Since there can be no
doubt about my sincerity, there's surely no point in withholding
your love, my angel?

LIDIYA: You think not? I'm in a foul temper today, I'm not in the
mood for love. This while back I've been hearing of nothing but
riches – my husband has goldmines, you've got mountains of the
stuff, Telyatev's practically a millionaire, and even Glumov, it
seems, has suddenly become a rich man. All my admirers rave
about my beauty, they all promise to shower me with gold, but
neither my husband nor any of my worshippers will advance me as
much as pin-money. I can't even go out, I've got to ride in a hired
carriage, with a couple of broken-down nags.

KUCHUMOV: But that's terrible! Anyway, in half an hour's time it'll
all be sorted out. It's my fault, I confess, I'm the one to blame.

LIDIYA: I mean, I'm living apart from my husband, you visit me
here every day at an appointed hour – what will people think, what
will they say?

KUCHUMOV: Well, what's done's done, my dear – they'll talk
anyway, no matter how virtuously you behave. In my opinion, you
might as well be hung for a sheep as a goat, but to be accused
unjustly, now that is a terrible business, *idolo mio*. Anyway, as I
say, in half an hour's time... well, there might be some unforeseen
circumstances, some absolutely essential outlay, and there might

not be that much money in the office. Anyway, in a day or two's time, or at the very most, a week, you shall have it all, even more than your heart's desire.

LIDIYA: *(stands up)* A week! I want it all here in ten minutes! Do you hear what I'm saying? Otherwise I won't even let you in the house!

KUCHUMOV: Ten minutes? I'm not Mercury, I can't fly at that speed. Beside which I might be held up.

LIDIYA: Nobody's going to hold you up. You have the money in a drawer, and no doubt the letter from Vasilkov in another drawer. Goodbye!

KUCHUMOV: Well, I'll have to justify myself, clearly, but it'll be a long time before I forgive the way you've spoken to me. *(wags his finger at her reprovingly, then exits)*

LIDIYA: This is where my confidence is beginning to waver. I can feel a cold shiver down my spine. Is Kuchumov deceiving me or isn't he? *(decisively)* He is. He hasn't kept a single one of his promises. So now what's left for me? Despair and suicide, or maybe... No, that's suicide too, only slower and more painful...

Andrei enters.

ANDREI: Mister Telyatev, ma'am.

LIDIYA: *(deep in thought)* Show him in.

Andrei exits. Enter Telyatev.

LIDIYA: I haven't seen you for ages. Where on earth have you been?

TELYATEV: Well, you know, the man with nothing to do is always busy. So why are you so serious? Oh dear, oh dear! *(peers at her intently)*

LIDIYA: What do you mean? What are you doing?

TELYATEV: Look, there's a wrinkle, right there, on your forehead – just a teeny one, but a wrinkle just the same.

LIDIYA *(alarmed)* No, it can't be.

TELYATEV: Have a look in the mirror. Oh dear, oh dear – and at your age, too. What a shame!

LIDIYA: *(in front of the mirror)* Is that all you can say! Oh, I'm fed up!

TELYATEV: You shouldn't think so much, my dear Lidiya. Above all else, guard against thought, and may God preserve you. That's how our women keep their looks, they never think about anything.

LIDIYA: Oh, Telyatev, it's a wonder I haven't gone grey, in my position. How can I not think? Who's going to do my thinking for me?

TELYATEV: Why, what more could you ask? Your position's absolutely sound: you're living on your own, in a splendid apartment, you're free as a bird, you're rich, I've heard you say so yourself, you have heaps of admirers and a non-existent husband.

LIDIYA: *(overjoyed)* What, has he shot himself?

TELYATEV: No no, he's changed his mind.

LIDIYA: Oh. What a pity. Can I trust you with a secret?

TELYATEV: Of course you can.

LIDIYA: You know how to keep secrets?

TELYATEV: No, I don't. Actually I lose them immediately, which is much better. They go in one ear, and fly straight out the other the same instant. Ask me an hour later, and for the life of me, I can't remember a blessed thing.

LIDIYA: Well, we're in pretty dire straits. We've virtually nothing to live on.

TELYATEV: Well, it's a rare family that hasn't got *that* kind of secret.

LIDIYA: Telyatev, listen to me – you're quite impossible. I left my husband because of... No, I'm too ashamed.

TELYATEV: Oh, don't be silly, go on, say it. Ashamed to tell me? Huh, I'm one of those chaps women are never ashamed to talk to.

LIDIYA: Well, I suppose I'm not ashamed with you either. Anyway, I left my husband because I had hopes of Kuchumov. He promised to lend me forty thousand roubles.

TELYATEV: What a queer old bird – why didn't he make it eighty thousand?

LIDIYA: He could've made it eighty?

TELYATEV: Oh, absolutely! Two hundred even – well, he could've promised, but paying out's a different story! You'd be lucky to find as much as ten roubles in his pocket!

LIDIYA: That's slander. Why, he bought my father's estate, and that was worth plenty. I even saw him give *maman* six hundred roubles.

TELYATEV: Well, I can't say anything about the estate, but I do know where he got the six hundred from. He spent five days chasing around Moscow trying to raise that money, which he eventually managed to borrow for one month, at a charge of two thousand roubles. I thought he wanted the money for your husband, since he lost to him at cards ages ago, and hasn't paid up yet.

LIDIYA: *(in despair)* Oh stop, stop, this is killing me!

TELYATEV: Why? Kuchumov's a decent chap, don't worry. We all love him, it's just that he's a bit forgetful. He actually did have a large fortune at one time, but he tends to forget it's all spent. And that's easily done: I mean, he still gives wonderful dinner-parties, balls, suppers, goes about in magnificent carriages, only everything belongs to his wife and it's held in trust for her nieces. He himself gets issued with no more than ten roubles for his bar bill. On his name-day or on holidays they'll give him fifty roubles, or now and again a hundred. Huh, you should see him then! Drives up to the club, sits at the head of the table, orders up his truffles, champagne, oysters, and what a fuss he makes! Has all the waiters run off their feet, about half a dozen of them hopping around him. And God help the poor chef!

LIDIYA: *(turning pale)* What am I going to do? I'm up to my ears in debt.

TELYATEV: That's no reason to despair. Honestly, who isn't in debt these days?

LIDIYA: Oh, Telyatev, you've got heaps of money, take pity on me! Don't let me perish!

Telyatev bows his head.

Telyatev, please, help me save our family's honour. I could even love you for it, you're so good and kind.

Telyatev's head sinks even lower.

Jean, I'm going under, you must save me! If you'll only get me out of this mess, I'll be yours, I promise.

Places her hands on his shoulders and bows her head submissively.

TELYATEV: Well, this is terribly sweet of you, my dear, and I'd be perfectly happy to assist, but... well, you see, I'm not a free agent any longer.

LIDIYA: *(looks into his eyes)* What? Are you married? Or getting married?

TELYATEV: No, I'm neither. Actually, they're taking me to the debtors' prison tomorrow.

LIDIYA: Debtors' prison, what do you mean?

TELYATEV: Just that. They're coming with a policeman to take me down.

LIDIYA: No, that's not possible. What's happened to all your money? You gave my husband a loan, I know you did.

TELYATEV: Well, so what? It was somebody else's money, what do I care?

LIDIYA: And you've no money of your own?

TELYATEV: Frankly, I can't remember when I ever had. Anyway, I discovered yesterday that I'm in debt to the tune of some three hundred thousand. Everything you've ever seen in my possession belongs to somebody else: horses, carriages, apartments, clothes. No money changed hands, bills were simply made out in my name, then credit notes, then I started getting summonses, and finally court orders. I must've borrowed vast amounts from the moneylenders. So, all my creditors will be calling on me tomorrow, it'll be an awesome sight. Furniture, carpets, mirrors, pictures – they were all hired, and they've already been whipped away. The carriage and horses are gone, and the tailor's coming to take back my suits first thing tomorrow! My creditors'll die laughing, I'm sure of that. I shall receive them in my dressing-gown, naturally, since that's the only thing I can call my own. I shall offer them a cigar, I've still got a dozen or so left. They'll look at me, and at my bare walls, and they'll say: "What the hell, Telyatev old chap, enjoy yourself!" One of them's annoyed about his wife, of course, so he'll probably keep me in the hole for a couple of months, until he gets fed up paying for my grub. Anyway, they'll let me out and I'll be a free man again, and I'll have plenty of credit, because I'm basically a nice chap, and I've got eleven aunties and grannies still living, and I'm heir to the lot of them. I mean, you wouldn't believe how much I had to shell out on stamped paper alone, for all those credit notes. If it were sold by the pound, it'd fetch more than they'll get out of me tomorrow!

LIDIYA: And yet you're so calm?

TELYATEV: Why on earth shouldn't I be? I've got nothing on my conscience, and nothing in my pockets. My creditors have had at least three times what I owed them ages ago. They're suing me for form's sake, that's all.

LIDIYA: So where can I borrow money? I mean, serious money, lots of it – hasn't anybody got any?

TELYATEV: Yes, of course they have.

LIDIYA: So who are these people?

TELYATEV: Well, business types, only they're not in the habit of flinging it around.

LIDIYA: They're not? Oh dear, that's a pity.

TELYATEV: It certainly is. Even the money's smarter these days – it all goes to these business chaps, and not to the likes of us. Money was a bit dumber in the old days. And that's just the sort of money you need.

LIDIYA: What sort?

TELYATEV: Crazy money. That's the only sort I ever had, you can't keep it in your pocket. Easy come, easy go. You know, it's just dawned on me why our money was like that – it's because we didn't have to earn it ourselves. Now, money you get by your own labour, that's smart money. That stays where it's put. We try and attract it, but it won't come. It says, "No, I know the kind of money you want, and I'm not coming near you." And you can beg all you like, it won't come. Which is a bit offensive, really, that it doesn't want anything to do with us.

LIDIYA: I'll become an actress.

TELYATEV: You need talent for that, my dear Lidiya.

LIDIYA: I'll go to the provinces.

TELYATEV: What's the point of that? Fascinating some ridiculous peasant, or tiresome petty bourgeois. What sort of career's that?

LIDIYA: Telyatev, you've got to help me, I need money!

TELYATEV: Please, allow me... *(leads her to the window)* You see ?

> 'Twas a little tiny house
> With a little tiny wall,
> And three little windows,
> Looked down on them all...

Now, there's your money, Lidiya.

LIDIYA: My husband?

TELYATEV: Yes, indeed. He's not only wealthier than any of us, he's so rich it'd make your head spin even to think of it. You see, the rich man these days isn't somebody with lots of money, it's the man who knows how to make it. I mean, if your husband has three hundred thousand in cash, say, then you can bet your life he'll have a million within the year, and in five years' time – five million!

LIDIYA: No, it's not possible. I don't believe you. Get out of here, go on. He must've put you up to this.

TELYATEV: No, Lidiya, please, listen. When you walked out on him, he and I had dinner at the Troitzky. He just sat there, not looking at anybody, not eating or drinking. Then these odd-looking coves walked up to him, whispered something in his ear, and it was as if he 'd come to life again, Next somebody brought him a telegram, he read it, and his eyes started to shine, honestly. "No," he says, "I won't shoot myself, it's a stupid idea. Let's have some fun, tonight we celebrate!" Well, anyway, I congratulated him, we embraced, and off we went on the town. I introduced him to a few of my old friends – well, not old, if you see what I mean – some of them are still quite young, and rather pretty...

LIDIYA: *(at the window)* Wait! Whose is that carriage? It's beautiful! Surely that's not the one maman has hired for me? Why, it's absolutely charming, the height of luxury!

TELYATEV: No, I'm afraid not. That's the carriage your husband gave one of my friends, along with the horses, and he's engaged a proper coachman too, the sort you can even show off at the Zoological Gardens. That's her coming out of his house now, the little blonde thing, with the cornflower blue eyes.

LIDIYA: What! Oh, I think I'm going to faint. That's not a carriage, that's a dream. You could just die of sheer happiness sitting in a carriage like that. What's the matter with me? I hate him, and yet I seem to be jealous. I could cheerfully kill that blonde. Just look at that tiny little turned-up nose of hers!

TELYATEV: That's not jealousy, my dear, that's envy.

LIDIYA: Is he in love?

TELYATEV: What, with the carriage?

LIDIYA: No, the blonde.

TELYATEV: Good heavens, no. Being in love and giving out money – that's altogether much too expensive. Do you want to hear what your husband told me about himself?

LIDIYA: Yes, tell me.

TELYATEV: Well, he's studied a good deal, although I can't for the life of me remember what. I mean, there are all sorts of sciences, my dear Lidiya, which you and I have never even heard of.

LIDIYA: Go on, tell me about him, I want to know!

TELYATEV: Anyway, he travelled abroad, to see how they ran their railways, then came back to Russia and leased a patch of ground from a contractor. He and his workers all lived together in huts, along with his man Vasily. You know Vasily, of course – an absolute treasure.

LIDIYA: You don't say.

TELYATEV: Anyway, his first venture was a success, he took on something a bit bigger, then a bit bigger still. And now he gets telegrams like these. "Well, Vanya," he says to me, "I'm not going to accept less than a million." And I tell him, "No, don't even think of it." I mean, what the hell, it's no skin off my nose.

LIDIYA: Oh God, I'm dying.

TELYATEV: Why, what's the matter with you?

LIDIYA: *(lies down on the couch)* Call *maman!* Call her quickly!

TELYATEV: *(at the door)* Madame Cheboksarova!

Cheboksarova enters.

LIDIYA: Oh, *maman,* for God's sake, help me!

CHEBOKSAROVA: Lidiya, what's the matter? What is it, my dear child?

LIDIYA: Help me, *maman,* for the love of God! Run and fetch my husband, tell him I'm dying.

TELYATEV: Take my horses, dear lady, you'll get there quicker!

CHEBOKSAROVA: *(peers at her daughter)* Yes, yes, I can see you're not well. I'll go right away. *(exits)*

Andrei enters.

ANDREI: Mister Glumov, ma'am.

LIDIYA: *(sits up)* Now, should I see him or not? I mean, I don't know if my husband *will* come, and a drowning man'll clutch at a straw. *(to Andrei)* Show him in.

Andrei exits. Enter Glumov.

GLUMOV: So, what's the matter with you?

LIDIYA: Oh, I'm a little out of sorts. Anyway, how are you? From what I hear, you're rich these days.

GLUMOV: Well, not yet, but I have hopes. I've taken up a very lucrative position.

TELYATEV: Oh, and perfectly suited to his abilities.

GLUMOV: Sheer good luck, that's all. A certain elderly lady's been trying for ages to find a what d'you call it... not exactly a business manager, but a sort of...

LIDIYA: Private secretary?

GLUMOV: Exactly. She wanted an honest man, to whom she could entrust both...

TELYATEV: Her person and her fortune?

GLUMOV: Just about, yes. She owns houses, estates, heaps of
businesses – I mean, how on earth can she manage all that herself?
She's fallen out with all her heirs. I'm trying to turn everything
into investment capital, put it into things I've got complete
confidence in, and for that I'm getting a very healthy commission.

TELYATEV: Truly a noble, trusting woman. You must admit,
Glumov, you don't find too many of those.

GLUMOV: Yes, I suppose she's the last of a dying breed. And I
know all their names by heart.

TELYATEV: We were just talking about crazy money, and how it's
practically extinct these days, but you're luckier than us, you've
actually found some.

GLUMOV: Well, I had to look long and hard for it.

LIDIYA: So anyway, you've plenty of money now?

GLUMOV: Mm... plenty's a relative term, of course. It wouldn't be
enough for Rothschild, but it'll do me nicely.

LIDIYA: Well, you can surely lend me twenty thousand?

GLUMOV: My dear Lidiya, nobody ever lends money to pretty
young women, because it's so indelicate to have to remind them, if
they forget to pay it back, and it's even more indelicate to sue
them. Better to politely refuse, or else simply give them the money.

LIDIYA: All right, then, just give me it.

GLUMOV: No, I can't do that, I'm sorry. You remember you told
me I'd never get to kiss your hand? I have a long memory.

LIDIYA: Here, kiss it.

GLUMOV: No, it's too late now, or too early, rather. Wait a year for
me, and I'll come and kiss both your hands. I'm leaving for Paris
tomorrow with my dear employer. She hasn't a clue about money,
either roubles or francs, and I shall be her banker. She also suffers
from asthma, and general all-round obesity. The doctors here have
given her less than a year to live, and in Paris, what with trips to
take the waters, and the very last word in medical attention, she'll
die even sooner. So you see I've no time to waste. I shall run
myself ragged for a year looking after my sick old lady, and then I

shall enjoy the fruits of my labours, spending a tidy sum of money, possibly with your assistance, if the idea appeals.

LIDIYA: Oh, you're a wicked, wicked man!

GLUMOV: Well, that's what you always liked about me, wasn't it? In that way we're very alike, you and I.

LIDIYA: Yes, but this time you've gone too far, so goodbye, sir!

GLUMOV: Goodbye. I shall leave in the fond hope that you'll miss me while I'm away, that you'll learn to appreciate me, and when we do meet again, we'll greet each other like kindred spirits.

LIDIYA: That's enough!

GLUMOV: *Au revoir!*

TELYATEV: Goodbye, Glumov. *Bon voyage!* Remember me while you're in Paris. I think my ghost still haunts every street crossing there.

GLUMOV: Goodbye, Telyatev. *(exits)*

> *Cheboksarova enters with medicine bottles, followed by a Maid, who places pillows on the couch and then exits.*

CHEBOKSAROVA: Lidiya dear, you must lie down, do you hear? There's no sense in tiring yourself out. It's quite obvious from the way you look, that you're suffering dreadfully. That's what I told your husband. He's coming right away. Now, here are your smelling salts and those drops you always take.

LIDIYA: *(lies back on the pillow)* What kind of reception did he give you?

CHEBOKSAROVA: Very polite. Rather cool, I'm afraid. He asked if you were seriously ill, and I said you were, extremely. Really, Telyatev, why are you laughing?

TELYATEV: I can't keep a straight face. I've either got to laugh or cry.

CHEBOKSAROVA: It's Lidiya's nature, you don't know anything about her, it's her constitution, she's so highly-strung. She's such a nervous person, really she is – she's been that way since she was a child.

TELYATEV: Forgive me, dear lady, I know nothing whatsoever about her constitution, that's a complete mystery to me.

LIDIYA:　Telyatev, you're such an idiot, you'll make me laugh too.

CHEBOKSAROVA:　That's just what you'll do, and her husband'll walk in any minute.

TELYATEV:　Are you ordering me to hide?

LIDIYA:　*(wearily)* No, stay where you are, Telyatev. I like having you around, you're good for me.

TELYATEV:　Oh well, if that's what you want, I'll not only stay, I'll remain standing before you as if nailed to the floor. You can look at me all you like then. Only if you don't mind, I'd prefer a walk-on part in this little comedy.

　　　Andrei enters.

ANDREI:　Mister Vasilkov.

LIDIYA:　*(in a weak voice)* Show him in.

　　　Andrei exits. Cheboksarova adjusts the pillows, while Telyatev dabs his eyes with a handkerchief. Vasilkov enters.

VASILKOV:　*(after a general bow)* You sent for me?

LIDIYA:　I'm dying.

VASILKOV:　In that case it's a doctor or a priest you need, and I'm neither.

LIDIYA:　You walked out on us.

VASILKOV:　No, you walked out on me, and without so much as a goodbye.

LIDIYA:　Do you want me to say goodbye?

VASILKOV:　If you wish.

LIDIYA:　Never part in anger, they say. That means asking forgiveness.

VASILKOV:　Ask.

LIDIYA:　The only thing I'm guilty of is leaving you without realising how little money I had. The rest is your own fault.

VASILKOV: We're quits, then. It was my fault, and you left me. What else is there to say? Goodbye.

LIDIYA: No, please, stay!

VASILKOV: What do you want?

LIDIYA: Look, you're getting off scot free, but I might have to pay a very harsh penalty. I'm up to my ears in debt, they'll put me in jail amongst all kinds of shopkeepers and the like.

VASILKOV: Oh I see, that's what's bothering you! That's the sort of dishonour you're afraid of? Oh, well, you needn't worry. Plenty of decent people wind up in the Moscow Pit, as they call it, but you can always get out of there. The sort of pit you should fear is that bottomless pit that goes by the name of corruption, in which a woman can lose her good name, her honour, even her looks. Yes, you're afraid of the pit, but you're not afraid of that abyss, from whence there is no way back onto the strait and narrow path!

LIDIYA: Who gave you the right to speak to me like that!

VASILKOV: Who gives a sighted man the right to show a blind man the way? Who bids the wise man counsel the foolish, or the learned to teach the ignorant?

LIDIYA: Well, you have no right to teach me, sir!

VASILKOV: Indeed I have. Pity gives me the right.

LIDIYA: How dare you speak of pity! You see your wife in this situation and yet you won't pay so much as a piddling debt for her.

VASILKOV: Throwing good money after bad, not likely.

CHEBOKSAROVA: I don't understand your way of thinking. This is a new one on me, a very strange idea altogether. Paying for your wife – you call that throwing your money away?

VASILKOV: What sort of wife is she to me? Anyway, she told me herself she had more money than I had.

CHEBOKSAROVA: Yes, that's what she *said*. Women say all sorts of things when they're provoked. And no matter how a wife insults her husband, you still ought to have more sympathy for the wife. We're such weak creatures, so highly-strung – any sort of row takes so much out of us. A quick-tempered woman will readily do something stupid, but she's also quick to regret it.

VASILKOV: Yes, well, she doesn't say she regrets it.

LIDIYA: I do, I do regret it. I'm sorry for what I've done.

VASILKOV: It's a bit late, isn't it.

CHEBOKSAROVA: No, it's not. She might've got carried away, but she didn't let herself go completely.

VASILKOV: Yes, that much I do know. I've been paying your servants rather more than you have. What I don't know is what prevented her – whether it was her honour, or the fact that Kuchumov was strapped for cash. *(to Lidiya)* What is it you want?

LIDIYA: I should like to live with you again.

VASILKOV: Impossible. You change your mind so easily you'll be wanting to walk out on me again tomorrow. I've been disgraced once, and that's quite enough.

LIDIYA: But you must save me.

VASILKOV: And how am I going to do that? There's only one way. I can offer you honest work, and pay you wages for it.

LIDIYA: What sort of work, and what sort of wages?

VASILKOV: You can be my housekeeper, and I'll pay you a thousand a year.

LIDIYA: *(gets up from the couch)* Go to hell! Get out of my sight!

Vasilkov exits.

TELYATEV: *(takes his handkerchief away from his eyes)* Well, I see you're restored to health now – I can stop crying.

LIDIYA: This isn't funny, Telyatev! Go on, run after him, get him to come back, no matter what!

Telyatev hurries out.

CHEBOKSAROVA: Oh, he's as stubborn as a mule. Absolutely

unbearable. Really, no decent person would behave like that, he'd sooner kill his wife than make such a suggestion.

Vasilkov and Telyatev return.

LIDIYA: You must forgive me, I don't think I quite understand. Explain to me what exactly you mean by 'housekeeper', and what her duties might be.

VASILKOV: Certainly, I'll explain, but if you don't accept my offer, then I shan't be returning. A housekeeper is a woman who looks after a house, and that's not a demeaning job for anyone. These would be your duties: I have an old mother in the country who is an excellent housewife, and you would work under her supervision – she'll teach you everything, how to pickle mushrooms, how to make home brew, how to make jam – she'll hand over the keys of the pantry and the cellar, and she'll keep you under her eye. I need a woman to do all that, since I'm away so much on business.

LIDIYA: That's dreadful, absolutely dreadful!

VASILKOV: Do you want me to stop?

LIDIYA: No, go on.

VASILKOV: Well, once you've mastered the art of keeping a house, I'll take you into our local town, where you'll be able to dazzle all our provincial ladies with your fine clothes and manners. I won't begrudge you money for that, but I'm not going to overstep my spending limits. Anyway, I need a wife like that, the way my business has expanded. Later, if you're nice to me, I'll take you to St Petersburg. You'll be able to hear Patti at the opera, I'll happily pay a thousand roubles for a box. Through my business, I have connections with some very grand people in Petersburg. I'm a bit awkward and uncouth myself, and I need the sort of wife who can entertain, so we won't be embarassed to receive even a Cabinet minister. You have everything you need for that, except that you've got to unlearn a few bad habits you've picked up from Telyatev and suchlike.

TELYATEV: Well, honestly, how was I to know dear Lidiya would have such a glittering prospect before her – all the way up from country cellar to St Petersburg salon!

VASILKOV: *(looks at his watch)* Well, do you accept my offer or not? Bear in mind that you'll be housekeeper a long time to start with.

LIDIYA: Oh, God, have pity on me, have pity on my pride! I'm a lady, born and bred. Won't you make at least some concession for that?

VASILKOV: Absolutely none. Why should I take pity on your pride, when you had no pity on my simplicity, or my good nature? It's because I love you that I'm even offering you the title of housekeeper.

LIDIYA: Well, couldn't you at least call it something else? It's so hurtful to my ears.

VASILKOV: No, it's a perfectly good word.

LIDIYA: I'll have to think it over.

VASILKOV: Do so.

TELYATEV: I wish someone would make *me* their housekeeper!

   Andrei enters.

ANDREI: Ma'am, the bailiffs are here to make an inventory of the furniture.

LIDIYA AND CHEBOKSAROVA: Oh, my God! Oh, no, no!

TELYATEV: What are you afraid of? Cheer up, ladies! Two of my friends had their furniture ticketed yesterday, today it's your turn, tomorrow it'll be mine, and the day after it'll be that Kuchumov of yours. It's a sort of epidemic these days.

LIDIYA: *(to Vasilkov)* Help me, please! I can't bear the shame. I agree to everything. What else can I do? I wanted to shine like an inextinguishible star, but you want to make me into a meteor, that flares up for a brief moment before dying out in some swamp. Anyway, I agree, I agree, but save me, please, I beg you!

   Vasilkov exits with Andrei. Andrei then re-enters.

ANDREI: Mister Kuchumov, ma'am.

LIDIYA: I think I'll see him.

TELYATEV: Yes, do.

LIDIYA: *(to Andrei)* Show him in.

Andrei exits. Enter Kuchumov, singing as usual.

KUCHUMOV: *Io son ricco...* What's the matter?

LIDIYA: The bailiffs are making an inventory of my furniture. Have you brought the forty thousand?

KUCHUMOV: *Io son ricco...* No, I haven't – actually you wouldn't believe what bad luck I've had.

Vasilkov enters, and stands in the doorway.

My valet – I tell you, I loved him like a son – he's robbed me, stolen all my money, and cleared off – to America, no doubt.

TELYATEV: Well, I feel sorry for him, frankly. With the money he stole from you, he'll do well to get as far as the next station, let alone America!

KUCHUMOV: It's no laughing matter. Anyway, I've sent off telegrams all over the country. They're bound to catch him soon, I'll get my money back and then I'll give it to you, my dear child.

TELYATEV: He didn't take it all, surely? You must have something left.

KUCHUMOV: Well, of course I have. I never leave home without a thousand in my pocket.

VASILKOV: Good. That means you can give me the six hundred roubles you lost to me at cards.

KUCHUMOV: Oh, you're here? Well, that's splendid – I've been meaning to settle up with you for ages. Gambling debts are my first priority. *(takes out his wallet)* Eh? What sort of nonsense is this? No, I must've mislaid it somewhere, it'll be in my left-hand pocket. Oh God, I've put on the wrong coat. Well, anyway, you can get the money I owe you from Madame Cheboksarova.

VASILKOV: Fine, I'll do that. Now, Lidiya, I've paid off your debts. We'll have to leave for the country.

LIDIYA: Whenever you wish.

VASILKOV: I'll be leaving tomorrow, so be ready.

LIDIYA: *(gives her hand to Vasilkov)* Thank you for allowing me a whole day for my tears. I have so much to cry over. The broken dreams of my youth, my mistakes, my humiliations. I need to weep for what I can never bring back. My goddess of untroubled delights has been tumbled from her pedestal, and in her place stands that rough-hewn idol of toil and industry, whose name is budget. Oh, how I pity these poor, delicate creatures, these carefree darling girls. No more exquisite young husbands, with no heads for figures! Oh, you ethereal creatures, give up your impossible dreams, forget that young man who can squander money with such style, and marry the man who can earn it, with no style whatsoever, and who calls himself a businessman.

TELYATEV: That's pretty hard on us idle types, I must say.

KUCHUMOV: *(sings) Io son ricco...*

TELYATEV: No, you're wrong. *Noi siamo poveri.*

LIDIYA: There's another sacrifice I'm making for you.

VASILKOV: I don't want any sacrifices.

LIDIYA: I see I've met my match. Very well, I'll come clean. I accept your offer because I consider it good business.

VASILKOV: Bear in mind, I'll never go beyond my means.

LIDIYA: Oh, you and your budget!

VASILKOV: It's only crazy money that doesn't keep to a budget.

TELYATEV: And that's the gospel truth, sir. That's just what I've been saying.

VASILKOV: *(to Telyatev)* Well, goodbye, my friend, I feel heartily sorry for you. Tomorrow you'll be out on the street, I dare say.

TELYATEV: Mm, you wouldn't like to lend me some money? No, no, don't bother. God knows, you'd be throwing it away. Anyway, dear Savva, people like Telyatev and Kuchumov and me, we'll never go under in a place like Moscow. Even when we're flat broke we'll still have both honour and credit. It'll be a long time before any shopkeeper won't count himself privileged to wine and dine us at his own expense. With our tailors, well, it's a different story, but even a shabby old hat and coat can be worn with such distinction, that people make way for you in the street. Goodbye,

Savva dear friend. Don't feel sorry for us. Even in the meanest
rags, virtue will out! *(embraces Kuchumov)*

> *Lidiya shyly goes up to Vasilkov, puts her hand on his shoulder
> and lays her head against his chest.*

THE END

(Beshennye den'gi, 1870)

INNOCENT AS CHARGED

CHARACTERS

LYUBOV (Ivanovna Otradina, a young woman of gentle birth)
KRUCHININA (Yelena Ivanovna, a famous actress, i.e., Lyubov, 17 years later)
TAISA (Ilyinishna Shelavina, a young woman, Lyubov's friend)
MUROV (Grigory Lvovich, a young man, a provincial official)
ANNUSHKA (Lyubov's maid)
ARINA (Arkhipovna Galchikha, a countrywoman)
DUDUKIN (Nil Stratonych, a wealthy gentleman)
NINA (Pavlovna Korinkina, an actress)
MILOVZOROV (Petya, an actor, 'juvenile lead')
NEZNAMOV (Grigory, a provincial actor)
SHMAGA (A provincial actor)
IVAN (A hotel porter)

-----oOo-----

ACT ONE
(In place of a Prologue)

The action takes place in a modest apartment on the outskirts of a large provincial town; doors at stage right and left lead to inner rooms, and upstage, a window and the hall door; the furnishings are simple but tasteful, and the room is clean and comfortable. Lyubov is seated at the table, stitching a collar, while Annushka sits beside her, sewing a new dress.

ANNUSHKA: *(biting off her thread)* There you are, ma'am – finished. We've cut it and sewn it ourselves, and no worse than any dressmaker, I reckon.

LYUBOV: No worse, indeed.

ANNUSHKA: It's turned out really stunning, too.

LYUBOV: Well, hardly stunning... No, when I was at the dressmaker's yesterday, to get a pattern for this collar, I saw a dress there... now that *was* stunning. They were making Taisa Shelavina's wedding-gown.

ANNUSHKA: Yes, I heard she was getting married, but I've not seen the dress. It'll be expensive, I suppose.

LYUBOV: Oh yes. Six hundred roubles, at the very least.

ANNUSHKA: Never! Six hundred roubles! What, six of those big hundred-rouble notes?

LYUBOV: Well, it's all in white satin – you can imagine how many yards that takes. And genuine Brussels lace.

ANNUSHKA: Six hundred-rouble notes! Oh, dear! You could have a whole wedding outfit made up for that kind of money, even for a fine lady, but to spend that on one gown!

LYUBOV: Well, why shouldn't she dress in style? She's rich enough.

ANNUSHKA: Yes, but you'd think she be a little more discreet, and not show off her money like that.

LYUBOV: Oh, what nonsense you talk, Annushka.

ANNUSHKA: Well, there's some strange goings-on in this world, right enough.

LYUBOV: What's strange about that? It's an everyday occurrence. She inherited the money – it was left to her by wealthy relatives.

ANNUSHKA: Yes, and how'd she come to inherit when she hasn't got any relatives, except for two old aunts?

LYUBOV: How do you know that?

ANNUSHKA: It's the talk of the town, ma'am, everybody's on about it.

LYUBOV: Yes, foolish talk, that's all.

ANNUSHKA: Must be something in it, ma'am, or they wouldn't do it. Why should they? No, Taisa Shelavina used to live here with her aunt, and hard up they were, everybody knew them, I knew them well myself. Wasn't that long ago, either, about three years. Then they got to know some rich gentleman, an old man he was, owned goldmines out in Siberia, they said, and he takes the pair of them off with him to Moscow. Anyway, the aunt comes back soon enough, but Taisa and the old man go off on the grand tour. He ups and dies then, leaves all his money, and his goldmines, to Taisa Shelavina, and that's how she got rich. So she comes back here, and now she's putting on the style. Treats that old aunt of hers like a servant.

LYUBOV: Honestly, Annushka – a young girl like you – you shouldn't repeat everything you hear, it's shameful.

ANNUSHKA: What's shameful about it, if it's the truth? It's not the talking about it that's shameful, it's the doing of it!

LYUBOV: Well, anyway, it's better to keep quiet about these things. She's an old friend of mine, we went to school together. And we still see each other.

ANNUSHKA: And d'you think she really appreciates you, ma'am? D'you think she values your friendship? I mean, that's a whole month now, and she hasn't once looked in to see you.

LYUBOV: She hasn't the time, she's too busy with her marriage plans.

ANNUSHKA: Yes, and you had to find out she was getting married from her dressmaker! And she calls herself your friend. She ought to have come to you right at the start: 'I'm thinking of getting married to so-and-so,' she should've said, 'What d'you reckon?' That's what decent people do.

LYUBOV: Who's she marrying? You haven't heard?

ANNUSHKA: No, some say he's an officer, others say he's some sort of government agent.

LYUBOV: What do you mean, government agent?

ANNUSHKA: Some sort of civil servant, you know. I wouldn't mind seeing the wedding, but it seems they're getting married some place out in the country, about thirty miles off by train, then another dozen or so on top of that.

LYUBOV: Annushka, where do you get all this information?

ANNUSHKA: Oh, we find things out quicker than you, ma'am. I got it off the girls at the dressmaker's. Yes, if everything was above board, she wouldn't be getting married out in the wilds, like she was in hiding.

LYUBOV: Even so, you really shouldn't speak ill of her. Talk like that could upset things for her, spoil her chances.

ANNUSHKA: Spoil her chances! With the kind of money she's got, people'd be running after her no matter what she was like. No, her sort get all the luck, while the good girls just have to sit and wait. It's about time you had a decent man, ma'am. Somebody should've snapped you up by now. There's Grigory Lvovich, for instance, if only...

LYUBOV: 'If only' what?

ANNUSHKA: Well, you've no dowry, ma'am.

LYUBOV: You think that's all that's holding him back?

ANNUSHKA: Well, what else can it be? You know what people are like these days. All they're after is money. Even supposing you haven't a dowry, you're still a lady, you've had a good education, you know all sorts of things. Just because your parents died and didn't leave you anything – I mean, whose fault's that?

LYUBOV: That's true. You've hit the nail on the head, Annushka. Still, just wait till I get rich, then I'll find a husband.

ANNUSHKA: And why on earth shouldn't you get rich, ma'am? Your aunt's got plenty of money.

LYUBOV: In the first place, she's a very distant relative, and in the second place, she's got children of her own. Actually, she wrote to me from the country, she's going to be in town today, and she'll drop in for tea. You'd better boil up some cream, she absolutely dotes on it. No, Annushka, I'll just have to get rich without aunts.

ANNUSHKA: What, giving private lessons? In a place like this? You won't get rich that way.

LYUBOV: I suppose not. It's a thriving town, as they say, but there's not much call for education.

ANNUSHKA: No, what do they want with learning! With all the money they've got, they can get by perfectly well in blissful ignorance!

LYUBOV: Well, I won't get rich, but maybe some kind gentleman'll take me without a dowry. What do you think? I have a certain one in mind.

ANNUSHKA: Please God, ma'am. Only you never know with men these days...

LYUBOV: What do you mean?

ANNUSHKA: Well, they're all over you to begin with, then as often as not they'll leave you in the lurch.

LYUBOV: How do you know that?

ANNUSHKA: I've got eyes in my head, I can see what goes on. *(begins folding up the dress)* Shall I hang this up in the wardrobe, ma'am?

LYUBOV: No, no, leave it here. I want to try it on again before I put it away.

ANNUSHKA: I'll get on with my work then. There's nobody in the kitchen, and I don't want people walking in.

LYUBOV: *(looking out of the window)* You'd better see to the door first – Grigory Lvovich is coming – then you can get on with your work.

Annushka opens the door, admits Murov, then exits right.

LYUBOV: Oh, darling, I'm so happy to see you!

MUROV: Lyuba, my dear! You must've got up early – you've

dressed and done your hair as if you're expecting somebody.

LYUBOV: I don't know why you're surprised. I'm always up early, and you said yourself that you'd be here first thing this morning, that there was something you wanted to talk over with me.

MUROV: That's right, I completely forgot. Yes, I did say that.

LYUBOV: You know, for some reason or other you've started coming early, as if you're afraid of being seen.

MUROV: Well, honestly! Of course I'm afraid of being seen here – not for my sake, but for yours. It's quite simple – I just don't want people talking about you.

LYUBOV: Oh, darling, I am grateful, but you weren't always so afraid. I mean, we can't keep it a secret forever, can we. People are starting to drop hints: 'Grigory Lvovich'll be getting married soon, don't you think, ma'am?' It'd be better out in the open, that would stop all the gossip.

MUROV: It would indeed, my dearest, but unfortunately that's just not possible at present.

LYUBOV: Why not? Why isn't it possible? What do you mean? I can't believe this.

MUROV: Mother's dead set against it, and I don't know whether she ever would agree, but I daren't make a move without her consent.

LYUBOV: What business is it of hers? What does she want?

MUROV: What she wants is that I should marry some rich young woman, with good connections.

LYUBOV: Well, this is all news to me. I've known you now for four years, and this is the first I've heard of it.

MUROV: I haven't even raised the subject with mother until now.

LYUBOV: What do you mean? You'd no right to keep silent, you had a duty to tell her about me.

MUROV: I know, I know, but what could I do? It's my whole upbringing that's at fault – I've been oppressed and downtrodden all my life. I'm sorry, but I was just too afraid. Well, anyway, I simply got fed up with being constantly under her thumb. I mean, judge for yourself: I'm a grown man, yet I daren't make a move without permission, I've got to beg her for every rouble I spend...

LYUBOV: So? Go on...

MUROV: Well, I asked her to give me my share of the estate, or else a decent allowance, say, three or four thousand a year. She told me she wouldn't give me so much as a kopeck, until I married the girl of her choice.

LYUBOV: And what did you say? Tell me!

MUROV: Oh God, don't ask me, please! My head's still spinning...

LYUBOV: But I've got to know your intentions, you surely realise that? I can't go on like this.

MUROV: My intentions?

LYUBOV: Yes, yes, your intentions!

MUROV: *(embarassed)* Well, obviously... I mean, you know what they are... You don't think I'd... I mean, in my position... I do have an obligation...

LYUBOV: Yes, yes, you do! And I hope you know what that obligation is. Oh, darling, I can't lose faith in you, that would be agony for me, just torture... You've got to keep telling yourself, every minute of the day – we have a son! You see him so rarely, but I was at that Arina's place yesterday. And he's beginning to understand – he puts his little arms round me, he hugs me and calls me 'Mama'. And he's kept apart from me, he's with that ignorant, greedy woman... I can't bear it, I can't sleep at night, I think about him all the time: is he getting enough to eat, is he sleeping properly? Oh, Grisha, Grisha – if you could only just see him, you'd be so proud of him! He's such an angel!

MUROV: You love our little Grisha very much, don't you.

LYUBOV: Of course I do. What sort of question's that? Of course I love him, the way only a mother can – the way a mother must.

MUROV: Yes, yes... Of course. But, Lyuba... suppose the poor little mite was suddenly left without a father?

LYUBOV: What do you mean, without a father?

MUROV: Oh, God... I mean, anything could happen. I travel
around so much, I might get killed by a horse... or on the railway,
for instance, there could be an accident...

LYUBOV: What on earth are you talking about? Have you come to
torment me today, or what?

MUROV: Lyuba, you've got to be prepared for the worst. It's on my
mind, that's all – what'll you do about Grisha, if you don't have me?

LYUBOV: Oh, stop it, please – you're getting on my nerves.

MUROV: Oh, of course, your nerves – that's the trouble with you
women, your blessed nerves!

LYUBOV: Look, if you're asking me a serious question, I'll give you
an answer. You needn't worry, Grisha won't go without. I'll work
day and night for him, to make sure he wants for nothing. D'you
think I'd let him go hungry, or naked? No, never. And he'll have
books and toys, expensive toys, too. He'll have the same as any
other child. Why shouldn't he? It's not his fault. And if I'm not
able to work, if I should fall ill, well, then... I wouldn't be ashamed
to beg in the streets for him! *(breaks down)*

MUROV: Oh, Lyuba, Lyuba...

LYUBOV: Well, you asked me, didn't you? You wanted to know
what I'd say. What did you expect, what other answer would I
give? Do you really think I'd abandon him?

MUROV: Oh, my poor darling... forgive me, Lyuba. I'd no idea it
would upset you so much. Let's talk about something else – we'll
change the subject.

LYUBOV: Yes, let's, please.

MUROV: So, what have you been up to?

LYUBOV: I've been making a new dress.

MUROV: For whom?

LYUBOV: Myself.

MUROV: Is it pretty?

LYUBOV: Pretty cheap. But it'll do me nicely. I don't have any goldmines.

MUROV: You don't need them, Lyuba, you're pure gold anyway. What goldmines are you referring to?

LYUBOV: Oh, you wouldn't believe it! I saw a dress yesterday, the last word in luxury. Someone's wedding-gown, trimmed with real lace.

MUROV: Whose?

LYUBOV: Taisa Shelavina's.

MUROV: What? Whose did you say?

LYUBOV: Taisa Shelavina's. Why, do you know her?

MUROV: No, no... I've heard of her, that's all.

LYUBOV: She's very pretty... and rich, unlike myself. But she was poor when she was young. I've known her for ages, we went to school together.

MUROV: Really?

LYUBOV: Yes, she was extremely lazy at school, a dunce, really, and now she's become rich and found herself a husband. Even as a girl she was full of surprises.

MUROV: In what way?

LYUBOV: Oh, she had very little shame. She's kindhearted, though, you'd have to give her that. We hadn't seen each other for about three years, and when we did meet she was almost in tears. She's been here twice, offering me money. I didn't take it, of course. But one good thing is that she's promised to find me two pupils, and a proper job. That's terribly important to me. I won't need to break into what little capital I have, I can save it for my son... or maybe even for my dowry. Listen, Grisha, you must introduce me to your mother – I can make her like me, I know I can. I'm wasting away here. I've a good mind, I'm quite knowledgeable – I can sparkle when I want to, and I'm sure I can win her round.

MUROV: Yes, I don't doubt it.

LYUBOV: Well, that's splendid, then. There's a family I've recently been introduced to, and I know your mother visits them too.

MUROV: Yes, yes, that's ideal – only not just yet, a bit later perhaps.

LYUBOV: Why so?

MUROV: Well... the thing is, you see... I'm afraid I've got some bad news for you, darling.

LYUBOV: Oh God, what next? Tell me, quickly! This has been a dreadful day...

MUROV: No, no, don't be alarmed – it's nothing serious. It's just that we'll have to be apart for a while.

LYUBOV: Why?

MUROV: I've got to go away.

LYUBOV: Go away where?

MUROV: To Smolensk, then on to St Petersburg – some business of my mother's.

LYUBOV: Will you be gone long?

MUROV: I can't say for sure. A couple of months anyway, maybe longer. Depends on how the business goes in the Senate... I'm taking leave of absence from work.

LYUBOV: And when do you have to go?

MUROV: This evening, I'm afraid.

LYUBOV: So soon? Why didn't you tell me earlier? I'm not ready for this, not at all... I was so happy today, I'd no idea I'd be parted from you, and now suddenly this... this misery... *(breaks down)*

MUROV: What d'you mean misery? What are you crying for? I'll be back in no time, you'll see.

LYUBOV: And what about little Grisha? Don't you feel for him?

MUROV: Isn't your love enough for him? Oh, honestly, you'd think I was going to my death! Lyuba, stop it, please. It's bad enough having to leave you like this, without you breaking your heart...

LYUBOV: Well... all right... I won't cry... *(she hugs him)* Oh, Grisha darling, how much longer will you torture me like this? One day soon we'll be together for always, won't we? Say it'll be soon, please, Grisha...

MUROV: Yes, of course... soon, I promise.

LYUBOV: Oh, you poor dear – what about money? Have you enough for the journey?

MUROV: Yes, plenty.

LYUBOV: I don't believe you. Your mother's not exactly generous. *(takes a purse out of her desk)* Here, take this, it's a hundred roubles – take more, if you want. I don't need it, I'll get paid for lessons, and I'll soon have a permanent job. After all, what am I going to do while you're away? I'll have to keep myself busy.

MUROV: No, no – I can't, I won't take money from you.

LYUBOV: Why not, for heaven's sake? It's not as if as we're strangers. Isn't it our duty to share and share alike? Look at me, Grisha... *(gazes steadily into his eyes)* Grisha, don't you love me any more? Do you want to leave me?

MUROV: What? What nonsense is this you've got into your head?

LYUBOV: Well, take it, then... Would you have refused it from your wife? Take it as a gift from me.

MUROV: All right... I'll take it. Only if I find I've enough money of my own, you'll allow me to return your gift.

LYUBOV: We'll see. And here, darling, take this locket. *(takes a locket from her neck)* Wear it always. There's a lock of our little Grisha's hair inside. It'll remind you of us.

MUROV: Thank you, dear Lyuba. Well, so be it...

LYUBOV: Oh, this is torture, parting like this!

MUROV: If it's such torture, we'd better do it quickly. Goodbye, Lyuba – I have to go...

LYUBOV: No, wait! You'll think of me often, won't you – you'll write?

MUROV: Yes, yes, without fail. Who else should I be thinking of, apart from you?

LYUBOV: Write to me as soon as you get to St Petersburg!

MUROV: You know I shall.

LYUBOV: Goodbye, Grisha darling. And God bless you. *(she embraces him)*

MUROV: Lyuba, please – I must go... *(looks out of the window)* What's that? There's someone drawing up outside.

LYUBOV: *(looks out)* It's Taisa Shelavina – that's her carriage.

MUROV: *(alarmed)* Oh, my God – that's awkward...

LYUBOV: What's the matter? Why are you so worried? You've nothing to fear from her, she's not one to judge other people.

MUROV: Why shouldn't I be worried? No, no, I don't want her to see me here. It's out of the question, she's such a gossip...

LYUBOV: So you do know her? You said just now you didn't.

MUROV: I've heard, that's all... people have said... She's coming, Lyuba, you'd better hide me!

LYUBOV: What on earth for? This is very strange.

MUROV: She's here... I'll go into this room... *(exits through door at left)*

LYUBOV: Well, do so, if you wish, but I don't understand...

   Taisa enters, carrying a large box.

TAISA: Lyuba, dearest!

LYUBOV: Taisa, how nice to see you. What have you got in the box?

TAISA: It's my wedding-gown. Yes, I'm getting married, didn't I tell you?

LYUBOV: No, but I've heard, anyway. I've even seen your wedding-gown, at the dressmaker's.

TAISA: It's an absolute dream, isn't it. Wouldn't you like to see m⁄ in it? Here, I'll put it on, let you see it...

LYUBOV: No, no, please, not here – someone might come in.

TAISA: I'll try it on in the bedroom, then... *(makes to exit by the door left)*

LYUBOV: No, please don't, honestly. I know how nice it is.

TAISA: Oh, well, if you don't want me to... What's the matter with you today? Get up out of bed on the wrong side, did we?

LYUBOV: I'm not feeling too well. And I had to get up early, I've been sewing all morning... *(indicates the dress)*

TAISA: So, you've made yourself a new dress? Oh, you poor thing – and there I am hopping around all over the place, having fun, while you're sitting here hard at work. Life's so unfair, isn't it. I mean, you're a thousand times better and cleverer than me, yet you live like this. Meanwhile I've become rich, for no reason at all.

LYUBOV: For no reason?

TAISA: None whatever. Riches beyond the dreams of avarice, right out of the blue. An old man suddenly goes gaga and leaves me all his money. I'm deeply grateful – yes, I'll say prayers for him for evermore. Thanks to his generosity, I've even found myself a husband.

LYUBOV: Congratulations!

TAISA: Hardly in order, my dear.

LYUBOV: What, don't you love your fiancé?

TAISA: I'm not sure I know how to. I can't quite figure him out. I don't believe a word he says, frankly.

LYUBOV: Is he rich?

TAISA: Rich? That's a good one. He's as poor as a church mouse.

LYUBOV: He must be handsome, then.

TAISA: I wouldn't say that – he's not bad, I suppose.

LYUBOV: He's from a good family – high-ranking?

TAISA: High-ranking? Oh, yes, indeed – His Excellency Count For Nothing.

LYUBOV: So what on earth's the attraction? Why are you marrying him?

TAISA: I'll tell you why. I'm a rich woman now, but I've no idea how to live like one. I mean, I know how to squander my money in shops, I've enough brains to do that, but when it comes to incomings and outgoings, running an estate, I'm absolutely clueless. I've inherited all these stocks and shares, and I keep turning them over, then putting them back in the box – I've so much money it'd take a lifetime to count it. Honestly, I learned to count using my fingers, andI haven't got enough of those! And what am I supposed to do with all these estates and factories and things? I could hand them over to bailiffs and agents and the like, but they'd size me up in no time, and start robbing me blind. Anyway, I've got the solution now – I can have a bailiff for free, and a husband to boot – a smart young man, what more do I need? And on top of that he's sworn his Bible oath to obey me to the letter.

LYUBOV: You can be assured of a good husband then, someone who'll respect you.

TAISA: Well, however he turns out, it's all settled now. We're leaving for St. Petersburg right after the wedding, he's transferring to the civil service there. I'm still young, and not bad-looking, we'll have a rare old time, you wait and see.

LYUBOV: Your fiancé's in the civil service?

TAISA: Yes.

LYUBOV: Where does he work?

TAISA: I've honestly no idea. All over the place, I should think, running errands for his boss. I'll show you what he looks like, shall I? I've brought a photograph...

LYUBOV: Oh, show me, please.

TAISA: I put it in my pocket, I think... *(rummages in her pocket)* Ah, here it is. It's a bit crumpled... *(hands the photograph to Lyubov)* There you are!

LYUBOV: *(glances at the photograph)* Oh, God!

TAISA: What's the matter?

LYUBOV: Nothing, nothing – I leant my hand on the table, and a pin pricked me, that's all...

TAISA: Oh, you poor thing – does it hurt?

LYUBOV: Here, take it. *(hands her back the photograph)*

TAISA: Well, what d'you think of him?

LYUBOV: I don't know what to say. Appearances can be so deceiving. *(she sinks down onto a chair)*

TAISA: Yes, that's true. But if he deceives me, it'll be the worse for him. I'm not one to be trifled with. I wouldn't hesitate for a second, no, sir – I'd show dear Grigory the door and no mistake! Anyway, I must be off. I'd love to stay a while, but I've got heaps of things to do in town. You must come to the wedding, do, please!

LYUBOV: No, no – thanks all the same.

TAISA: Lyuba, darling, you don't look well. Why don't you have a lie down, and I'll send for a doctor? If there's anything you need, you know you've only to ask – I'd do anything for you. Well, anyway – goodbye, my dear. *(kisses Lyubov and exits)*

> *Lyubov accompanies her to the door, then, barely able to stand up, she leans on the table and stares fixedly at the bedroom door. Murov appears in the doorway.*

LYUBOV: *(pointing to the outer door)* Get out!

MUROV: Lyuba, listen to me...

LYUBOV: Get out!

MUROV: *(holding out the money)* Your money...

LYUBOV: *(takes the money and lays it on the table)* Get out, I tell you!

> *Arina enters.*

LYUBA: What are you doing here, Arina?

ARINA: I've come to see you, ma'am.

LYUBA: What have you done with my child? What are you doing here in town?

ARINA: That's what it is, ma'am... *(wipes her eyes with her apron)* It's the child...

LYUBA: What? What is it?

ARINA: He's dying, ma'am...

LYUBA: What? What are you talking about? Annushka! Annushka!

Annushka appears in the doorway at right.

My shawl! Bring me my shawl! And run for a cab!

ARINA: I came in one, ma'am – he's waiting outside.

Annushka exits.

LYUBOV: Oh, my God! What's wrong with him, tell me, tell me, for God's sake! There was nothing wrong with him yesterday.

ARINA: It was so sudden, ma'am... He just started wheezing, gasping for breath, and then he turned blue all over.

LYUBOV: Get the doctor, quickly! Get the doctor!

ARINA: The doctor's with him now, ma'am. The local man just happened to be in our village, and I called him in. It was him as sent me to fetch you.

LYUBOV: What did he say?

Annushka enters with the shawl.

ARINA: It's not good, ma'am – he says it's a right serious ailment. *(wipes her eyes)* Says he won't last another hour.

LYUBOV: Oh, my God! *(flings her shawl around her)* Come on, hurry! Hurry! *(to Murov)* Well... you're a free man now...

MUROV: I'll follow you out... *(they exit)*

END OF ACT ONE

ACT TWO

The scene is a hotel room, decently furnished, with a fireplace; up-stage, a door leading to the corridor, at right, a door into an adjoining room. Between Act I and Act II seventeen years have elapsed. Ivan is dusting the furniture, as Dudukin opens the door.

DUDUKIN: *(in the doorway)* May I come in?

IVAN: Please do, sir.

DUDUKIN: *(enters, carrying a small package)* Well, is Madame Kruchinina up yet?

IVAN: She's already had coffee, sir.

DUDUKIN: Kindly ask her if she'll see me.

IVAN: 'Fraid she's gone out, sir.

DUDUKIN: Damn, what a pity! And I've brought her some tea, I just picked it up at the market. Some fresh caviar too, the kind she likes.

IVAN: I see. Well, I'll give them to her maid, sir. Or if you don't mind waiting, she'll be back soon.

  Takes the package, exits left, and immediately returns.

DUDUKIN: You wouldn't know where she's gone?

IVAN: She's gone to see the Governor, sir.

DUDUKIN: What for?

IVAN: Couldn't rightly say, sir. Maybe it's to do with her benefit performance – that's the first thing with actors always, whenever they...

DUDUKIN: That's nonsense. What benefit? I've heard nothing about any benefit, and I'd be the first to know. Who's driving her there? Is it Stepan?

IVAN: That's right, sir.

DUDUKIN: So, has he got the bay horse on the outside?

IVAN: He has, sir.

DUDUKIN: Good, good. Because if he puts the little grey mare there, she's skittish and tends to lash out – she'll get her hind leg caught up in the traces, for sure. She's going with a man, so that'll be all right, but women are such frail creatures. It's their nerves, you see.

IVAN: We does our best, sir. God preserve her.

DUDUKIN: And what about dinner? Have you any sort of greens?

IVAN: Huh, chance'd be a fine thing! Nothing but lettuce, sir, and tough as old boots. Does anything in this place get done proper? People stays here, we gets nothing but complaints, sir, I can tell you. But what can the likes of us do about it, if the owner himself don't care?

DUDUKIN: Well, all right, then, I'll send you some fresh lettuce and cauliflower. But make sure you give it to nobody but Madame Kruchinina, I'm not feeding the entire hotel. And you can tell the cook I said that.

IVAN: Yes, sir. But I don't know why you're bothering, sir. I mean if our owner don't know what decent people wants, then hell mend him, I say, he's only cheating himself.

DUDUKIN: That's right, it's a piggery he's got here, my friend.

IVAN: That's absolutely true, sir, you've hit the nail right on the head.

DUDUKIN: My God, she's a world-famous actress!

IVAN: Oh yes, sir, all the gentlemen as have seen her, they've been singing her praises, sir, she's fair got 'em going!

DUDUKIN: Well, I couldn't care less about your owner, but it's a disgrace to our town: I mean, I'm a resident here. And Madame Kruchinina's likely to talk about us, in some other provincial town somewhere, about how we've no idea how to accommodate people, or feed them, and that won't be very nice, will it!

Nina Korinkina enters. Ivan exits.

NINA: Oh, you're here? Well, of course you are, where else would you be?

DUDUKIN: Darling, how lovely!

NINA: What d'you mean darling? Cut the familiarity, I have a proper name, you know.

DUDUKIN: Well, Nina Pavlovna, allow me to point out that your annoyance is uncalled for. I'm here on business, that's all, doing my duty.

NINA: Oh yes? Duty, is it? And what's that exactly, might one ask?

DUDUKIN: There's a famous actress just arrived, it's her first visit to our town, and she doesn't know anybody. So, as a representative of the local intelligentisia, I'm here to...

NINA: Oh, don't talk rubbish. Intelligentsia? A new bit of skirt's arrived, that's all, and you've turned to jelly. *(laughs)* Duty! That's some duty you've taken on yourself.

DUDUKIN: What, are you jealous, my precious?

NINA: Jealous on your account? Don't make me laugh. I'm embarassed for you, that's all. The minute you clap eyes on a woman you start drooling, it's disgusting!

DUDUKIN: So, was that all you came to see me about, my angel?

NINA: Huh, my angel, is it! *(stamps her foot)* Well, you just listen to me. Some of the actors are meeting at my place right now, and we want a serious talk with you about a certain matter, so you'd better be there. I've been looking everywhere for you, driving all over town.

DUDUKIN: So what exactly is this congress of yours, and what's on the agenda?

NINA: You heard what Neznamov was up to yesterday?

DUDUKIN: Yes, I not only heard, I was almost an eyewitness to the whole edifying spectacle. I got there just too late, which I greatly regret.

NINA: Yes, well, he beat up Mukhoboev in the theatre buffet, during the performance.

DUDUKIN: And a damn good thing, too.

NINA: Mukhoboev's a well-respected man, he's even got hopes of becoming mayor.

DUDUKIN: I don't doubt it. But is that what the people hope?

NINA: Anyway, that's two circle seats gone, and a large slice of the stalls, at every benefit night. Now, I doubt if he'll even set foot in the theatre. So, we're meeting to draft a letter to Mukhoboev, to the effect that we disown Neznamov, and we're going to demand that the manager dismiss him. I'm telling you, I don't want to work with Neznamov ever again.

DUDUKIN: Really, why are you getting so het up about him, my lovely charmer?

NINA: Because he's impossible, he's quite unbearable! He's got a wicked sharp tongue and a thoroughly bad character. I mean, whenever any of the cast get together, especially if he's had a glass too many, he just goes on and on, and you can be sure he'll start sniping at somebody or other. And the things he says to the women! He's quite insufferable! I could cheerfully kill him.

DUDUKIN: What, does he insult you? Does he invent slanders about you? You'd certainly kill for that.

NINA: Well, no, I suppose he doesn't invent things. What he says is true enough, but why does he do it? Who asked him? He's the youngest person in the company, he's there to learn. We get together to have a good time, not to listen to him preaching. I mean, if you know something, you should keep it to yourself. All he does is poison our little community. I tell you, I'd be delighted to see the back of him. For somebody so young, practically still a boy, to be so bad-tempered!

DUDUKIN: He's been badly used, that's why he's bad-tempered. D'you think his life's been a bed of roses?

NINA: Don't try and defend him, please. So, you'll be staying here, then? Right, you can have half an hour with Madame Kruchinina, quarter of an hour would be plenty. Then you can look in at the shop and collect my shoes, buy some sweets at the confectioner's, and be at my place at twelve o'clock on the dot. Twelve o'clock, do you hear? Five minutes late and I'll lock the door on you.

DUDUKIN: Really, for how long?

NINA: For ever! I'm standing here talking to you, and Milovzorov's waiting for me in a cab.

DUDUKIN: What, you can't go out without an escort?

NINA: That's not jealousy, surely. Well, that's a new one. I mean, he is our juvenile lead, we make love every day on stage, it's time you got used to it.

DUDUKIN: Well, let him be your lover on stage and stay there. You'd be better taking along a comedian for company, they're more fun.

NINA: Huh, fun's all very well for you, you're only interested in trivia, but I'm a serious-minded woman. Anyway, twelve o'clock on the dot, see you get there. Goodbye.

DUDUKIN: Right, right, I'll take wing, shall I?

Nina exits. Enter Ivan.

IVAN: Madame Kruchinina's here, sir.

DUDUKIN: Excellent!

Kruchinina enters.

KRUCHININA: My dear Dudukin, how nice to see you! Excuse me for a second, will you, while I take off my hat?

IVAN: There was some actors here asking for you, ma'am – twice.

KRUCHININA: Actors?

IVAN: Dunno, ma'am – they wasn't top rank, anyhow.

KRUCHININA: So where are they now?

IVAN: They're still here, ma'am, in the billiard room.

KRUCHININA: Oh well, they can carry on playing, send them in later. *(exits left)*

DUDUKIN: You're a disgrace, man – you don't know the actors?

IVAN: What's their names? Oh, I did know, but I've forgot. One of 'em's wearing somebody else's coat, too big for him, like...

DUDUKIN: Shmaga, is it?

IVAN: That's the one, that's him.

Kruchinina re-enters. Ivan exits.

KRUCHININA: Honestly, Dudukin, you should be ashamed of yourself. Bringing me more gifts? You're really spoiling me. I can't take these, it's not right. That's tea and caviar you've brought me today.

DUDUKIN: Well, you've got to eat something. Our hotels are in a dreadful state. Anyway, what sort of trifles are these? Tea, caviar, all these bouquets and wreaths I've been sending – they're not even worth talking about. It's a small price to pay for all the happiness, all the pleasure you bring to us with your talent.

KRUCHININA: Everyone says you're the soul of kindness.

DUDUKIN: Well, I do possess that quality, but I must say it's inherited from my parents, and no particular merit of my own. Anyway, it's not that important an attribute. If I didn't have my kind heart, I shouldn't be worth much, I can tell you!

KRUCHININA: Oh, it's a wonderful thing to have, believe me.

DUDUKIN: Yes, but I got it cheap, you might say, it didn't cost me any effort.

KRUCHININA: It's dear just the same.

DUDUKIN: Whatever you say, I won't argue with you. I know my limitations, I've no talent for anything, not even practical matters, so in order not to be completely idle, I've made it my occupation, if you like, to brighten up the lives of actors.

KRUCHININA: And actresses?

DUDUKIN: And actresses. I mean, for example, a touring company comes to our town, to entertain people who do absolutely nothing, they're interested in nothing, they want nothing, and the actors are stuck here like crabs on a sandbank. People round these parts are for the most part solid, sober citizens, wealthy philanthropists and the like, staid in the extreme.

KRUCHININA: What more could you ask?

DUDUKIN: Yes, but as far as their morals, and mental development is concerned, they're still in the most primitive state of ignorance, and they have only the haziest notion of the very existence of the dramatic art. And actors are very special folk – proletarians, as they say in the West, or as we call them in Russia, "birds of heaven". Where there's grain scattered for them they eat, where there's none they starve. How can you help feeling sorry for them?

KRUCHININA: Well, yes, but I imagine it's rather more than pity that attracts you to actresses.

DUDUKIN: That's true, my dear lady. You're absolutely correct. Yes, there's not much of the saint in me, but plenty of the old Adam. I'm your common or garden naughty old man, there's no shortage of us in this town. Anyway, you were at the Governor's house?

KRUCHININA: Yes, I went there to thank him. There was a bit of a row in the theatre buffet last night during the show, and a young actor called Neznamov's being blamed for it. The manager came running into my dressing-room in a state of alarm, and declared that Neznamov was in dire straits, he's only been kept on in the company thanks to the Governor's forbearance, and he'd already told him he'd be expelled from the town if he caused any more trouble, since that wasn't the first time, and his passport isn't in order, either. Anyway, the Governor came backstage after the show, and I asked him there and then to pardon Neznamov. He said Neznamov ought to be taught a lesson, but for my sake he'd let the incident pass, provided it ended peaceably. And so it's turned out, apparently. Tell me what you know about these ongoings, and this Neznamov. He's still quite young, I believe?

DUDUKIN: Well, I can give you a very brief biography, as he himself told it to me. He has no knowledge of either his mother or his father, and he was brought up in some far-off place practically on the edge of Siberia. He lived there with a childless couple, reasonably well-to-do, middle class types, and for long enough he looked on them as his parents. They loved him, treated him very well, though they weren't above flinging his origins in his face, when they got angry with him. Naturally, he'd no idea what they meant at first, and it was only later that he managed to work it out. They even got him an education: he went off to some cheap boarding-school and managed to acquire quite a decent education, at least for a provincial actor. Anyway, he lived like that until he was fifteen, then his sufferings began, which he still can't recall without a shudder. This civil servant, his father, died and the widow married a retired surveyor, which was the start of endless drinking bouts, fights and arguments, mostly directed at him. He was driven out into the kitchen, and took his meals with the servants. Often he'd be flung out of the house at night, with nowhere to sleep but under the stars. Sometimes the rows and beatings got so bad he'd walk out of the house himself, and go missing for a week or more, living with casual labourers, tramps and beggars. From that time onwards, he heard nothing but dog's abuse from people. Living like that made him very bitter and withdrawn, so that he'd bite you as soon as look at you. Anyway, one fine morning they flung him out of the house for good. He joined a company of strolling players, and travelled with them on to the next town. However, when it was discovered that he'd no papers, he was sent back home under police escort. It turned out all his documents had been lost, and they kept harassing him non-stop, until eventually they issued him with some sort of copy on petition. Anyway, that's allowed him to travel with various managers from one town to the next, but under the constant threat of the police at any time sending him back home.

KRUCHININA: He's called Grigory...

DUDUKIN: That's right, Grigory.

KRUCHININA: And how old is he?

DUDUKIN: Oh, about twenty-three.

KRUCHININA: Not less?

DUDUKIN: No, certainly not less. Why does he interest you?

KRUCHININA: Oh, just coincidence... Anyway, don't mind me, it's just my imagination. Forgive me for interrupting.

DUDUKIN: Well, as far as yesterday's little scene is concerned, it's a familiar story. Things like that happen all the time with us. One of our most respected citizens, Mukhoboev, was so taken with your performance yesterday that he got drunk by the first act. He started carrying on in the buffet, pestering everybody, buying them drinks, hugging and kissing them. Then Neznamov appears, and he even attaches himself to him. Anyway, Neznamov makes to leave the buffet, in order to get rid of him, and Mukhoboev loses his rag, starts cursing and swearing at Neznamov in the most offensive manner.

KRUCHININA: What on earth for?

DUDUKIN: Because he refused to drink with him. I'm doing him the honour, he says, of buying this doorstep brat a drink, and he has the effrontery to turn me down!

KRUCHININA: What do you mean, 'doorstep brat'?

DUDUKIN: Well, abandoned as a child, I suppose, left on somebody's doorstep or under a hedge.

KRUCHININA: But that's terrible! Are there really people like that, I mean, capable of that kind of senseless behaviour?

DUDUKIN: Unfortunately, yes, a fair number. Anyway, an insult like that had to be answered, and Neznamov just about made mincemeat out of friend Mukhoboev. He was absolutely furious at first, wanted to make an official complaint, have Neznamov sent to Siberia, but some good people talked him out of it, and they were eventually reconciled, over a round of drinks. However, the noise had attracted the police, and the whole business might've turned out very badly for Neznamov, if it hadn't been for your intervention. But what a performance you gave last night! No wonder people were getting drunk from sheer joy. You really conveyed that poor mother's feelings so well!

KRUCHININA: Well, I *am* an actress, after all.

DUDUKIN: Yes, but to put over her situation so convincingly, you've surely got to have experienced it, you've got to have lived through it yourself, or at least something similar.

KRUCHININA: Oh, my dear Dudukin, I've lived so through many things, had so many experiences, that there's virtually no dramatic situation new to me.

DUDUKIN: So, your laurels didn't come cheap?

KRUCHININA: No, the laurels come later, first it's tears and sorrow.

DUDUKIN: But the mother's emotions, her passionate love for her son, her desperation...

KRUCHININA: I've been a mother too, I've watched my son die, just like that English lady I played last night. Only my son died when he was still a baby... *(breaks down, weeping)*

DUDUKIN: Oh God, now I've made you cry. I'm sorry, please forgive me.

KRUCHININA: It's all right. It's good to cry sometimes, and I don't do that very often nowadays. I'm actually grateful to you for reviving memories of my past life. There's a great deal of sorrow there, but even the most bitter sorrow can be welcome. I don't try to escape from the past, in fact I consciously try to keep my memories alive. And if I cry a little, well, that's no great tragedy. Women enjoy a good cry. Anyway, I went for a drive around your town yesterday. It hasn't changed much. I recognised many of the buildings, and even the trees, so there was a great deal to remind of my former life, good and bad alike.

DUDUKIN: So this isn't your first visit here?

KRUCHININA: Indeed no, I was actually born in this town, and spent almost all my youth here. I'd intended just to pass through at first, on my way to Saratov and Rostov, but your manager discovered I was in the area and asked me to give a few performances, to improve the box-office, which I gather has been falling off, and I'm not sorry now that I agreed to stay.

DUDUKIN: So, did you leave here a long time ago?

KRUCHININA: Seventeen years to the day.

DUDUKIN: And you haven't met any old friends or relatives? No-one's recognised you?

KRUCHININA: I haven't any relatives. And I lived here very quietly, with scarcely any friends, so there's really no-one to recognise me. I drove past the house I used to live in yesterday, and asked the coachman to stop. I took it all in again – the porch, the windows, the shutters, the fence, I even peeped in at the garden. Oh God, you've no idea what memories flashed through my mind. I've too vivid an imagination, I'm afraid, at the cost of my better judgment.

DUDUKIN: Well, that's no vice, dear lady – that's true of many women.

KRUCHININA: At the drop of a hat, I can be whisked back in time seventeen years, to imagine myself sitting in my old room, sewing. Suddenly, I feel depressed, and I snatch up my shawl, put it over my head, and hurry out to see my little boy. I play with him, we talk together. I can picture him so vividly. That's probably because I never saw him dead. I never saw him in his little coffin, or in the grave.

DUDUKIN: But how did that happen? I'm sorry, I don't mean to pry.

KRUCHININA: No, I don't mind being so open with you, you're a good man. Anyway, what happened was that they told me my son was sick, at the very moment I discovered that his father had been unfaithful to me, and was secretly intending to leave me for another woman. I was already reeling, utterly destroyed, and now on top of that, my son's illness. I rushed to his bedside, and found my baby already showing no sign of life. He was beginning to go blue, like a corpse, and he had stopped breathing. All I could hear was a kind of wheezing sound, coming from his throat. I fell on him, hugging and kissing him, and I must have lost consciousness. They took me back home like that, in a dead faint, and by evening it was obvious I had a bad case of diphtheria. I was ill for about six weeks, and I could still barely stand up when an old aunt, the only relative I had, and a distant one at that, took me to live with her in the country. Eventually I was handed a letter there, in which I was informed that my son had died, and been buried by his father – that my little angel was now in Heaven, praying for his parents. The letter had been written some time before, but they had kept it from me. Later on, I went with my aunt to the Crimea, where she had a little house, and we lived there for three years in perfect solitude.

DUDUKIN: And what happened after that?

KRUCHININA: Oh, nothing of any great interest. My aunt and I travelled extensively, I lived abroad quite a long time. Then my aunt died, and I inherited a substantial part of her estate. I was a reasonably wealthy woman, quite independent, but I was so idle, I'd no idea what to do with myself. Anyway, I gave it a great deal of thought, and decided to become an actress. I've played mostly in the South, though, and never once in this part of the world. Now I've turned up here quite by chance, and I'm remembering so vividly my youth, and my son – for whom I can still cry, as you see. I'm a strange woman, don't you think – completely at the mercy of my emotions, which can take such a grip on me that I now and again even experience hallucinations.

DUDUKIN: You should try and get treatment, dear lady. These days there are some excellent remedies for an over-active imagination. They work wonders, by all accounts.

KRUCHININA: But I don't want to be cured. I enjoy my affliction. I enjoy conjuring up the image of my son, talking to him, and believing that he's still alive. Sometimes I'm actually in a state of fright, trembling all over, expecting him to appear before me at any moment.

DUDUKIN: Supposing he did appear? Surely you wouldn't even recognise him?

KRUCHININA: No, I'd recognise him all right. My heart would tell me.

DUDUKIN: Yes, but you're imagining him as an infant, and if he
was alive now, he'd be twenty. Just imagine your dreams were to
come true, and you saw your son again... Say someone told you he
was coming here this very minute...

KRUCHININA: No, don't! *(covers her face with her hands)*

DUDUKIN: In your mind's eye you see a smiling, angelic little face,
with lovely fair silken curls...

KRUCHININA: Yes, that's right – silken curls...

DUDUKIN: Instead of which, in walks some shaggy-haired layabout
like Neznamov, reeking of cheap cigarettes and brandy.

KRUCHININA: Stop it, please. That's enough. It's no laughing matter.

DUDUKIN: I'm not laughing, dear lady. I'm just trying to make you
see the truth of the matter. It's no use brooding over something
that happened seventeen years ago. It's not healthy. You stay at
home too much, you need cheering up, a bit more fun in your life.
(looks at his watch) Oh dear, I'm afraid I've got quite carried away.
(stands up, looks at the mantelpiece) Well, anyway, you've had
plenty of visitors.

KRUCHININA: They're only cards. Ivan puts them out on the
mantelshelf, but I hardly ever receive anyone.

DUDUKIN: *(glancing at one of the cards)* Mm... there's one here from
Grigory Murov.

KRUCHININA: What? What was that name?

DUDUKIN: Murov. Grigory Murov. If you'd known him in the old
days, you certainly wouldn't recognise him now. He's an
important man these days, terribly rich, one of the most influential
people in the whole region. Anyway, I must say goodbye, though
you be perfection among women... *(kisses Kruchinina's hand)*
That's what I'm going to call you – perfection.

KRUCHININA: Goodbye, my dear Dudukin.

   Dudukin exits.

Ivan!

Ivan enters.

No matter whether I'm in or out, you must never admit Mr Murov to my rooms, do you understand?

IVAN: Yes, ma'am. *(exits)*

KRUCHININA: So, Murov's grown rich, become a great man, pillar of the community. And what a pathetic, shamefaced, insignificant creature he was when we saw each other for the last time, when I flung him out of my house. I can still picture it all so clearly, as if it had happened only yesterday. And the night before that fatal day I had been to see my little Grisha. *(covers her face with her hands)* Arina was holding him up at the window, partly wrapped in her shawl. When I approached, he began tapping with his little fingers on the glass, and trying to hide under the shawl. Then he peeped out again and went into fits of laughter. He was jumping around so much that Arina could scarcely hold onto him, waving his arms, his little cheeks burning bright red. Oh, I can see him! There he is, I see him even now!

> *Enter Neznamov and Shmaga, who is eating the remains of a sandwich.*

KRUCHININA: *(steps back in alarm)* Oh!

NEZNAMOV: What's wrong, did I give you a fright?

KRUCHININA: I'm so sorry...

NEZNAMOV: Don't be frightened. I'm your colleague in art, or maybe I'd better say trade. What d'you reckon – art or trade?

KRUCHININA: Whatever you like. It depends on your point of view.

NEZNAMOV: Well, no doubt it suits you to call your acting art, and who's to stop you? But frankly, I think of my acting as a trade, and a pretty lousy one at that.

KRUCHININA: You walked in so unexpectedly...

NEZNAMOV: Yes, this is the second time we've been here today.

KRUCHININA: That's right, they told me.

NEZNAMOV: So, we weren't all that unexpected. I say 'we' because I'm with my friend. Allow me to present – Shmaga the actor!

Comedian in real life, villain on stage. Oh, don't imagine he plays murderers, that's not his line at all. He actually plays all kinds of parts, even distinguished Papas – it's just that he murders every play he's in! Well, go on, Shmaga, take a bow!

Shmaga bows.

KRUCHININA: Well, gentlemen, what can I do for you?

NEZNAMOV: We'd like a talk with you. Of course, you can fling us out right now, you'd be perfectly entitled to, so feel free.

KRUCHININA: Good heavens, why should I do that? Come in, gentlemen, please. Sit down.

NEZNAMOV: Right, let's sit down, Shmaga. It's not every day we're received so graciously.

They sit down. Shmaga casually sprawls in an armchair.

Actually, the matter only concerns myself, but I'm volunteering Shmaga to represent me, since he's so eloquent.

SHMAGA: We've heard from our dear patron Dudukin, that you had a word backstage with the Governor .

KRUCHININA: That's right.

SHMAGA: And you spoke up for my friend Grisha here?

KRUCHININA: I did. And the Governor promised that he wouldn't take any action against Mr Neznamov this time.

SHMAGA: I see, I see – so tell me, please – exactly what gave you the right to speak on behalf of Grisha? He didn't engage you as his counsel, did he?

KRUCHININA: Really, I don't understand what it is you want of me, gentlemen. I was told Mr Neznamov was in very serious trouble.

NEZNAMOV: So what if I was? What business is that of yours?

KRUCHININA: Well, I'm sorry, but if I have the opportunity to get somebody out of trouble, without too much effort, then I'll do so without a thought. I don't consider it a right, but an obligation – a duty, if you like.

NEZNAMOV: *(mocking)* Making people happy – a do-gooder, no less.

SHMAGA: And without too much effort, note. No, you can make whoever you like happy, but not actors, d'you hear? *(jabs his finger at her, then slumps back even deeper into the armchair)* Actors are too proud!

KRUCHININA: *(rises)* Well, that's too bad, but I'm afraid I act as my conscience directs me. I simply follow my heart, I have no ulterior motives, and I don't think I need justify myself, no matter what you think of me.

NEZNAMOV: See? I told you to fling us out. You'd have saved yourself some trouble.

KRUCHININA: No, why should I? I I'm not even going to throw you out now. I've had plenty of abuse, and insults, all kinds of misery in my life, I'm well used to it. Right now I'm very hurt, but I'm also interested. Fate has thrown us together, and I need to find out more about you, your thoughts, your outlook on life. So tell me, please, what's on your mind.

NEZNAMOV: Oh, yes, my dear lady, I' ll tell you. I mean, you're already complaining you've been hurt. But you've known plenty of other feelings, you've had it good, a sweet life, so why not a little pain, for the sake of variety? Yes, and you just imagine a man, who from the very day of his birth has known no other feeling but pain, who hurts all the time, all over. I'm so sick at heart, that every single glance, every single word, causes me pain. I feel pain whenever people talk about me, whether it's good or ill, it makes no difference. And what's even more painful, is when they pity me, when they're kind to me. That's like a knife in my heart. All I want from people is to be left in peace – that they should forget I even exist!

KRUCHININA: I didn't know.

NEZNAMOV: Well, now you do, so you can scatter your blessings a little less generously in future. Think twice. No doubt you wanted to save me from being run out of town. What for? You think you've done me a favour? Not in the least. I've been down that road before, it's nothing new to me. I've had to march under guard while I was still only a child, and through no fault of my own, either.

SHMAGA: Yes, because he'd no documents, he didn't have a passport. Forgot to hang onto his label, as it were, didn't know his proper name – no dad, so no patronymic – didn't know how to give his betters their place at the top table, and all that.

NEZNAMOV: You see? Even he makes a fool of me. And he's right. I'm
   nothing, less than nothing, and he's at least something, a member of
   society, with a name, and a passport, even. And on his papers it says:
   "Son of retired office clerk; expelled from college for bad behaviour;
   employed as copy clerk to the Orphans' Court, dismissed for
   dereliction of duty; charged with complicity in the theft of a woollen
   greatcoat, and released on suspicion." Now that's the kind of
   document you can be proud of! That's a proper passport. He's a lucky
   man, he can look anybody straight in the eye and say who he is and
   what he is. And I'm supposed to be delighted, that thanks to your
   intervention, I can stay here, in this rat-hole? They're trying to get rid
   of me in the theatre, and they'll do it soon enough. And what sort of
   figure will I make then, d'you think? A tramp, with nobody to call my
   own, and no fixed occupation. And with a title like that you can't live
   anywhere, not in any town. Or rather you can, but only as a guest of
   the state – locked up, in other words. I'm not a thief, I've no
   inclination to that sort of work. I'm not a highwayman or a murderer, I
   don't have the right bloodthirsty instincts. Even so, I feel as if I'm on a
   slippery slope, and whether I will or no, I'm headed straight for prison.
   People like me are best left alone: charity only makes them more bitter.

KRUCHININA: But why, for God's sake, why?

NEZNAMOV: Well, for instance, look at us. You mean nothing to me, I
   really don't care whether you live or die. We're ships that pass in the
   night, and that's how it should be. But here you are, thrusting your
   benevolence on me, and expecting me to be grateful for it. And even
   supposing I don't thank you, I'll still get no peace. The other actors'll
   take every opportunity to fling your charity in my face: "Yes, you
   wouldn't be here, if it wasn't for Kruchinina. If it wasn't for her,
   you'd be tramping the roads!" They'll keep on at me, till eventually
   I'll come to loathe you. And that's not what I want, I'd rather remain
   indifferent to you. I can understand how tempting it is to play Lady
   Bountiful, especially when people shower you with compliments all
   the time, and you're used to getting your own way, but you can't
   always expect gratitude. Now and again you'll run into hostility.

KRUCHININA: Actually quite often. I know that.

NEZNAMOV: And it doesn't put you off?

KRUCHININA: I'm never put off. The urge to do good's very strong.

NEZNAMOV: That's odd. It might be a good idea to restrain it.

KRUCHININA: Well now, gentlemen – I've heard you out with great

patience, and I'm sorry for the trouble I've caused by intervening on
your behalf. However, I'm afraid, Mr Neznamov, that you've rather
abused that patience. You might've confined yourself to your own
affair, but you've taken the liberty of judging my actions and offering
me advice. You're still quite young, you really know nothing of life.
The people you mixed with as a child, and indeed even now, are
very far from the best sort. And you've no right to make such
sweeping generalisations, when you've hardly ever met decent
people, or lived amongst them. You've only ever seen life from the...

SHMAGA: From the gutter?

KRUCHININA: That's not what I was going to say.

SHMAGA: Why not? It's the truth, isn't it?

NEZNAMOV: Who cares? It's only words.

KRUCHININA: I'm more experienced than you, and I've lived
longer. And I know that there's a great deal of nobility in people, a
great deal of love and self-sacrifice, especially among women.

NEZNAMOV: Really?

KRUCHININA: You've never witnessed it?

NEZNAMOV: Can't say as I have, no.

KRUCHININA: That's very sad.

NEZNAMOV: So where are these rare specimens to be found?

KRUCHININA: Everywhere, if you care to look. They're not rare,
there are plenty of them. And you don't need to look far – you've
heard of the sisters of mercy?

NEZNAMOV: Yes.

KRUCHININA: And what do you think makes them endure the most
incredible hardship and deprivation, danger, even?

NEZNAMOV: I've no idea.

KRUCHININA: And not only the sisters of mercy, there are many
women who've devoted their entire lives to looking after orphans,
sick people, people who can't fend for themselves, or who are

suffering through no fault of their own. And that's not all – there are loving souls who don't even care whether a person is suffering through their own fault or another's – they're ready to help anybody, even people who... who...

NEZNAMOV: Stuck for a word? Go on, say it, feel free.

KRUCHININA: Even those who are hopelessly depraved. What do you know about love?

NEZNAMOV: What I've read. In novels.

KRUCHININA: Has no-one ever loved you?

NEZNAMOV: What can I say? Not really. No, I'm impossible to love.

KRUCHININA: What d'you mean?

NEZNAMOV: Look, you can't love somebody who's hopelessly depraved, can you? What would be the point? Maybe to reform him? Well, in the first place, not everybody *can* be reformed, and in the second place, not everybody *wants* reforming, thank you very much.

KRUCHININA: They can still be loved.

NEZNAMOV: I doubt it.

KRUCHININA: And do you imagine the sisters of mercy, out of their love, only look after those people they can cure? Not at all – they take even more care of the hopelessly incurable, show them even greater love. I trust you'll admit now that there are women who do good with no thought of reward, from only the purest motives. That's true, isn't it? Isn't it?

NEZNAMOV: *(glumly)* I suppose so.

KRUCHININA: Anyway, I've said my piece. You're a bit put out, and annoyed. But once you've calmed down, just have a think about what you've said.

NEZNAMOV: Oh, come on, Shmaga, let's go. We've done what we came for – we've been rude to the nice lady, but what more can you expect from the likes of us?

SHMAGA: No, being rude's your forte, not mine – I'm the soul of tact. Just what was this conversation we've had? This is a mere prelude, the serious talking's still to come. I have another theme, which I'd now like to introduce in a minor key. However, I'd feel more at ease without witnesses.

NEZNAMOV: No, no – say what you have to. I know your tricks.

SHMAGA: Ma'am, we came to this hotel to discuss the matter you know about, but you were busy somewhere else. Anyway, you know what young people are like – there's a bar, a billiard room, various temptations... and of course, a shortage of funds. I mean, you know what us poor actors are like. In a word, we ran up a bill at the bar.

NEZNAMOV: *(severely)* What! What are you saying?

KRUCHININA: Don't worry, I'll see it gets paid. *(to Neznamov)* No, please – don't make a fuss, let me have this pleasure at least.

SHMAGA: Well, ma'am... *Merci beaucoup!* Anyway, it's only right, you shaould pay, it wasn't our fault you weren't here. And we couldn't wait outside in the lobby. As I said, we're actors, our place is at the bar.

NEZNAMOV: Right, you've had your say, that's enough. Come on, let's go.

SHMAGA: Hey, Grisha, leave go! Let me go, I'm telling you! *(to Kruchinina)* Anyway, I'm bound to inform you, ma'am, our future welfare isn't provided for either. I mean, you're a famous actress, you're getting almost half the the box office receipts, but it's a moot point who's responsible for the success of the play, or who's bringing in those receipts – it could be you, it could be us, nobody knows. So it wouldn't harm you to share with your colleagues...

> *Neznamov silently grips Shmaga by the collar, and propels him to the door. Shmaga turns and twists vainly in his grasp.*

Grisha! Grisha!

NEZNAMOV: *(thrusts Shmaga through the door)* Now, get out!

> *Shmaga hurriedly withdraws.*

KRUCHININA: You're ashamed of your friend?

NEZNAMOV: No, of myself.

KRUCHININA: Why do you take up with people like that?

NEZNAMOV: Who else is there, for somebody in my position? All right, you wouldn't exactly describe him as a moral giant. He'd sell his best friend up the river without a second thought, but really, in my experience, that's a fairly widespread failing among actors. And he does have a few priceless attributes – for instance, he'll go out in the freezing cold in a light summer coat without even flinching. He never complains of hunger, when he's got nothing to eat, and he never loses his temper, however much he's abused, and even beaten. I dare say he's angry deep down, but he never shows it.

KRUCHININA: He wears a summer coat even in winter?

NEZNAMOV: Well, you've seen him, haven't you. That's his entire wardrobe.

KRUCHININA: *(takes a ten-rouble note out of her purse)* Please, give him this from me.

NEZNAMOV: What's this? No, no, don't do that – he'll drink that up in no time.

KRUCHININA: Well, let him, if that's what he wants.

NEZNAMOV: You're throwing your money away.

KRUCHININA: You mean he won't be pleased to get it?

NEZNAMOV: Huh, won't he just!

KRUCHININA: Well, then, if he's pleased, that'll please me too. I enjoy giving. Now, listen, this is what I was going to ask you – you couldn't perhaps buy him a decent overcoat? I'll pay whatever it costs. Would you do that for me? It's not too much trouble?

NEZNAMOV: It's no trouble at all. *(bows)*

KRUCHININA: Goodbye, then.

NEZNAMOV: *(after a pause)* If I may be allowed to kiss your hand...

KRUCHININA: Oh, please...

NEZNAMOV: Look... if you're giving me it out of pity... If you really do object, I'd be glad if you'd say so, straight out.

KRUCHININA: No, of course I don't. I'm delighted.

NEZNAMOV: You know, I'm basically a bad lot – a worthless down-and-out.

Neznamov takes Kruchinina's hand.

KRUCHININA: *(softly, averting her eyes)* Don't say that. I can't bear to hear it.

Neznamov kisses her hand. She presses his head to her breast and hugs him fiercely.

NEZNAMOV: What are you doing? What was that for?

KRUCHININA: Oh, forgive me!

NEZNAMOV: You're asking my forgiveness? God help you! *(exits)*

IVAN: *(outside the door)* No, go away! Go on! The mistress is seeing nobody, I've told you!

KRUCHININA: Who is it, Ivan?

Ivan enters.

IVAN: It's some half-witted old beggar-woman, ma'am – she keeps hounding people.

KRUCHININA: Well, I'll give her something.

IVAN: Ma'am, she'll think you're a soft touch, you'll never get rid of her. Better I show her the door... *(exits)*

KRUCHININA: *(glances through the door)* Oh, my God, it can't be! It's her! Ivan, Ivan, bring her in!

Ivan re-enters with Arina.

Arina! Arina, don't you recognise me?

ARINA: Why, of course I do, your highness. Same as last year – you didn't forget to show mercy to a poor old woman then either, a poor miserable creature.

KRUCHININA: No, no – take a good look at me, please! Look hard!

ARINA: Oh, I'm sorry, my dear, it's gone clean out my head. It was the year before last, it was a pair of nice warm boots you gave me... Oh yes, I remember now...

KRUCHININA: Ivan, who is she? What's her name? Arina Galchikha, surely.

IVAN: Indeed it is, ma'am.

KRUCHININA: Ivan, leave us.

Ivan exits.

Where did you bury my poor Grisha? Arina? *(takes her by the shoulders)* My baby! Where did you bury my baby!

ARINA: Oh God, I ain't been in that line of work for nigh on fifteen year. That's right, I used to take in little 'uns, for money, made a decent living, too, and now I beg for my bread. I've got no folks, no family, no friends...

KRUCHININA: Take a good look at me, Arina, please, for pity's sake!

ARINA: Eh? Mother of God... it can't be... surely it's not... you're not... Lyubov Ivanovna?

KRUCHININA: Yes, yes, it's me! It's me, Arina!

ARINA: Oh God, now I remember – oh, you was so kind to me, ma'am, a real angel!

KRUCHININA: Arina, take me to his grave. Please, let's go right now!

ARINA: Eh? What grave, ma'am? Where?

KRUCHININA: My son, Arina, I had a son.

ARINA: That's right, a son, yes, so you had... What was his name now? Oh, God, I'd so many little 'uns. You remember General Bistrov? I looked after his little 'un as well, took in everybody's.

KRUCHININA: Arina, you're not making sense.

ARINA: And then there was them merchant folks, lived up by the church, fierce rich they was – she couldn't have got by without me. I helped her out too.

KRUCHININA: Arina, I'm talking about my son! My son!

ARINA: That's just what I'm saying – your son, too. And that widow woman, lived in that big house other side of the river, the one with the attic. That's where she kept...

KRUCHININA: Arina, for God's sake! My son! Grisha!

ARINA: Grisha? Oh yes, yes, now I remember...

KRUCHININA: *(sits Arina down on a chair)* He fell ill, you remember? He came down suddenly with a terrible disease. He could scarcely breathe – now do you remember? And he died.

ARINA: No, no, he got better. God saved him, he got better.

KRUCHININA: Arina, what are you saying? Have pity on me, for God's sake!

ARINA: I'm telling you he got better, ma'am!

KRUCHININA: So what happened to him? What happened, Arina?

ARINA: Oh, God, I fell on hard times, ma'am. I had a decent life them days, everything was just fine, and now I've got nothing. Ma'am, if you could spare me a few old clothes...

KRUCHININA: Oh, for God's sake, if it's money you want – here, take it, take it all, just tell me! *(puts money on the table)* Where's my Grisha, what did you do with him?

ARINA: Oh, ma'am... God punished me, that's what happened, that's what I was punished for...

KRUCHININA: What do you mean? Punished for what? You said he got better...

ARINA: Yes, yes, that's true, he did get better, in no time at all, ma'am. *(eyeing the money)* Yes, the Lord looks after His own, and here's me a poor wretch...

KRUCHININA: I've already said, the money's all yours, if you'll only tell me – please, I beg you...

ARINA: Tell you what, ma'am?

KRUCHININA: About Grisha! My little Grisha!

ARINA: The little fair-haired boy?

KRUCHININA: Yes, yes. You say God punished you because of him
  – what do you mean?

ARINA: Oh, no... oh, ma'am... now I remember...

KRUCHININA: Oh, God in Heaven, now she remembers! Well, go
  on, go on! *(kneels before Arina and gazes intently into her eyes)*

ARINA: Yes, the very second he starts pulling round, he cries all the
  time for his mama, keeps asking for her...

KRUCHININA: *(her voice breaking)* For his mama, you say?

ARINA: That's right – reaches out his little arms and says, "Mama!
  Mama!"

KRUCHININA: Oh, my God! Oh, my God! Mama! Mama! Go on,
  go on...

ARINA: Well, I thinks, what am I going to do with him? I can keep
  him by me, but fat chance I'll get paid for that. Anyway, there's
  that couple – I don't remember their name – but God didn't give
  'em no children. And she comes to me and says, "You get hold of
  some poor orphan for me, and I'll love him like my own son. So,
  anyway, I gives him to her – got a lot of money off her, too... I
  mean, for bringing him up, I says, that's two years I got nothing for
  him, so pay up, I says! And she did. So then I goes to Grigory...
  what's his name? Well, you know who I mean... Anyway, I goes to
  Grigory and says I've give the child away. Well done, he says,
  that's just fine. And he gives me a heap of money too.

KRUCHININA: Then what happened?

ARINA: Why, nothing – turned out nicely, didn't it.

KRUCHININA: Did you see him? Did you go to visit him?

ARINA: Oh, I seen him all right... Yes, and not that long ago, neither.

KRUCHININA: *(alarmed)* You've seen him, recently?

ARINA: Oh yes, running about the garden, he was, pushing his little cart. In a little blue shirt...

KRUCHININA: *(moves away from her)* What are you talking about? He's twenty now!

ARINA: Twenty? Twenty years old? No, he's a little boy.

KRUCHININA: Yes, yes, Arina – oh, God, what are you saying?

ARINA: Oh, ma'am, forgive me. It was the money made me say it... You begged me to talk, so that's what I did, I just said them things to put your mind at ease, I don't know nothing, it's all gone blank... This head of mine's all muddled up, I can't think straight no more... Ma'am, if I could just have a little breather...

KRUCHININA: Yes, yes, go and have a lie down... *(shows Arina into the next room)*

ARINA: If there's anything I know... I'll try and remember... *(exits)*

KRUCHININA: *(sits down at the table)* Oh, how cruel, how dreadfully cruel! I grieve for my son, I'm brokenhearted, and they tell me he's dead. I cry for him endlessly, I try to escape, to find some corner of this world where I might forget my sorrow, and he keeps holding out his little arms to me, calling "Mama! Mama!" Oh God, how cruel! *(slumps forward, sobbing)*

END OF ACT TWO

ACT THREE

The scene is a ladies' dressing-room in the theatre, the wallpaper torn in some places, peeling off in others; at the rear, a door leading onto the stage; a table with an old worn armchair, the remainder a motley collection of furniture. Nina Korinkina is sprawled in the armchair, deep in thought. Milovzorov enters.

NINA: Who's that?

MILOVZOROV: It's only me, darling.

NINA: Close the door!

MILOVZOROV: What for?

NINA: People keep snooping about, eavesdropping.

MILOVZOROV: It's your nerves, my dear.

NINA: Of course it is. It'd get on anybody's nerves. I don't understand it, everybody seems to have gone mad. Honestly, sane people just don't do these things.

MILOVZOROV: Who are you talking about?

NINA: I'm talking about the audience, at last night's show. I mean, what's so special about Madame Kruchinina, that they should go berserk like that? Well, go on, tell me. I'm asking you, what's so special about her?

MILOVZOROV: Well, her subtle French style of playing...

NINA: You idiot! Get out of here! What've you come into my dressing-room for? To talk rubbish, I suppose. Well, I can do without that. I think you try to annoy me on purpose.

MILOVZOROV: What, can't I have my own opinion?

NINA: No, of course you can't, because you don't know anything about it. Besides which, it's disloyal of you. If the audience want to go mad, well, let them, but not you, surely. You've got your own actress, you should be sticking up for me! You just don't appreciate me, or what I've done for you. I mean, really, who do you think you are? You ought to be...

MILOVZOROV: But, darling, I do, I do appreciate everything you've
done for me.

NINA: It's me that taught you how to behave on stage, how to hold
yourself, how to stand, how to walk. You just remember what you
were like – a wretched little hairdresser!

MILOVZOROV: And I'm grateful to you, honestly, but why all the
name-calling? It's a bit strong, darling. *(tries to kiss Nina's hand)*

NINA: Huh, all lovey-dovey, are we? Get away from me! *(stands up)*
You know, there's nothing special about her, nothing at all. Oh, she
has feeling, but so what? That's quite commonplace, plenty of women
have feeling. And as for her acting, well, I've seen the great French
actresses, and she's nothing like them. And what really annoys me
is the pretence she puts up, all that false modesty, she carries on as
if she were a schoolgirl, as if she were some sort of nun, for God's
sake. And everybody falls for it, that's what really annoys me.

MILOVZOROV: Well, she is modest, you've got to allow her that.

NINA: You're sticking up for her again? No, no, you can say what
you like about her modesty to other people, but not me, I know
different. I know too much about her.

MILOVZOROV: Yes, and I do.

NINA: All right, then, what do you know?

MILOVZOROV: Probably the same as you. Dudukin told me.

NINA: Oh, that's nice! He swears me to silence, then goes off
blabbing to everybody. Well, that's just fine, if he can talk, I've no
intention of shutting up. Why should I keep other people's secrets?

MILOVZOROV: Anyway, it all happened ages ago, and after that she...

NINA: What do you mean, "after that"? Honestly, you get on my
nerves, you do. Are you really so stupid as to believe her? That's
quite funny, actually. She tells everybody that she's spent years
abroad, companion to some old lady or other, and that she's been
left all her fortune, out of gratitude. I mean, what sort of halfwit
would believe that? Some elderly gentleman, yes, but not a lady.
That would be more like the thing. You do get old fools like that,
it's well known, just ripe for the picking. But an old lady? Oh yes,
they've been known to leave their fortunes abroad, it's not

unheard of, but not to female companions! And besides, if she's
got money, what's she doing becoming an actress? Why's she
traipsing across Russia, stealing the bread out of our mouths? It's
obvious she just can't stay in one spot – some sort of scandal
happens in one place, she has to move on to the next, then another
scandal, and she moves on to a third, and so on.

MILOVZOROV: From what I hear, she does a great many good deeds.

NINA: Yes, to get herself talked about. You can do what you like if
you've got money. All right, she spoke up for Neznamov, but you
ask her why she did that. She doesn't even know herself. She'll
clear off, and we're stuck with that useless creature!

MILOVZOROV: It's just a pity she's leaving so soon, otherwise he'd
show her what he was really like.

NINA: Yes, well, he still can. I've had an idea at the back of my
mind since yesterday. The only trouble is that I can't depend on
any of you lot.

MILOVZOROV: Oh, come on, darling, why d'you say that? You
know I'd do anything for you.

NINA: You really mean that? Word of honour?

MILOVZOROV: Cross my heart!

NINA: Then listen – I'm going to ask Dudukin to invite her to his
house this evening. There's no performance, of course, and we'll
invite Neznamov too, get him thoroughly drunk. All we'll have to
do is wind him up, and let the music begin!

MILOVZOROV: Chances are he won't go to Dudukin's house – he
doesn't like company.

NINA: Well, I'll work on him somehow. And you can prepare him
beforehand, feed him with some topic of conversation. Give him
the whole story on Kruchinina, why should you spare her feelings?
And you needn't try and duck out of this one, my darling. I have
to know, once and for all, if you're friend or foe.

MILOVZOROV: Mm – I'm a little wary of taking him on – he's so
much cleverer than me.

NINA: Well, that's your business. Really, how can you have the audacity to play great heroic lovers on stage, if you're afraid to sacrifice yourself, even just once in your life, for me, for everything I've done?

MILOVZOROV: All right, all right, darling, I'll do it.

NINA: Just think, what a carry-on there'll be! Wonderful!

DUDUKIN: *(off-stage, at the door)* May I come in?

NINA: Yes, of course you may. What sort of question's that? *(aside to Milovzorov)* Stand back a bit...

Dudukin enters.

MILOVZOROV: Good morning, Nil! *(takes a cigarette case out of Dudukin's side pocket, helps himself to some cigarettes and transfers them to his own case, while Dudukin pays no attention.)*

DUDUKIN: *(to Nina)* Well, how are you feeling, my darling? You seemed very out of sorts last night.

NINA: What gave you that idea? I'm perfectly well, thank you.

DUDUKIN: Good, good, I'm delighted to hear it.

MILOVZOROV: You're well supplied with these?

DUDUKIN: Oh, take them, my dear chap, don't stand on ceremony.

MILOVZOROV: Now, whenever did I do that? You hurt my feelings, sir. *(puts the cigarette case back in Dudukin's pocket)*

DUDUKIN: *(to Nina)* Permit me to press your snowy white little hand to my unworthy lips... *(kisses her hand)*

NINA: Yes, I'm in perfect health, Dudukin, but I'd advise you to consult a doctor without delay. I'm beginning to have serious doubts about you.

DUDUKIN: Oh? Why's that? No, I can't complain. I'm not aware of any sort of ailment.

NINA: I'm afraid you're finally losing your mind. Don't your hands hurt after yesterday's little show?

DUDUKIN: Oh, I see, I see. Yes, I did go rather over the top, didn't

I. But really, what a performance! You were on stage, Petya, you can say – that scene she played opposite you, for instance...

MILOVZOROV: Oh well, I bring out the best in any actress – I have such passion.

DUDUKIN: Passion? You messed up your lines twice last night, it was unbelievable.

MILOVZOROV: Oh, come on, Dudukin, I was fired up, you go too fast, you get tongue-tied at times.

DUDUKIN: And the way you pronounce foreign words! God only knows what you'll come out with.

MILOVZOROV: Well, the parts are badly written out. And anyway, why should I make an effort? All right, you know the difference, but as for the rest... It makes no odds to them, the sort of audiences we play to.

DUDUKIN: Yes, well, those of us who *do* understand are driven to distraction. I sit there thinking, "Merciful God, just where is he getting those words from!" For all I know you might as well be speaking double Dutch! I mean, no offence, my dear chap, but...

MILOVZOROV: Oh, none taken, to be sure. No, you're absolutely right, Dudukin. Other people have said the same thing, but for the money I'm getting, why bother to put myself out?

DUDUKIN: *(to Nina)* And as for you, my unspeakably lovely lady, please don't be angry with me. I adore beauty in all its forms, but people of taste have a quite different attitude towards beauty in art, from that in real life. You have no grounds for jealousy.

NINA: What? Who told you I was jealous? I'll prove the opposite, this very minute!

DUDUKIN: Please do, my angel!

NINA: I mean, you show your admiration for Madame Kruchinina, you send her flowers, you take up collections for her – d'you think she actually needs these things? She's had all that stuff before. You just haven't a clue, have you, about how to really please her. She's staying in dingy rooms in a squalid little hotel, and there's no performance tonight – what d'you think she'll be doing? Two or three moth-eaten fans'll drop in to see her, and go into stupid ecstasies – if you'll forgive my saying – and d'you think she'll enjoy that? You haven't actually introduced her to anybody, and she only sees the actors at rehearsals. So why don't you throw a party at your house tonight, with a decent supper, just a few select people, and invite her so she can meet them ? You invite your friends, and you can leave the actors to me – I'll know who to ask. Well, d'you like my idea? Does that sound like jealousy?

DUDUKIN: No, it certainly doesn't! A first-rate idea, excellent! *Merci,* my little treasure. What is it they say? A woman's mind... a woman's mind...

MILOVZOROV: A woman's mind is a genuine find.

DUDUKIN: Yes, that's absolutely true. I'd never have thought of that. I suppose we're such an ungrateful lot, Petya, we just don't kiss the ladies' hands enough.

> *Shmaga enters wearing a new overcoat and a hat at a jaunty angle. He bows.*

SHMAGA: *(to Dudukin)* My beloved patron, enlightened champion of all the arts! You couldn't oblige me with a cigar, could you?

DUDUKIN: Of course. Any particular brand?

SHMAGA: Oh, I only ever smoke the one sort.

DUDUKIN: And which might that be?

SHMAGA: Other people's.

> *Dudukin gives him a cigar, which Shmaga wraps in paper and puts in his pocket.*

This is for after, at lunch.

MILOVZOROV: Shmaga, you haven't seen Neznamov, by any chance? Is he going to be at rehearsal?

SHMAGA: How should I know? I'm not his nursemaid.

NINA: I thought you two were inseparable?

SHMAGA: Well, these things happen. Even husbands and wives split up, so why not friends?

DUDUKIN: Wonders'll never cease! So what's come between you?

SHMAGA: *(importantly)* We couldn't agree on our convictions.

NINA: You're joking. What sort of convictions did you two ever have?

DUDUKIN: True enough, Shmaga, I can't say I noticed them before.

SHMAGA: You're wasting your time. I have very firm convictions.
Yesterday, against all expectations, I suddenly acquire some
money, right out of the blue, you wouldn't believe it.

MILOVZOROV: Oh yes, we can see that, from the new outfit.

SHMAGA: And so firm are my convictions, that I'm convinced I
need to drink it up as quickly as possible. And you say I have no
convictions? What do you call those, eh? Anyway, I tried to talk
Grisha into heading for the tavern – The Boon Companions,
actually – but he didn't share my convictions.

DUDUKIN: He refused? Honestly?

NINA: Oh, rubbish, he's made the whole story up.

SHMAGA: He not only refused, he insulted me, verbally no less, and
would've gone on to blows, if God hadn't taken pity on me. So,
it's all over. Grisha's dead, as far as our little society is concerned.

MILOVZOROV: Your what?

SHMAGA: The Boon Companions. And I've lost my best friend.

DUDUKIN: What's happened to him?

SHMAGA: It's quite simple. He's lost the thread.

MILOVZOROV: What d'you mean, lost the thread? What thread?

SHMAGA: The thread of his life, for heaven's sake! Everybody has a
thread running through his life. Yours, for instance, is to play the
lover both on stage, and off – that's the thread you follow, and
we've got to follow our own.

NINA: Leading to the Boon Companions, I suppose?

SHMAGA: Of course. And when a man loses the thread, he's done for. The established order decrees that Neznamov must go to the tavern, but he's taken up philosophy instead. Now, philosophy makes a man melancholy, and what could be worse than that?

DUDUKIN: Neznamov, and philosophy? I don't believe it.

NINA: Maybe he's under a spell – d'you think?

SHMAGA: Oh, he's that all right.

NINA: Whose spell?

SHMAGA: Our visiting celebrity.

NINA: Oh, that's rubbish! Clear off, go on.

SHMAGA: It's the absolute truth, I tell you.

NINA: Well, you're witness to this, Milovzorov.

MILOVZOROV: I am, indeed.

SHMAGA: Anyway, it's all over... Goodbye, my dear friend! He's lost the thread.

MILOVZOROV: And you're not losing yours?

SHMAGA: Not a chance. What good would it do me? And now I should like to offer my services to our beloved patron...

DUDUKIN: Why, thank you, my friend. What services are we talking about?

SHMAGA: Well, I suspect you're about to stand us lunch, I mean the leading actors, and that being the case, if you give me the money, I shall take it upon myself to serve you by purchasing the pies, sausages, caviar, and so forth.

NINA: Only not in here, please.

SHMAGA: Good God, no! It's lunch for the leading actors, so we'll go to our dressing-room.

MILOVZOROV: And where might that be?

SHMAGA: Upstairs, in the attic – it's the general room where the spear-carriers get their beards glued on.

DUDUKIN: Well, go on then, do your service. Just wait for me a minute or two on the stage, I want a word with Madame Kruchinina.

MILOVZOROV: And if you see Neznamov, send him in.

SHMAGA: *(pointing to the door leading onto the stage)* There he goes now.

Dudukin and Shmaga exit.

NINA: *(at the door)* Neznamov, come here a minute!

Neznamov enters.

NEZNAMOV: What is it?

MILOVZOROV: Hello, Grisha!

NEZNAMOV: Hello.

NINA: Where've you been hiding from us?

NEZNAMOV: From whom? Who's 'us'?

NINA: Well, from me.

NEZNAMOV: *(looking her over)* I've never been part of your circle. That happiness has been denied me.

NINA: And whose fault is that? You didn't want to be, you're so uncivil, Neznamov. You surely don't expect the woman to make all the running? I mean, that can happen, but it's extremely rare. A man ought to...

NEZNAMOV: I'm sorry, I can't. I'm not qualified for the position.

NINA: What position?

NEZNAMOV: Faithful swain or gigolo. That's *his* job. *(indicating Milovzorov)* Now, what is it you want?

NINA: Oh, nothing in particular. Just that you shouldn't be so standoffish, don't give us the cold shoulder. Really, what sort of company is Shmaga, for goodness' sake?

NEZNAMOV: No, excuse me, please – just leave Shmaga out of it.
For a start, he's good fun and witty, and you're all such bores.
And for another thing, he might be the scum of the earth, but at
least he's honest – he admits it, while you people, if you'll pardon
my saying, are utterly phoney.

NINA: Well, my God, I'm not claiming we're all saints, we have our
shortcomings, phoney and whatever else you want to call us. But
you might at least forgive us as you forgive Shmaga, and don't
judge us so harshly!

NEZNAMOV: 'Forgive us', 'Don't judge us' – I've no wish to judge
or forgive any of you – who am I to judge? I'm simply keeping out
of your way, and I'll go on doing so, otherwise you're very likely to
make a complete fool of me.

NINA: Oh, really, what nonsense!

MILOVZOROV: Yes, come on, Grisha – good heavens, why are you
so mistrustful?

NEZNAMOV: What's this, then – a duet?

NINA: You're much too nice to be running around with Shmaga.

NEZNAMOV: Nice? Since when? What sort of song is this? I mean,
you don't even like me.

NINA: No, that's true, I didn't.

NEZNAMOV: And now you've fallen for me?

NINA: Well, that's asking too much. People surely don't say such things
straight out? *(laughs)* I'm not going to make a declaration in public.

NEZNAMOV: Well, I'll take you at your word sometime in private.

NINA: Ah, that's another matter.

NEZNAMOV: Look, let's get to the point – what is it you want?

NINA: All right, I'll tell you... only I know what you're like, you're so
cranky and stubborn. But for once in your life, please, don't refuse.

MILOVZOROV: Oh, good heavens, no, be a good chap.

NEZNAMOV: Well, go on, then.

NINA: I hardly know where to begin, you frighten me so. Well, the fact is... Dudukin has invited us to a party this evening.

NEZNAMOV: So? What's that got to do with me?

NINA: Oh! You see what I mean? You see why I'm frightened? Well, here goes – no matter what... Right, then – I want you to accompany me to Dudukin's, stay with me there the whole evening, and then see me home! Now, there you are, what do you say? Oh, you're such an oaf!

NEZNAMOV: What exactly are you up to?

NINA: Oh, come on, Neznamov, be a sweetheart, do.

MILOVZOROV: What's this 'Neznamov' business? Call him Grisha.

NINA: Grisha, then. You'll do this much for me, Grisha darling, won't you? *(puts her arms round him and kisses him)*

NEZNAMOV: Look, what is this? This is something new, surely.

NINA: Darling, it comes from the heart. From the *heart,* Grisha.

NEZNAMOV: From the heart, eh? That's different. But what about him? He's your boyfriend, isn't he – your 'steady'.

NINA: He's taking somebody else. Anyway, I'm fed up with him.

NEZNAMOV: Well, all right, if you want. I'm free this evening. It'll be pretty boring, though.

NINA: Then we'll try and liven it up for you. Oh, you're so sweet – thank you so much, darling! *(blows him a kiss and exits through the door to the stage)*

NEZNAMOV: So, what was that little performance all about?

MILOVZOROV: Oh, no performance, my dear chap, absolutely above board.

NEZNAMOV: What does she suddenly want with me, eh? It's not as if she couldn't have got somebody else.

MILOVZOROV: Who else? One of our old stagers or comedians? You can't rely on them, they don't even know themselves what state they'll be in by evening. Maybe it's just a whim. Women get all sorts of passing fancies.

NEZNAMOV: A whim? I don't think I like whims.

MILOVZOROV: Well, you show me a woman without them, dear boy.

NEZNAMOV: And how do you know all this? You've known lots of women, have you? What sort? You judge all women by the sort you get in music-halls, who smile at the audience and sing a refrain after every line. What's going on at Dudukin's tonight?

MILOVZOROV: Oh, nothing special. All the smart set'll be there, and the actors, everybody you know. Oh, and Kruchinina's coming.

NEZNAMOV: She's coming? Why didn't you say so earlier?

MILOVZOROV: Why should I? What's so extraordinary about that, that I should make a special point of it?

NEZNAMOV: Tell me what you think: isn't Madame Kruchinina an exceptional woman?

MILOVZOROV: She's an actress, that's all.

NEZNAMOV: But an exceptional actress?

MILOVZOROV: Mm, audiences like her.

NEZNAMOV: What about you?

MILOVZOROV: Well, they do say she's not as good as Sara Bernhardt.

NEZNAMOV: They say! Haven't you got eyes, or a mind of your own? Well, let me tell you this – she is a most extraordinary actress *and* an extraordinary woman!

MILOVZOROV: Actress, maybe, but woman...? *(smiles and shrugs his shoulders)*

NEZNAMOV: *(sternly)* What do you mean, woman? Explain yourself!

MILOVZOROV: I just mean she's like any other woman.

NEZNAMOV: Listen, you know me – I'm none too generous with praise, but I'll tell you this much: I've spoken with her only once, but when I did, all that absurd posturing of ours, all that bragging and boasting, the contempt we affect for the rest of the world, it all seemed so trivial and pathetic – I felt so insignificant I could cheerfully have sunk through the floor. We shouldn't even open our mouths in her presence. Fools like us should just stand there, with our heads bowed, and seize hold of her every wise, simple word, like manna from heaven!

MILOVZOROV: No, not me – I take everybody as they come.

NEZNAMOV: You're a wretch.

MILOVZOROV: I mean, this is philosophy, dear boy.

NEZNAMOV: Oh, shut up. Just assume you haven't heard a word I've said, I've been talking to the wall. You don't happen to know how long Madame Kruchinina will be staying here?

MILOVZOROV: I imagine she'll be leaving quite soon.

NEZNAMOV: Why's that?

MILOVZOROV: Well, let's say certain factors have come to light... youthful indiscretions...

NEZNAMOV: Look, I'm warning you – you speak about that woman with respect, d'you understand?

MILOVZOROV: I'd be only too delighted to oblige, dear boy, but you can't shut everybody up, and I'm only repeating what others have said.

NEZNAMOV: No, no, you've made up some sordid story yourself, and you're retailing it everywhere. I know you, that's just your style. Well, you can tell them all from me, that I won't allow her to be slandered, I'll... I'll...

MILOVZOROV: You'll beat them up? Yes, I'm sure you would, dear boy.

NEZNAMOV: No, I won't beat them up...

MILOVZOROV: You won't? You'll go easy on them?

NEZNAMOV: I'll kill them stone dead!

MILOVZOROV: *(alarmed)* Good God! How's a person supposed to speak to you? The hell with that, don't ask me any more, I'm clearing off!

NEZNAMOV: No, wait! Finish what you started! Only I want the truth, d'you hear, nothing but the truth!

MILOVZOROV: You see? You're forcing me to tell you, and as soon as I open my mouth, you'll start...

NEZNAMOV: No, go on, go on, tell me! I've got to know everything. So much depends on what... Oh, you won't understand, that's what worries me. I mean, I was an orphan, cast out into this cesspool, this dog-eat-dog world of heartless people, ready to sell each other for a rouble, and then suddenly I find real sympathy, and warmth, and from whom? From a famous woman, a celebrity – someone whom everybody considers it a privilege even to talk with. Can you believe it? For the first time in my life, last night I witnessed a mother's love!

MILOVZOROV: That's infatuation, dear boy. You're in love, Grisha, surely?

NEZNAMOV: No. And I can see there's no point in talking to you. Can't you leave off that ridiculous stereotype of yours for even a second? It's not love, it's reverence.

MILOVZOROV: All right, you say you understood a mother's love for the first time? Well, let me tell you, you're making a big mistake.

NEZNAMOV: What are you talking about? What nonsense is this?

MILOVZOROV: If it's a mother's love you're looking for, try anywhere but her.

NEZNAMOV: Look, don't test my patience!

MILOVZOROV: The main charge against her is that she abandons her children.

NEZNAMOV: What do you mean?

MILOVZOROV: Well, right here in this town, for instance, a number of years ago – she abandoned her child to the vagaries of Fate, and went off with some gentleman or other. And they say it's happened more than once.

NEZNAMOV: Who says?

MILOVZOROV: Everybody, dear boy, I'm telling you. You ask Dudukin – he spoke with her on that very subject, and she herself admitted it.

NEZNAMOV: No, stop, stop! That's impossible, that's not in the least like her. Her voice, her conversation, everything about her – she's so patently sincere, and kindhearted...

MILOVZOROV: And you've simply melted, gone weak at the knees. She's an actress, dear boy, a consummate performer.

NEZNAMOV: All right, she's an actress, but I still don't believe you.

MILOVZOROV: Well, that's up to you – I'm not going to try and convince you.

NEZNAMOV: *(deep in thought)* An actress, eh? Well, you can keep your acting for the stage. Folk pay good money for a clever impersonation. But in real life, playing on the hearts of simple, trusting people, people who don't want acting, but the plain truth... that's a hanging matter! That's fraud, and we don't need that – just give us the truth, the honest truth! An actress! *(after a pause)* Where's Shmaga?

MILOVZOROV: He's upstairs in the dressing-room, drinking vodka.

NEZNAMOV: A noble occupation. Oh, how I wish this would all turn out to be rubbish!

MILOVZOROV: But if it's true?

NEZNAMOV: Well, then, I'll know how to punish myself for being so gullible. Yes, and more than myself will suffer!

Exits. Enter Nina.

NINA: You'd better get out. Kruchinina's coming, she wants to rest. How did it go with Neznamov?

MILOVZOROV: I hit the mark, I think.

NINA: Well, he went out looking thoroughly down in the mouth. So we can expect a good show tonight.

MILOVZOROV: Oh yes, with a superb grand finale. Neznamov does like saving his best effects to the last. *(exits)*

Kruchinina enters.

NINA: Oh, come in – I'm just leaving. You must excuse our dressing-rooms, they're quite dreadful. At least you can sit down in mine, you can't even turn round in the others.

KRUCHININA: Yes, mine's rather inconvenient, and draughty.

NINA: And of course I can receive visitors here.

KRUCHININA: Well, I've no visitors, anyway.

NINA: You don't know that. There are always members of the public wandering about backstage, one of them might just drop in! Anyway, till we meet again at Dudukin's. Milovzorov will call for you.

KRUCHININA: Yes, I've already asked him.

> *Nina gives her her hand and exits. Kruchinina sists down at the table, takes out her script and begins reading. Murov enters. Kruchinina turns round, stands up and nods in acknowledgment of Murov's bow.*

MUROV: *(smiles)* Allow me to introduce myself... Murov, Grigory Murov. *(bows)* I looked in at your hotel twice yesterday, but unfortunately for me you were out. I was at the theatre a couple of days ago, and I can't begin to tell you what an impression your performance made on the audience. Anyway, you know that without my saying, but I was struck by the extraordinary resemblance you bear to a woman with whom I was once acquainted.

KRUCHININA: What is it you want of me?

MUROV: I'd like to know if I was mistaken or not. Stage lighting, make-up and so on, can change a face so that it's possible to find a likeness where none exists.

KRUCHININA: Well, you see me without make-up. What do you find now?

MUROV: I'm even more struck. Such a trick can't come from nature. When I look at you, I must either disbelieve my own eyes, or else – if you'll pardon me – I must ask a question.

KRUCHININA: Go ahead.

MUROV: Aren't you Lyubov Otradina?

KRUCHININA: Yes. I am Lyubov Otradina.

MUROV: Where have you come from? Where have you been all this time, what have you been doing? What sort of life have you had?

KRUCHININA: I can't see that there's anything you need know about that, since it in no way concerns you.

MUROV: But where did you get the name Kruchinina? Why have you turned up here under someone else's name?

KRUCHININA: When I went on the stage I was beginning a new life, so I changed my name – it's common practice. I took my mother's name. Have you any further questions?

MUROV: You're anxious to get rid of me, to end our conversation and show me the door.

KRUCHININA: No, I'm waiting till you finish your interrogation.

MUROV: I've finished.

KRUCHININA: Good. Now I'll begin mine. Where is my son? What did you do with him?

MUROV: I wrote to you, didn't I? I told you he'd died. Surely you received my letter?

KRUCHININA: Oh yes, I received it all right, but you lied to me. He recovered, and when you wrote to inform me of his death, he was alive and well.

MUROV: Well, if you knew this, why didn't you come and take him?

KRUCHININA: I learned about it only yesterday. And I couldn't have come then in any case, I was desperately ill myself. I was half-dead when they took me away. And you knew that perfectly well. Why did you lie to me?

MUROV: One false step always leads to another. I was afraid you would return, people would talk, my wife would get to hear about it, and it would cause a row in the first weeks of our marriage.

KRUCHININA: Well, it doesn't matter, it's all over now. But what did you do with my son? The truth, please – I know a few things myself.

MUROV: We found some decent people, reasonably well off, and I handed him over to them in person. I left that little locket with him, the one you gave me.

KRUCHININA: He has that? I put a wisp of his golden hair in it, along with a note.

MUROV: A note?

KRUCHININA: Nothing, really. Just the date of his birth.

MUROV: And that 's all?

KRUCHININA: Oh, I don't remember.

MUROV: I wasn't aware of that. I thought it was just a little gold trinket, it didn't seem to have any sort of information. Well, it doesn't matter now. Those good people promised me they'd never take that locket away from him. They probably thought of it as some kind of lucky charm or talisman, with mysterious powers, the sort of thing you hang round children to ward off illness.

KRUCHININA: So, what happened next?

MUROV: Well, they brought him up, educated him and so on, and meanwhile grew rich. They expanded their trade, opened up large stores in several provincial towns, built themselves a fine house – I can't exactly remember where, possibly Syzran, or Irbit, or Samara – no, I think it was Taganrog – and moved down there to live.

KRUCHININA: And this was a long time ago?

MUROV: About eight years.

KRUCHININA: Have you had any news of him since?

MUROV: No. They asked me to break off all communication with him. We've brought him up, they said, he bears our name, and he'll be our heir, so please leave us in peace. To be honest, if you look at it sensibly, what better fate could a fatherless child have? I felt extremely relieved – he was in an enviable position.

KRUCHININA: What was this merchant's name?

MUROV: Oh, I've forgotten – might've been Ivanov, or Perekusikhin. Something midway between Ivanov and Perekusikhin... Podtovarnikov, I think. I can look out the papers, if you wish. I'll be meeting a visitor to the town later today, in fact – someone who knows all the merchants down in that part of the world, so I'll be able to let you know. Are you going to be at Dudukin's?

KRUCHININA: Yes, I am.

MUROV: If you don't mind, I'd like to say a few words more.

KRUCHININA: Go on.

MUROV: Well, for the grief I caused you, I've been cruelly punished. My late wife made my life a living hell. Still, I won't speak ill of her, I deserved everything I got, and besides, she left me a huge fortune. Anyway, after my joyless existence, when I saw you again, my old passion flared with renewed force. I mean, I'm no longer a young man, I don't overstate my feelings, and I have learned to weigh my words carefully. So when I say 'with renewed force', it means just that, and there are no other words to express how I feel. Only now do I realise what happiness I lost – happiness so great that there's nothing I wouldn't do to recapture it. You have defeated me, overwhelmed me completely. I beg for mercy, pray for reconciliation. Let's make peace! I am the vanquished, you have the right to dictate terms, and I shall humbly and submissively accept them.

KRUCHININA: Oh, how it hurts me to hear these things! You thought nothing of the fresh, innocent love of a simple young girl, and now you're ready to grovel before a middle-aged woman, whose heart has grown cold, purely because she's a celebrity!

MUROV: Lyuba, please – surely there's some spark left of that old feeling?

KRUCHININA: There's no Lyuba here. This is Yelena Kruchinina.

MUROV: You were so rich in love then, so extravagant...

KRUCHININA: I've managed to unlearn those words.

MUROV: I beg your pardon. It was the woman I knew – now I see the actress. I shall try a different tack. Would you do me the honour of visiting me at my country estate? Would you do me the honour of remaining there as mistress of it? In a word, would you do me the honour of becoming my wife?

KRUCHININA: And I shall answer all your questions with another – where is my son? Until I see him again, there can be no futher conversation between us. Now, I'm due on stage. *(exits)*

MUROV: Goodbye. *(follows Kruchinina out)* I'm a patient man, I never give up hope.

> *Murov exits. Enter Neznamov, downcast. He stands by the door, staring fixedly out at the stage.*

NEZNAMOV: Shmaga! Shmaga, come here! Come here, I tell you!

SHMAGA: *(off-stage)* You won't hit me?

NEZNAMOV: Not likely. I wouldn't dirty my hands.

> *Shmaga enters, and Neznamov grabs him by the collar.*

Right, come on, talk! What's all this behind my back, what are they saying about me?

SHMAGA: Stop, stop, you're choking me! Let go a minute, let me breathe! I'll tell you everything!

NEZNAMOV: *(releasing him)* Right, tell me.

SHMAGA: What's to tell? It's all rubbish, anyway.

NEZNAMOV: I know that.

SHMAGA: Well, if you know, why are you so angry?

NEZNAMOV: Never you mind. You just tell me what you've heard.

SHMAGA: Well, to tell you the truth, I haven't even been listening. Why should I? I mean, I'll get nothing out of them but nonsense, and I've got enough of that at home.

NEZNAMOV: Yes, well, they've been linking my name with Madame Kruchinina's, and whispering about us.

SHMAGA: Well, if it's rubbish, what does it matter if they're whispering, or shouting it from the rooftops?

NEZNAMOV: I mean, they're laughing at us. That's terrible, it's unbearable. At least on my side it was a deep, sincere feeling – why the hell did I tell them about it!

SHMAGA: Well, that's how it goes.

NEZNAMOV: And this party at Dudukin's, that they're making such a fuss about. Maybe they're planning something, some cheap trick.

Couldn't they be going to make a fool of a woman who deserves nothing but respect?

SHMAGA: Respect, you say?

NEZNAMOV: *(seizing his head in his hands)* Oh, God! I don't even know myself, if it's respect or contempt!

SHMAGA: Well, if you don't know, don't get involved with either her or them.

NEZNAMOV: No, stop! Just think for a minute, just imagine a poor wretch, the poorest of of the poor, who has never in his entire life had so much as a kopeck in his hands, and who suddenly finds a heap of gold...

SHMAGA: I can't imagine anything more fantastic!

NEZNAMOV: No, wait... just suppose that gold turns to ashes? What then?

SHMAGA: Well, if the man's extremely greedy, and the gold means that much to him, then after a transformation like that, he would instantly fasten a noose onto a stout nail, and begin slipping it around his neck.

NEZNAMOV: Right, then listen!

SHMAGA: *(waving his hand dismissively)* No, no, this is philosophy again. I'm sorry, Grisha, but you really do wear me out with this stuff.

NEZNAMOV: What, you don't think there's a difference between good and evil?

SHMAGA: Oh yes, there's some small distinction, but that's none of our business. No, Grisha, spare me your philosophy. Otherwise I'll become just as miserable as you. Come on, let's go to the Boon Companions instead.

NEZNAMOV: Barbarians! What are they playing at with my feelings! Yes, well, somebody's going to pay for my suffering – either them, or her!

They exit.

END OF ACT THREE

ACT FOUR

*A moonlit night. An open space in a large garden, surrounded by mature
lime trees; benches and ash tables, on wrought-iron legs. The terrace of a
large house, with French windows, projects onto the stage and on the
terrace are flower-beds and climbing plants. The house is ablaze with
light. Neznamov and Milovzorov are sitting on one of the benches, and
Shmaga on another. He is gazing now at the moon, now around him,
and sighing, striking one pose after another.*

MILOVZOROV: What are you sighing for, Shmaga? Is something
bothering you?

SHMAGA: I'm annoyed at the moon.

MILOVZOROV: You're what?

SHMAGA: Why does it keep staring at me? And such a stupid
expression! It's like some great round-faced peasant girl, standing
at a gate, and grinning her silly head off for no reason.

MILOVZOROV: Trouble with you, dear boy, is you've got no poetry in
your soul. Whereas I'm sitting here thinking, "What a glorious night!"

SHMAGA: Yes, on a night like this it'd be nice to...

MILOVZOROV: Take a trip down the Volga?

SHMAGA: No, to go for a drink.

MILOVZOROV: Oh, what rubbish! A tavern's fine in winter, when
there's a blizzard outside, or a hard frost. The sort of rooms we're
in are mostly cold and damp, and it's nice and warm in the tavern.

SHMAGA: And good fun.

MILOVZOROV: Yes, but they get dreadfully stuffy in summer.

SHMAGA: Well, you can always open a window, let some air in.
And there's your poetry. The moon shines straight onto your
plate, the lilacs and lime-trees are in bloom outside the window,
there's a scent of orange-blossom in the air...

MILOVZOROV: What, from the lime-trees?

SHMAGA: No, of course not – from the bottle on the table. And all the cocks are crowing – at least all the ones we haven't managed to roast yet.

MILOVZOROV: Cocks! That's not poetry, that's prose! Surely you mean nightingales?

SHMAGA: Well, that depends on how much money you have. If you're flush, you can sit there till the nightingales sing, if you're broke, you're finished by cock-crow. Nightingales sing to greet the dawn – oh, they'll give out a few notes in the evening, but you don't get the full works till sunrise. But the cock knows when it's midnight, he's as good as a stopwatch. The minute he starts crowing, us poor wretches get up and go, before they throw us out. *(gazes at the moon and sighs)* I'll tell you this much – this is torture. I mean, look at us, here we are at the rich man's table, and for what? To admire the scenery? To sit and gaze at the moon, like a wolf on a winter's night? Yes, and a wolf'll start howling after a bit. Hey, Grisha, come on, let's give them a duet. You start howling, and I'll join in with a few choice variations. Maybe our host'll get the message.

NEZNAMOV: You can't be that bad. At least you can still joke. I feel dreadful.

SHMAGA: Well, I'm not much better.

NEZNAMOV: Once you've reached the bar, all your troubles'll disappear.

SHMAGA: So what's stopping you?

NEZNAMOV: That won't cure me. It'll make things worse, if anything.

MILOVZOROV: Don't say that, dear boy.

SHMAGA: Go on, why not give it a try?

NEZNAMOV: No, don't ask. Otherwise I might just do that.

SHMAGA: Look, what's going on here? He invites people to his house, then leaves them twiddling their thumbs!

MILOVZOROV: Oh, come, that's not true, dear boy. Dudukin knows how to run these things. The solid citizens play cards, and the young chaps try to get off with the ladies.

SHMAGA: And what about the actors?

MILOVZOROV: Why should he worry about the actors? It's their job to be the life and soul of the party.

SHMAGA: Then you should get us in the mood beforehand, raise the tone a bit, fire our imaginations, then we might feel like livening up the party.

MILOVZOROV: Everything in its time, dear boy. They're drinking tea just now. Would you like some?

SHMAGA: Good God, no – drink it yourself! *(sighs)*

Nina enters.

NINA: Gentlemen, what are you doing out here on your own? *(to Neznamov)* Why are you sitting there sulking, why don't you come in and join us?

NEZNAMOV: What do you need me for?

NINA: Madame Kruchinina's been asking about you twice already. She speaks very highly of you.

NEZNAMOV: High or low, what's the difference? Frankly, I don't like people talking about me. Why can't they just leave me alone? It's not as if you've nothing else to talk about.

NINA: Honestly, you're so touchy! A person can't even say nice things about you. Kruchinina thinks you have real talent, and a lot of feeling.

SHMAGA: Feeling's the last thing an actor needs. if you ask me.

MILOVZOROV: Well, yes, comedians, fair enough – but there are other sorts of actor.

SHMAGA: Oh yes? So you play lovers every day, you make love on stage as a matter of routine – how much feeling do you have?

MILOVZOROV: Enough. Enough for our audiences, certainly, dear boy.

SHMAGA: Yes, enough for the audience, but how about for domestic consumption?

NEZNAMOV: What I'd like to know is how these great actors behave in their everyday lives? I mean, do they really go on pretending, the way they do on stage?

NINA: Very likely. You need a lot of experience, you need to have lived a long time, to learn how to distinguish genuine feeling from fake.

NEZNAMOV: You mean you have to wait until you're old? And meanwhile people can keep lying to you and making a fool of you? Well, I thank you most humbly. I'd better to trust nobody.

NINA: You're probably right.

SHMAGA: Grisha has feeling, that's true. Trouble is, he's got no sense. He doesn't know where to put it, where to direct his feeling.

NEZNAMOV: Well said.

SHMAGA: And what about you, Nina? Have you any feeling?

NINA: What sort of stupid question is that?

SHMAGA: Well, I can see people might not want to allow me, Shmaga the actor, into their respectable homes – that's fair enough, I'm not offended. But if they have done so – nay, invited me, even – then they've got to accept my way of life, and my personal habits. So if you have any feeling, Nina, you'll organise things so that...

NINA: Right, right, I get the message. I have feelings, it's all organised long ago. That's why I came out here, to invite you to the table.

SHMAGA: What! Good news like that and you've said nothing till now? It's just as well I haven't died of impatience, or this might've been a hanging matter. *(goes up to Neznamov)* Come on, Grisha – dump the philosophy, and let's go! What's scenery to us? Woods, mountains, the moon? I mean, we're not savages, we're civilised people.

NEZNAMOV: Yes, it's actually very boring. Come on then, my civilised friend – let's head for the bar! Let us go where my sorry fate beckons!

NINA: *(to Milovzorov, aside)* He's in good form. All he needs is a little gentle warm-up.

MILOVZOROV: I'll do my best.

> *They all head towards the house. Dudukin and Kruchinina come out to meet them.*

KRUCHININA: Where are you going, gentlemen? You're not running away from me, I hope?

NINA: Oh no, they'll be back in a minute. I'll bring them to you.

SHMAGA: There are moments in an actor's life when he flies like an arrow to his target, and nothing on this earth will stop him.

KRUCHININA: So when do these moments occur?

SHMAGA: When the cutlery starts clinking, and they call out: 'Dinner is served!'

NEZNAMOV: Come on, quit clowning!

Nina, Neznamov, Milovzorov and Shmaga all exit to the house.

DUDUKIN: You know, when Shmaga starts talking about food, he gets real feeling into it. He gives everybody an appetite. That's why we invite him.

KRUCHININA: Well, that's a talent of a sort, though I'm not sure it's one that should be encouraged.

DUDUKIN: What else can we do? Our provincial life here is so dreary we're very glad of a Shmaga. I'm no preacher – live and let live, is what I say. You're not bored with us yet? Not fed up with the place?

KRUCHININA: There's nowhere much better. It's the same everywhere. Still, I'll have to leave here quite soon.

DUDUKIN: Why is that?

KRUCHININA: I'm under too much strain here. Everything reminds me of my sorrowful past.

DUDUKIN: It's time you forgot the past.

KRUCHININA: I thought I had, then I ended up by chance in my home town, and it's revived all my painful memories.

DUDUKIN: Forget them, dear lady, you must. It's time you enjoyed your fame, your success – it's time to rest on your laurels.

KRUCHININA: I'd be only too glad to rest, but they won't let me. I almost died from shock yesterday.

DUDUKIN: Really? What on earth happened?

KRUCHININA: It turns out I've been deceived in the most cruel manner. When they wrote to tell me my son was dead, he was alive all the time, he had recovered. And he was handed over to foster-parents.

DUDUKIN: Who were they?

KRUCHININA: I don't know, nobody knows. I've asked everybody I can think of. Some people say they were merchants or tradespeople, just passing through, others say they were gentry, that they took the child and then left. But where they went, nobody knows. Vanished without trace.

DUDUKIN: And you won't find any trace now. You can be sure whoever wanted rid of the child would take damn good care to cover their tracks.

KRUCHININA: What, you think they did it on purpose, in order to get rid of him?

DUDUKIN: No doubt about it. I mean, why else would they write and tell you he was dead?

KRUCHININA: Yes, of course. Well then, you see? And you're advising me to forget it.

DUDUKIN: I am, yes – what's the point of brooding all the time, the same thing? It won't help, there's nothing you can do about it, and it might even drive you mad.

KRUCHININA: Yes, it might. I can understand how a person might easily go mad.

DUDUKIN: You have to resign yourself to your fate, dear lady. And if you're fated to find your son again, then he'll surely turn up.

   Murov appears on the terrace.

Anyway, let's enjoy life while we can. That's what life's for.

   Murov enters.

MUROV: They've just finished the last rubber of whist. They're trying to organise a new game.

DUDUKIN: Oh, excuse me, I must run – I'll get the card-players settled, and be back in a minute. *(exits)*

MUROV: Mind if I have a word with you?

KRUCHININA: You have something to tell me?

MUROV: Yes, I have. Unfortunately, it isn't very good news.

KRUCHININA: Go ahead, it doesn't matter. I'm not exactly used to good news.

MUROV: I've seen the man I was telling you about.

KRUCHININA: What did you find out from him?

MUROV: Well, it seems this merchant Prostokvashin...

KRUCHININA: I thought you said his name was Ivanov?

MUROV: No, that was a mistake. I remembered later. Anyway, this Prostokvashin left for Astrakhan about three or four years ago, along with his adopted son, something to do with his business. And apparently they both contracted some sort of infectious disease there and died.

KRUCHININA: If that's the truth, there must be a widow left. You'd have been better saying they all died.

MUROV: No, how could I? Why should she die too? I mean, really! No, the widow's alive, definitely.

KRUCHININA: So where is she? Tell me.

MUROV: Well, it seems she was so grief-stricken that she married a young man, one of their own clerks.

KRUCHININA: What's his name?

MUROV: Ah, now that I don't know. But it shouldn't be difficult to find out. You've only got to ask who the widow Nepropyokin married.

KRUCHININA: You've just this minute told me this merchant's name was Prostokvashin, and now he's Nepropyokin!

MUROV: Really? Did I say that? Well, I won't argue with you, I'm honestly terrible with names.

KRUCHININA: Look, I have one more question. Everything you've told me, then and now – is there a shred of truth in any of it?

MUROV: *(laughs)* You don't pull your punches, do you? Yes, there is, I assure you.

KRUCHININA: What, exactly?

MUROV: That your son's dead, that he's been dead many years, and it's time you put all that behind you.

KRUCHININA: You forget him if you can. I'm not stopping you.

MUROV: Lyuba, I'm giving you good advice. Concentrate on your acting career – lucky for you it's going so well. Honestly, you're not some seventeen year-old girl, it's time you put all that maudlin sentiment aside, you should use your head, take life more seriously.

KRUCHININA: How dare you! How dare you offer me advice!

MUROV: Well, you've forced me to it. You go all round the town, interrogating people, you find some half-witted old crone... I mean, that's not very nice for me, is it! I'm one of the biggest landowners in these parts, we're having elections soon, I'm up for a very important office, and here you are spreading rumours all over the place – next thing there'll be an almighty scandal!

KRUCHININA: I don't care a damn about you! I'm trying to find my son, and nobody's going to stop me!

MUROV: Hah! We'll see about that. Look, I'm asking you one more time to drop this absurd melodrama – we can make our peace on very favourable conditions, as far as you're concerned. And if you don't want that, then you might at least leave.

KRUCHININA: I don't want either one. I'm obliged to give two more performances here, which I'll do, and then I'll leave when it suits me.

MUROV: Obliged! What do you mean obliged! Box-office receipts, is that the attraction? I'll reimburse you, for God's sake, I'll pay both you and the management!

KRUCHININA: You've already paid me once, evil for good, and for the evil you've done me, you couldn't afford to pay me again. I'm not as wealthy as you, but I'd give a very great deal of money never to see you again, never to cross your path. And I've kept out of your way here, it's you who came looking for me.

MUROV: Well, I'd gladly leave here, you wouldn't have to pay me, but I can't. I live in this town, all my interests are here, but what is there for you? Nothing but an absurd fancy. And you can give free rein to your imagination anywhere. Listen, you'd better not make trouble for me – you'll come off worst, believe me. I'm a powerful man, I have influential friends.

KRUCHININA: You don't frighten me. You're capable of anything, I know that, but there's nothing you can dream up worse than you've done already,

MUROV: *(shrugs)* Well, it's up to you.

Dudukin enters.

DUDUKIN: Well, here I am again, at your service. Would you care for a walk through the garden?

KRUCHININA: No, thank you, it's a bit chilly. I'll go inside. You don't have to accompany me, I can find my own way.

DUDUKIN: As you wish.

Kruchinina exits.

MUROV: So... tell me, Dudukin – that young actor I saw you with just now, has he any talent?

DUDUKIN: Yes, I believe so. The pity is that there's no-one to teach him, he never sees any decent exemplars, stuck out here in the provinces. And it's now he should be learning, while he's still young.

MUROV: He doesn't look all that young.

DUDUKIN: Well, it's the disorderly life they lead, drinking sprees, late nights, it soon puts years on you.

MUROV: So how old would you say he was?

DUDUKIN: About twenty, I'd say – certainly not much more.

MUROV: Really? No, he's thirty, if he's a day.

DUDUKIN: Why do you ask?

MUROV: He's a bit too free with his opinions, talks too much, in a very loud voice.

DUDUKIN: Well, what do you expect? It's the way they are these days, they don't know how to behave.

MUROV: Anyway, have you finished making over your summer-house?

DUDUKIN: Yes, I have – and built out a little stage for the musicians.

MUROV: Who is that actor, incidentally? Where's he from?

DUDUKIN: His name's Neznamov, but I've no idea where he comes from. Why are you so interested in him?

MUROV: Oh, no reason. Just asking. There's something about him. It's obvious he's not from common stock.

DUDUKIN: Well, he himself knows absolutely nothing about his origins.

MUROV: You shouldn't really invite such people.

DUDUKIN: Oh, I don't know, they're good fun. And they're not harming anybody. Certainly, they're always very polite to me.

MUROV: That's not good enough. They should be polite to everybody. I pointed out to him that young people used to be much more respectful to their elders, and he had the effrontery to challenge me. No doubt, he said, that's because their elders had more brains, and were more deserving of respect. A really stupid response. So, you say he's twenty?

DUDUKIN: Yes, round about.

MUROV: Have you cleaned out your pond?

DUDUKIN: Indeed I have, and filled it with fish – you wouldn't recognise it.

MUROV: I'd love to see it.

DUDUKIN: Let's go, then.

They exit into the garden. Nina enters from the house, followed by

Milovzorov.

MILOVZOROV: Where are you racing off to?

NINA: I need to have a word with Dudukin.

MILOVZOROV: Well, you can do that later.

NINA: Oh yes? Feeling affectionate, are we?

MILOVZOROV: Yes, and that's the snag – just when I am feeling tender, and witty and eloquent, and so on – that's when you choose to run away from me.

NINA: And why shouldn't I? Anyway, I'm afraid I've no time for you just now. Where's Neznamov, is he still playing the innocent?

MILOVZOROV: Oh, no, he's come out of his shell. He and Shmaga are glued to the table. There's a crowd of people around them, Shmaga's tossing off witty remarks and Neznamov's making mincemeat out of anybody who tries to put them in their place, or attempts to score off them. They've got a proper little audience there, roaring with laughter. The table's heaped with food, and there's oceans of drink. Somebody shouts, "Hey, come on, Grisha, have a drink with me!" and "No, no – me!", shouts another. And Shmaga keeps chipping in, "Me too, for company!"

NINA: Anyway, here I am talking to you, when I really must see Dudukin.

MILOVZOROV: Well, that's him coming now, I think. Kruchinina's looked into the dining-room a couple of times. She heard Neznamov sounding off, and went back out again.

NINA: I'd better send Dudukin into her, in case she decides to leave. She's getting bored, I think.

Enter Shmaga.

SHMAGA: Well, now I can really enjoy the scenery. Even the moon looks a bit more intelligent.

MILOVZOROV: So where's Neznamov?

SHMAGA: The same place.

MILOVZOROV: You really shouldn't have left him, dear boy.

SHMAGA: You go and see him, if you're that keen. I mean, all right, he is my friend, but at times like this I give him a wide berth.

MILOVZOROV: Supposed to be your friend, and you're scared of him? That's charming!

SHMAGA: Well, you just poke your nose in, go on – here he comes now. Do you want me to set him on you?

MILOVZOROV: Good God, no – don't even think of it!

Enter Neznamov.

NEZNAMOV: *(to Nina)* Oh, you're out here?

NINA: That's right. Where would you like me to be?

NEZNAMOV: I don't care. Actually, I love you... I've fallen in love with you.

NINA: I most humbly thank you.

NEZNAMOV: So, do you love me?

NINA: What do you think?

NEZNAMOV: What do I think? I haven't a clue.

NINA: Guess!

NEZNAMOV: That's all I need, silly guessing games. Just tell me straight out, the truth.

NINA: Not a chance – you'll wait a long time for that. Anyway, what gave you the right to speak to me like this?

NEZNAMOV: Why shouldn't I?

NINA: Just don't dare, that's all!

NEZNAMOV: I'll dare if I like. You know, you're actually much nicer than I thought.

NINA: Really? So what did you think?

NEZNAMOV: You're seriously asking?

NINA: Yes, I am.

NEZNAMOV: I used to think you were totally uninteresting – a complete cipher, a nonentity.

NINA: Good God! I don't believe this! Well, in the first place, my dear sir, you're much too young to analyse and judge people – you're scarcely more than a boy.

NEZNAMOV: Oh yes, that's in the first place, is it? So what's in the second? You can't even come out with one, can you. Do you want me to show you how?

NINA: No, I don't.

NEZNAMOV: Well, you obviously can't. When a woman gets angry she always imagines she can reel off a horrific catalogue of home truths. So she starts off terribly pompously – "In the first place...", and then runs out of steam after half a dozen words. She's got nothing left in her armoury. So in the second place, they'll say, in the second place... and they haven't got a second!

NINA: Oh, you're disgusting!

NEZNAMOV: But even then she won't give up. When she's got nothing to say, when she's run out of ideas, she starts name-calling. "In the second place..." she'll say, "You're a fool, you're just ignorant!" Well?

NINA: Exactly! And in the second place, you are ignorant!

NEZNAMOV: *Merci, mademoiselle!* You lose your temper so naturally – bravo!

NINA: If you make one more stupid remark, it'll be even more natural! I'll give you such a slap...

NEZNAMOV: Why wait, why not do it now?

NINA: I don't want to, that's all.

NEZNAMOV: No, please, do! I beg you. What's stopping you? It's not as if it was hard work.

NINA: No. I'm not in the mood. It would be a joke now, and I want to be serious.

NEZNAMOV: Well, do it for a joke.

NINA: You never stop, do you. Right, then! *(gives Neznamov a playful pat on the cheek)*

NEZNAMOV: Ah, I see – so that's how it is? Well, you'd better watch out now. That now gives me the right to...

NINA: The right to what?

NEZNAMOV: To kiss you. How else would I repay an insult from a woman?

NINA: Good God, have you gone mad?

NEZNAMOV: Indeed I haven't, and the time for talking's past.

NINA: Neznamov, what are you doing! Don't be silly! Look, Dudukin's coming!

NEZNAMOV: Pat on his cue! Well, if it wasn't for that same Dudukin... Anyway, we'll be going home together.

   Enter Dudukin.

NINA: My dear sir, why have you left Madame Kruchinina? She's getting ready to go home, isn't she?

DUDUKIN: Home? No, surely not, not before supper. Be an angel, and see if you can keep her here.

NINA: She's not likely to do what I say.

DUDUKIN: Well, let's both go and talk her round.

NINA: Yes, let's. Hold on a minute... *(turns to address Neznamov and Shmaga)* Gentlemen, whatever you do, please don't say anything about children at supper – and not in front of Madame Kruchinina at any time.

NEZNAMOV: About children? Why not?

DUDUKIN: That's right, that's right! Under no circumstances, my dear sirs – not a word.

NEZNAMOV: That's strange, isn't it? Suppose I can't help it? I mean, if the notion suddenly pops into my head?

DUDUKIN: No, no, please – I'd take it as a personal favour if you'd say nothing. I am the host, after all, and I'm concerned to make sure nothing upsets my guests.

NEZNAMOV: All right – children are taboo. What about mature adults?

DUDUKIN: Please – I'd be much obliged.

SHMAGA: It's not on, Grisha – we'll just have to talk about grannies and grandads.

NEZNAMOV: *(laughs loudly)* Absolutely! You can rest easy, Dudukin – the only childhood we'll discuss will be second childhood!

Nina and Dudukin exit.

So, this is the latest? What sort of absurd edict is this? Some sort of party game? Supper with a set menu for conversation?

MILOVZOROV: My dear boy, surely you haven't forgotten what I told you?

NEZNAMOV: Oh, yes. Yes, I see now. *(takes his head in his hands)*

MILOVZOROV: So I was right. And you wanted to kill me.

NEZNAMOV: So what? What if I had killed you? Who would care?

Shmaga moves apart.

I wish to God somebody would kill me. Hey, Shmaga – what are you running away for? What are you scared of?

SHMAGA: *(at a distance)* Once bitten, twice shy, as they say.

NEZNAMOV: Come back, I need some of your chatter.

SHMAGA: What's the point? Witticisms just seem to evaporate in the fresh air, you'd have to weigh them down with something.

NEZNAMOV: Oh, we'll weigh them down, don't worry. Shmaga, dear friend, we've got to seize the moment. It's not every day that the likes of you and me are invited into polite society, or treated like human beings. And here we are, look at us, guests like everybody else.

SHMAGA: That's true, it's not like one of your jumped-up merchant's dos, where you've just got to beat up the host, you can't leave until you've done it.

NEZNAMOV: No, this is rather nice here. And actually you and I haven't been behaving too well, looks like we'll even start a row. Well, not exactly a row, but let's say an ugly moment might be on the cards.

SHMAGA: Yes, something like that. Still, what can we do? You can't change the habit of a lifetime.

> *Enter Dudukin, Kruchinina and Nina, followed by two footmen, one with a bottle of champagne, the other with a tray of glasses, which they set down on the tables. Murov emerges up-stage from the garden, and other guests come out of the house and position themselves in various small groups in the open area.*

DUDUKIN: *(to Kruchinina)* Well, my dear lady, we've waited what seems like an eternity to have the pleasure of your company in our little society – indeed, I shall mark the date of your visit in letters of gold on the wall, and yet you're intending to leave us?

KRUCHININA: I'm deeply grateful to you, sir, and I'd be only too glad to remain, but I'm afraid I can't. This is the only free evening I have, with a performance every day, and I must get some rest.

DUDUKIN: Well, you'll have time for that, you can rest at home, but do give us at least another half-hour

KRUCHININA: No, I can't, honestly. I'll say goodbye to my friends, find my escort, and be on my way.

DUDUKIN: Good heavens, we can't just let you leave without the proper formalities. We've got to do these things right. Please, dear lady, be seated – sit down here on the bench. Is everything ready, Nina?

NINA: It is indeed. *(to the footmen)* You can serve the wine.

> *The champagne is served.*

KRUCHININA: Really, my dear sir, you shouldn't – I don't even drink, it's bad for me.

DUDUKIN: There's no way out, dear lady – this is how we always take leave of our honoured guests. Please – if you'd be so kind, just a little drop...

Kruchinina accepts a glass of champagne.

Ladies and gentlemen, if you all have a glass... I propose a toast to Madame Kruchinina.

MUROV: I most heartily accept your proposal – I've not yet had an opportunity to thank Madame Kruchinina for the pleasure she's given us with her talent.

They all raise their glasses.

DUDUKIN: Ladies and gentlemen, I propose a toast to a true artist, who has stirred up the weed-choked, stagnant waters that are our provincial life. I am no great orator, so I shall speak simply. Among people like us, the provincial intelligentsia, there are only two occupations – playing cards and gossiping in clubs. Let us then honour a talent which has made us abandon our customary pastimes. Ladies and gentlemen, we are, so to speak, asleep – so let us be grateful to those chosen few, who from time to time manage to waken us up, and remind us of that ideal world we have all forgotten.

Shouts of "Bravo! Bravo!"

Talent is a precious thing in itself, but in combination with other qualities – with intelligence, kindheartedness, genuine goodness, it presents itself to us as a true phenomenon, before which we can only bow our heads. Ladies and gentlemen, let us drink to a rare talent, and a wonderful woman – to Madame Kruchinina!

They all clink glasses with Kruchinina and drink.

NEZNAMOV: *(clinks glasses with Shmaga)* Well, Shmaga, we'll drink to a talented actress, but wonderful women really aren't in our line. Besides which, who can tell whether they're wonderful or not?

DUDUKIN: Neznamov, really!

NEZNAMOV: Sorry.

KRUCHININA: I've already been sufficiently rewarded for my labours,

both materially and spiritually. Dear friends, the honour which you
bestow on me, I feel bound to share with my colleagues, and I
propose a toast to all those who serve the cause of art, to all honest
toilers in that noble profession, without distinction of degree or talent!

DUDUKIN: Well spoken! Bravo! Excellent! Nina, Milovzorov,
Neznamov, Shmaga – to your good health!

MUROV: Your good health!

SHMAGA: At long last, I've arrived! They're drinking my health!

KRUCHININA: And now, my dear sir, I really must be going.

NEZNAMOV: Good heavens, no! Please – you can't leave now.
There's another toast to be drunk. *(shouts)* Hey! Let's have some
more champagne! I mean, you must allow me to say a few words –
I won't hold you back, I promise. I only want to say what's in my
heart – I can't leave it unsaid.

KRUCHININA: Feel free to do so. I shall be only too glad to hear
you, and I hope everyone else will.

NEZNAMOV: Ladies and gentlemen, I have been granted permission
to speak, so please don't interrupt.

DUDUKIN: Well, get on with it.

MILOVZOROV AND SHMAGA: Speech! Speech!

NEZNAMOV: Ladies and gentlemen, I'd like to propose a toast to all
mothers who abandon their children.

DUDUKIN: For God's sake, sir, stop it, now!

KRUCHININA: *(stricken)* No, go on, go on.

NEZNAMOV: May they pass their days in joy and happiness, and may
their paths be strewn with roses and lilies. May nothing and nobody
cast a blight on their delightful existence. May nothing and nobody
ever remind them of the bitter fate of their wretched orphans.
Indeed, why should they be troubled? Why should their peace of
mind be disturbed? They did all they could for their beloved
offspring. They wept over them, as much as they had to, kissed
them more or less tenderly. "Farewell, my darling, live as best you
can! But it'd really be better if you died." There's no getting away

from the truth – dying's the best thing that could happen to such new arrivals into this world of ours, the best they can hope for. But not all are granted that happy fate. *(bows his head for a moment, deep in thought)* Some mothers are a bit more feeling – they don't stop at tears and kisses, they even hang some sort of gold trinket round their child's neck. Wear this, in remembrance of me! But what's the wretched child supposed to remember? Why should he remember? Why leave him with a constant reminder of his shame and misery? There are enough people as it is, all too willing to do that, to remind him he's a foundling, a doorstep brat. Oh, if they only knew, those mothers, how many tears are shed in vain over their little trinkets by those abused and insulted children! "Where are you rejoicing now?" they say, "Why don't you answer me? Won't you shed even one tear for me, in my despair, to ease my suffering?" Oh yes, souvenirs like these scorch the breasts of those who wear them.

Kruchinina rushes towards Neznamov and tears the locket from around his neck.

KRUCHININA: It's him! It's my son!

She collapses unconscious onto the bench. The other guests crowd round her.

DUDUKIN: Oh my God, she's dying! A doctor, call a doctor! You're her son, and you've killed her!

NEZNAMOV: I'm her son?

DUDUKIN: Yes. She's been trying to find you for years. They told her you were dead, but she never gave up hoping for some miracle. She dreamed about you night and day, even spoke with you.

NEZNAMOV: Had she no other children?

DUDUKIN: No, of course not.

NEZNAMOV: So why did they say these things to me? *(turns to the others)* Why did you lie to me?

NINA: Sshh, be quiet – she's starting to come round.

NEZNAMOV: Well, I won't look for revenge, I'm not an animal. I'm a child now. I've never been a child. Yes, I'm a child. *(kneels down before Kruchinina)* Mother! Mama! Mama!

KRUCHININA: *(coming to)* Yes, yes, he held out his little arms, and said, "Mama! Mama!"

NEZNAMOV: I'm here.

KRUCHININA: Yes, it's him... it's Grisha, it's my Grisha! Oh, what joy! How wonderful to be alive! *(she strokes Neznamov's hair)* Friends! Please, don't hurt him, he's a good boy. And now he's found his mother again, he'll be even better.

NEZNAMOV: *(quietly)* Mama, where's my father?

KRUCHININA: Your father? *(looks round the company. Murov turns away)* Your father... *(tenderly)* Your father isn't worth looking for. But I should like him to see us. Just to see us – he'll have no share in our happiness. Why do you need a father? You'll be a fine actor, we have enough money... As for a name, you can take mine, and bear it with pride. It's no worse than any other.

DUDUKIN: I was afraid you had died!

KRUCHININA: No. Nobody dies of happiness. *(she embraces her son)*

THE END

(Bez viny vinovatye, 1884)